MAJOR ISSUES IN AMERICAN HISTORY

GENERAL EDITOR
A. S. EISENSTADT, Brooklyn College

CONDUCTING THE DIPLOMACY OF THE NEW NATION, 1793–1815
Patrick C. T. White

THE NEGRO QUESTION: FROM SLAVERY TO CASTE, 1863–1910
Otto H. Olsen

CREATING AN AMERICAN EMPIRE, 1865–1914
Milton Plesur

THE NEW IMMIGRATION
John J. Appel

REFORMING AMERICAN LIFE IN THE PROGRESSIVE ERA
H. Landon Warner

THE UNCERTAIN WORLD OF NORMALCY: THE 1920s
Paul A. Carter

*CONDUCTING THE
DIPLOMACY OF THE
NEW NATION, 1793–1815*

A JEROME S. OZER BOOK
published by PITMAN PUBLISHING CORPORATION
*New York * Toronto * London * Tel Aviv*

CONDUCTING THE DIPLOMACY OF THE NEW NATION, 1793–1815

EDITED BY

Patrick C. T. White
University of Toronto

TO MY WIFE

FOREWORD

The study of history in our classrooms too often proceeds merely from the perspective of the present. Hindsight becomes the great arbiter for settling the past's problems. In our standard textbooks, we judge rather than encounter the past; we instruct it with lessons learned from later developments. In such textbooks, the study of history tends to become a tidy arrangement of certain consequences that arose out of certain causes. As a result, the student can grasp only meagerly the sense that every past was its own present, alive with its own problems, wavering among the alternatives for solving these problems, uncertain about the future. With the security of hindsight and distance, the student is not sufficiently able to consider that a decade he sees as *then* was once a vital and challenging *now*, that its roads into the future were many, that there was nothing inevitable about the one it followed, and that many voices spoke and many forces were at work in affecting its decision to travel one road or another.

The study of American history has tended in recent decades, in yet another way, to remove the classroom from the past itself. It is not merely that we have been proceeding, in our textbooks, to perceive the past from a perspective that is settled and certain, but also that, in our supplementary materials, we have been reading not the past itself but how our major historians are perennially changing their interpretations of it. In this way, too, we are supplanting a study of the past with a study of latter-day commentators on it and, all too often, of commentators on the commentators. The original, vital language of the past itself has, it is fair to say, lost a good deal in the translation.

The *Major Issues in American History* series undertakes above all to restore the fresh, lively contact between the student of the past and the past he is studying. Each of the volumes in the series consists of fifteen or more essays written by earlier generations of Americans on issues of great importance in their times. The different volumes of the series tap a variety of primary sources, but mainly the rich store of our great periodical literature, in which the foremost leaders of American life, our publicists, literary figures, and statesmen addressed themselves to the major problems confronting their respective eras. The men and women who speak in these selections offer various reasons or qualifications for doing so: their intimate knowledge of the problem they are speaking of, their sophisticated perception of its nature, their deep persuasion about its urgency, their strong convictions about how to resolve it.

The selections in each volume seek to lay out the larger dimensions of the major issue with which it is concerned, to recapture the sense of the issue's contemporaneity and urgency, and to afford answers to questions such as the following: What are the nature and significance of the issue? How and why did the issue arise? How should it be resolved? What alternatives are there to achieve its resolution, and what difficulties does the pursuit of each of these alternatives present? Every age is alive with problems, doubts, and controversies, and the selections in each of the volumes seek to convey what these were, in the full measure of the immediacy and liveliness with which the age experienced them. In sum, the central aim of the series is to vitalize the study of the American past by means of *important contemporary essays on major issues.*

Each of the volumes has been edited by a specialist on the issue with which the volume is concerned. Each volume has several principal features designed to enhance its use by the student in his pursuit of a meaningful, rewarding study of the American past. The editor's introductory essay undertakes to present the issue in a broader perspective, indicating how it arose, what were its essential themes and substance, how the controversy it engendered proceeded, what proposals were made for its resolution, how it was ultimately settled, and what were its impact and historical significance. The headnotes for each of the selections extend the introductory essay, offering details about the author of the selection, what occasioned its writing, what the other sides of the controversy were, and the specific historical context in which the selection appeared. The bibliographical essay at the end of the volume offers a critical appraisal of the literature, primary and secondary, dealing with the issue under discussion. Selective rather than comprehensive, it affords the student the basis for a further exploration of the subject. Each volume has, moreover, a chronology which sets the major issue in the context of its times, relating it to the principal events of the age. It is a special point of the series, finally, that the selections have, wherever possible, been reprinted in their entirety. It is important that a spokesman of an earlier age be permitted to present his views in all their completeness and that the student give the past the full hearing it merits.

The *Major Issues in American History* series is meant for use in both basic and advanced courses in American history. The series extends the study of the American past in several ways. It takes the student beyond the confines of the textbook, with its pat formulations and neat divisions, to the reality of the past. Without in any way discounting the importance of what they are saying, it also takes the student beyond the perennial controversies among latter-day and recent historians about what the past signified. It sets the student down in the lively context of a major issue or crisis which earlier Americans had to face, and it compels him to take his place among them in facing and resolving it. Above all, it encourages him to venture out on his own into the realm of the American past and to develop those qualities of perception and judgment that make the study of history the challenging enterprise it is.

A. S. EISENSTADT
Brooklyn College

CONTENTS

PREFACE

Conducting the foreign policy of a nation is a delicate and difficult task which calls for firmness, wisdom, and a nice sense of timing. Even during periods of tranquility these qualities are desirable, but in times of stress and danger they are doubly necessary. Fate did not give to the newly independent United States a period of grace during which she could consolidate her position and secure her institutions. Instead she was immediately confronted by challenges from Great Britain and Europe which threatened her very survival. That she surmounted these difficulties says much for the quality of her people and the character of her governments.

But success was not easily achieved, for men differed deeply and passionately over the measures which should be taken and the course of action which should be pursued. This volume attempts to show how foreign policy was conducted and how honest men differed sharply over ends and means. By letting contemporaries speak for themselves, so often eloquently and effectively, it is hoped that students will gain a better and deeper insight into the great issues with which America grappled.

I should like to express my thanks to Jerome S. Ozer and his successor as editor at Pitman, Philip C. Flayderman, for the warm cooperation given me in the making of this book. They and their staff have always been efficient and helpful. I owe a particular debt to Professor A. S. Eisenstadt, Department of History, Brooklyn College, who is general editor of the series of which this book forms a part. His advice and help proved to be invaluable and were given generously and thoughtfully. I am deeply grateful to him. Finally, I should like to thank my wife whose patient assistance was indispensable.

PATRICK C. T. WHITE
University of Toronto, 1970

A SELECTIVE CHRONOLOGY

1793

February 1   France declares war against Great Britain.

April 8   Citizen Edmund Genêt, French Minister to the United States, arrives in Charleston, S.C.

April 22   President Washington issues the Neutrality Proclamation.

June 8, Nov. 6   British Orders in Council authorize the seizure of neutral cargoes bound for France or French-controlled ports.

August 23   Washington asks for the recall of Genêt.

1794

April 16   John Jay named as special envoy to Great Britain to negotiate outstanding disputes.

November 14   Jay's Treaty signed in London.

1795

October 27   Pinckney's Treaty negotiated with Spain. It provided for American freedom of navigation on the Mississippi River and for the right of deposit at New Orleans.

1796

August 23   President Washington issues his Farewell Address.

1797

May 31   C. C. Pinckney, John Marshall, and Elbridge Gerry appointed to negotiate with France. These commissioners were met with demands by French agents (X.Y.Z.) for a monetary settlement before negotiations could begin.

1798

Spring   Beginning of the undeclared war with France.

1799

September 30   Convention of 1800 signed with France.

1800

December 3   Thomas Jefferson elected President.

1801

October 1   Peace of Amiens signed, bringing a temporary peace between Britain and France.

1803

April 3   United States purchases Louisiana from France.

May 18   France declares war against Great Britain.

1805

July 23   *Essex* Case; the British Court of Appeals upholds the Rule of 1756.

1806

November 21   Berlin Decree; Napoleon declares the British Isles under a French blockade.

December 31   Monroe and Pinckney Treaty with Britain signed, but rejected by Jefferson because it contained no reference to impressment.

1807

January 7   British Orders in Council bars American shipping from French coastal trading.

June 22   H.M.S. *Leopard* attacks the U.S.S. *Chesapeake.*

December 17   Milan Decree states that any neutral ship submitting to a British search would be treated as if it were British property.

December 22   Embargo Act prohibits American vessels from sailing to foreign ports.

1808

April 17   Bayonne Decree orders the seizure of all American ships in French ports.

December 7   James Madison elected president.

1809

March 1   Non-Intercourse Act repeals the embargo and opens trade with all nations except Britain and France.

April 19   Madison opens trade with Britain because of the agreement signed with Erskine, the British minister in Washington.

August 9   Non-Intercourse Act reapplied to Britain when Britain repudiated the Erskine agreement.

1810

March 23   Napoleon's Rambouillet Decree orders the seizure of American ships entering French ports.

May 1   Macon's Bill No. 2 opens commercial intercourse with Britain and France. In the event that one of these powers rescinded its decrees and the other did not follow suit within a specified time, non-intercourse would be applied to the offending power.

August 5   The Duc de Cadore's note announces France's repeal of her Berlin and Milan decrees effective on November 1, 1810 on the assumption that Britain would repeal her Orders in Council. If Britain failed to do this France then expected that the United States would apply the Non-Intercourse Act to Britain.

November 2	Madison announces the annexation of West Florida which had been held by Spain.

1811

March 2	Non-Intercourse Act applied to Great Britain.
November 4	Twelfth Congress convenes.
November 7	Battle of Tippecanoe fought.
November 29	Debate starts in Congress on proposals for military preparations for war with Great Britain.

1812

April 4	A ninety-day embargo applied to all ships in American harbors.
June 1	President Madison sends his war message to Congress.
June 16	Britain announces a conditional repeal of her Orders in Council.
June 18	Congress declares war. The vote favoring war was as follows: Senate: 16 to 13; House of Representatives: 79 to 49.
August 16	General Hull surrenders Detroit to British forces.
December 2	James Madison reelected President.

1813

April 27	American forces capture and burn York (later to be named Toronto), the capital of Upper Canada.

1814

August 8	Peace negotiations begin at Ghent, Belgium, with the United States represented by John Quincy Adams, Henry Clay, James A. Bayard, Jonathan Russell, and Albert Gallatin.
August 25	British forces capture and burn Washington.
December 15	Hartford Convention meets with representatives from Massachusetts, Connecticut, and Rhode Island as well as unofficial delegates from New Hampshire and Vermont. Its opposition to the war was expressed in a report issued when it adjourned on January 15, 1815.
December 24	Peace of Ghent signed; ratified by the United States on February 15, 1815.

1815

January 8	Battle of New Orleans fought.

INTRODUCTION

 "We wish," wrote Jefferson in 1793, "not to meddle with the internal affairs of any country, nor with the general affairs of Europe. Peace with all nations, and the right that gives us with respect to all nations, are our objects."[1] This view was widely shared in America, for successive administrations recognized that the United States needed tranquility at home and relief from foreign adventures abroad in order to achieve the kind of stability which would ensure her future. The function of American foreign policy was then, to protect the national interest and to avoid an entanglement in European affairs. This was to prove incredibly difficult to do for events conspired against the United States. Instead of peace in Europe, which would have provided the ideal conditions for American growth, that continent was torn by a violent and protracted war which continually placed the security and sovereignty of the United States in jeopardy.

The wars between Britain and France first broke upon the world in 1793 and confronted President Washington with a critical situation. America was bound to France by both sentiment and treaty: the former because France had aided America in her own struggle for independence and the latter, because in 1778 the United States had entered into the Franco-American Treaty of Alliance. But the making of foreign policy cannot be based upon sheer sentiment, and limited treaties should not be used to enlarge recklessly the obligations of its signatories. President Washington rejected, therefore, the urgings of those who insisted that France merited support and chose instead the prudent course of neutrality.

[1] Jefferson to Dumas, March 24, 1793, A. A. Lipscomb and A. E. Bergh (eds.), *The Writings of Thomas Jefferson* (20 vols., Library Edition, Washington, 1903), IX, 56.

But it was one thing to proclaim neutrality, and another to maintain it. As events unfolded America found herself pushed and pulled by Britain and France. Only the breadth of the Atlantic Ocean gave her the opportunity to protect her vital interests. And even the advantage of distance could not save her in the long run. For as the war in Europe increased in savagery and intensity, America found her position being attacked by first one and then the other of the major antagonists. Her immediate need, after Washington's Proclamation of Neutrality, was to resolve pressing disputes with Great Britain. These arose both from the maritime policies which Britain was pursuing and from the Treaty of 1783, portions of which had not been completely honored. John Jay was, therefore, sent to London to resolve these issues. Unfortunately, Jay had eloquence at his command but not power, and he was unable to gain the concessions which many thought were due America. As a consequence, the Treaty of 1794 was the subject of harsh and unrelenting criticism throughout the country, but the settlement was probably the best that the United States could have secured in the given circumstances.

While Jay's Treaty settled the issue of the northwest posts and while it established commissions to clarify the boundaries with British North America, it did nothing to resolve the disputes over maritime rights. The practice of impressment and the imposition of punitive Orders in Council by Britain continued to inflame Anglo-American relations. Even worse, France began to treat the United States contemptuously by seizing her ships, inciting her population to disorder, and humiliating her representatives in Paris. But impetuous responses to such provocation would not have served the interests of the United States. Washington, on the eve of his retirement from office, drove this lesson home in his Farewell Address, when he warned his countrymen against involvement in the affairs of Europe and cautioned them against an excess of partisanship. It was not an easy task for his successor, John Adams, to follow this advice, for the mood of the country was belligerent. Men like Robert Goodloe Harper of South Carolina argued that if the United States could protect its interests only by war, then war it should be. President Adams, in the heat of the moment, appeared to encourage the idea of war with France and, of course, the XYZ affair gave him ample reason for doing so. But he soon recognized the hazards involved in such a course of action and began to caution restraint. A settlement with France in 1800 which formally abrogated the Treaties of 1778 was ample reward for his prudence.

Even more important, however, was the Peace of Amiens in 1801, for it brought an end to the war in Europe and gave the United States immediate relief from the dangers surrounding her. Unhappily, Amiens proved to be just a truce, and a desperately short one at that, in a greater war. When that struggle engulfed Europe again in 1803, the United States faced all the old hazards as well as some new and dangerous ones. Time was to prove that these problems did not lend themselves easily to negotiation and could not be avoided by the pursuance of neutrality.

The United States was fortunate, however, that before she faced these problems, the Louisiana Purchase added so strikingly to her power and territory. While some Federalists expressed doubts about the constitutionality of this expansion, most Americans boisterously welcomed the President's initiative and faced the future with a renewed sense of enthusiasm. And this enthusiasm was needed, for the problems Jefferson faced mounted with each passing month.

The first and most intractable dispute involved impressment. After Britain's military defeat on the continent she was compelled to use her power on the ocean to forge a victory, and her naval strength rested, in the opinion of almost all Englishmen, upon the ancient practice of impressment. Furthermore, it was widely believed that this practice could be effectively implemented only if vessels were searched upon the high seas. The issue was made more complicated by the traditional view that allegiance and nationality could not be changed through the novel doctrine of naturalization. Thus Britain would seize from private ships American citizens of British birth as well as recognized subjects of her own nation. The issue was simply and clearly drawn. The United States could not tolerate a practice which placed her citizens in jeopardy and rendered the new Republic and its flag meaningless. And Britain could not give up a practice which she deemed to be, rightly or wrongly, absolutely vital to her survival.

Other problems were less fundamental but equally vexing. The right of a neutral during a war to trade in all commodities not contraband had long been recognized. But Britain challenged that principle as well as the centuries-old definition of what constituted contraband. Through a series of Orders in Council the government in London restricted American trade with French colonies and limited American access to Europe by blockading, not just ports, as had been the custom, but whole stretches of coastline. And she declared as contraband, not merely arms and accouterments of war, but also grains and foodstuffs. France's measures interfering with American trade were nearly as vindictive, but never as, deeply and immediately felt, for she lacked a navy strong enough to enforce her decrees on the high seas.

All these taxing problems were borne by Jefferson. By nature an idealist who hated war and a rationalist who believed that honorable men could meet and resolve their differences by reasoned argument, he was destined to learn the painful lesson, that in foreign affairs, power is often more important than logic and that the force of reason is mightily aided by strength of arms. Thus it was that when negotiations by Monroe and Pinkney in London in 1805 and 1806 failed to gain America relief from impressment or the Orders in Council, Jefferson tried economic coercion through non-importation and non-intercourse acts. But before these could be fully tested the *Chesapeake* crisis broke upon the United States.

The *Chesapeake* was an American frigate that had sailed from Norfolk in June, 1807. When she was some twelve miles offshore, she was stopped by a British vessel and ordered to surrender alleged British deserters in her crew. When this request was quite properly rejected, she was fired upon, and four of her crew were forcibly removed by a boarding party. A demand for war swept the country, but Jefferson resisted it and called instead for an apology from Britain, an end to impressment, and reparations for the damage done to the ship and her crew. When this demand was not promptly met Jefferson instituted a total embargo. This was a measure which he felt would uniquely meet the needs of the moment. It would punish the transgressors by denying them American goods and it would preserve the nation's shipping by removing it from the high seas where it had been the object of search and seizure. Unfortunately this measure, for which such high hopes were held, collapsed in total ignominy. It neither coerced Britain, who saw it as a measure of either weakness or cowardice, nor confined trade to America, whose merchants evaded it with the same ingenious skill that they had displayed in avoiding British customs officers prior to the Revolution. It was finally repealed in 1809 as Jefferson left office. His years in the presidency had tried him to the limits of his endurance. Yet he entered private life with the serene conviction that he had done all that was humanly possible to protect his country's interests and that any failure on his part was due more to circumstances beyond his control than to the ineffectiveness of the measures he had adopted. And perhaps he was right.

His successor, James Madison, was a lesser man for he lacked the breadth of vision and the power of mind which had characterized Jefferson. And while he brought to the presidency wide experience in public affairs he lacked the ability to make swift and wise decisions and the capacity to surround himself with talented and inventive subordinates. But the problems he faced were so enormous, and his range of options so limited, that it is doubtful whether even a more skilled leader could have altered the course of events. After a decade of compromise and negotiations many Americans were slowly but surely deciding that force should be met with force, and that, if America's sovereignty were to be protected and her honor upheld, Britain would have to be faced down.

This was a terrible choice to make and some still backed away from it, arguing instead that war would destroy the nation and shatter a great and noble experiment in the governance of mankind. But time was running out on them. The passage of Macon's Bill No. 2, a wretched and self-serving measure, only postponed the inevitable. Macon had first introduced a bill that would have allowed American ships to sail anywhere and that would have permitted the importation of French and British goods only in American bottoms. But this measure was deemed by some to be too hostile to Great Britain. It was modified, therefore, in a second bill which opened trade with both France and Britain. This act also stated that if one of these two powers rescinded its decrees and the other did not follow suit within a stipulated period of time, the United States would penalize the offending power with the non-intercourse act. The immediate result of the bill was, of course, the Duke of Cadore's letter which announced the French repeal of the Berlin and Milan decrees and demanded the fulfillment of the American pledge to institute an embargo against Britain if she did not promptly rescind her Orders in Council. As Britain believed, with good reason, that the French repeal was spurious, she refused to modify her position, but Madison accepted the Cadore letter at face value and acted accordingly. He has been harshly criticized for doing so, but he was prepared to grasp at straws to save America.

The drift to war now became almost irresistible. The War Hawks in Congress called for measures to arm the country for the event. War held no terror for them, for they were convinced that the battle would be short and victory certain. Britain was vulnerable in Canada and the painless occupation of that colony would deal such a fatal blow to England that she would readily come to terms with America. But others were not so sure. John Randolph of Virginia believed that war was always a chancy business and that success in it was always dearly won. But his opposition to the President was so intemperate and his failure to recognize the grave nature of the challenge to America so obvious, that his views were dismissed by his colleagues. The report of the Foreign Relations Committee of the House of Representatives, which appeared in December, 1811, issued a clear and resolute call for war. And if the President still harbored doubts about the wisdom of this, they were removed in the early months of 1812 when his fruitless discussions with the British minister in Washington showed that there was to be no modification in the practices which so angered the nation.

And so in June, 1812, Madison sent his war message to Congress. The debate over it was long and bitter and when the vote came it was far from unanimous. There were still some who argued again that the nation was not ready to confront Britain, that negotiations were still possible, that the wrong enemy had been chosen, or that war would destroy the union. But a clear majority believed, as did Calhoun, that this was America's second war of independence.

Hostilities began in an atmosphere of high optimism. Even Jefferson believed that the taking of Canada was a mere matter of marching. But war is a great destroyer of illusions. Within months of its declaration the United States had suffered a series of humiliating reverses in Upper Canada. Here, of course, was the problem. For instead of striking at Montreal and starving Upper Canada into submission the United States made the serious strategic error of moving her forces into the Niagara region. After occupying this area she planned to move her armies down the St. Lawrence River. The scheme failed disastrously and although, by 1814, the military situation had improved, the damage had been done. A speedy victory had eluded the President's grasp and all the terrible political consequences which flowed from this error now encompassed the administration.

Opposition to the war had existed in 1812, but now it became intense and passionate. New England provided much of it, and Daniel Webster expressed the feelings of many when he demanded that the government end its futile efforts to seize Canada and begin the arduous task of negotiating a just peace. He did not, of course, have everything his own way. Those who had plunged into the war in defense of America's honor and interests were not prepared to surrender these goals without a struggle. A more vigorous prosecution of the war and an end to the divisive tactics of the opposition would, argued Felix Grundy and his fellow War Hawks in Congress, bring victory to the United States.

But complete success was beyond the resources of America. She could not defeat Britain on the high seas, and the occupation of Canada, if it were at all possible, could only be accomplished after bloody and costly fighting. Britain's position was no better. She knew that any invasion of the United States promised doubtful success at prohibitive costs. Both circumstances and reason, then, called for a negotiated peace.

This was finally reached on Christmas Eve in 1814, but only after protracted and often bitter discussions. The problem in the negotiations lay in the extremity of the demands that each side first put forward. The United States wanted an end to impressment, the resolution of other maritime disputes in her favor, and the retention of the fishing liberties which she had secured in the Treaty of 1783. Britain's demands were equally unreasonable, for she wanted a neutral Indian barrier state south of Canada, an end to the American fishing liberties in British North America waters, and a boundary drawn upon the principle that each side should keep the territory currently occupied by its troops. Since neither side could accept such extravagant terms, and since both parties realized that the war was in a stalemate, a compromise settlement was finally reached. The Treaty of Ghent provided for a return to the *status quo ante bellum,* called for the creation of mixed commissions to resolve certain outstanding boundary disputes, and left to future discussions the difficult question of the fisheries.

If the United States had not won the war, she had emerged from it with credit. She had defended her borders with tenacity and increasing effectiveness. She had proven to herself and the world that republican institutions of government could survive the harshest of tests and she had shown that her economy was capable of growing under the most adverse conditions. And, perhaps most important of all, her people had come through a period of trial with a renewed sense of national purpose and dedication.

PART I

THE PROBLEMS
OF
NEUTRALITY

1
THE NEUTRALITY PROCLAMATION

 Some two weeks after Washington's Inaugural Address the French Revolution broke upon Europe. It was an event that was welcomed with as much enthusiasm in America as with passion in France. For to most people in the United States, the mob in Paris which stormed the Bastille was acting in as noble and enlightened a tradition as those who had fought in the Revolution of 1776. As long as the turmoil was confined to France it posed no serious problems for the United States, but when domestic strife turned into international war the President was faced with precisely the kind of problems which he had so ardently hoped to avoid. For he had long been convinced that the United States needed stability at home and relief from pressures abroad in order to develop her institutions and create the stability in her society which would guarantee her future security and greatness.

The eruption of war between Britain and France in 1793 placed the United States in a particularly cruel dilemma. There were some who felt that the Franco-American Alliance of 1778 obligated the United States to give aid to the government in Paris. But Washington himself was not prepared to jeopardize the future of his country by taking such a step. Instead the President called the Cabinet into session where it was agreed that a proclamation of neutrality (although that word was never used in the actual document) should be issued.

Alexander Hamilton (1755–1804), the Secretary of the Treasury (1789–1795), writing under the name of *Pacificus,* gave a powerful and cogent defense of the President's conduct. America's interests, as Washington correctly diagnosed and as Hamilton persuasively argued, were best served by a detachment from Europe's quarrels. Jefferson shared

9

the view that neutrality was imperative, but hoped that some concessions could be wrung from Britain in exchange for America's proposed
course of action. He also argued that the Franco-American treaties were
still binding upon the nation and that Washington should recognize
the new French government and accept its accredited ministers to the
United States.

PACIFICUS

NO. I

Alexander
Hamilton

June 29, 1793

As attempts are making very dangerous to the peace, and, it is to
be feared, not very friendly to the Constitution, of the United States,
it becomes the duty of those who wish well to both, to endeavor
to prevent their success.

The objections which have been raised against the proclamation
of neutrality, lately issued by the President, have been urged in
a spirit of acrimony and invective, which demonstrates that more
was in view than merely a free discussion of an important public
measure. They exhibit evident indications of a design to weaken
the confidence of the people in the author of the measure, in order
to remove or lessen a powerful obstacle to the success of an opposition to the government, which, however it may change its form
according to circumstances, seems still to be persisted in with un-
remitting industry.

This reflection adds to the motives connected with the measure
itself, to recommend endeavors by proper explanations, to place it
in a just light. Such explanations, at least, cannot but be satisfactory
to those who may not themselves have leisure or opportunity for
pursuing an investigation of the subject, and who may wish to perceive that the policy of the government is not inconsistent with its
obligations or its honor.

The objections in question fall under four heads:

FROM *The Works of Alexander
Hamilton,* Henry Cabot Lodge,
ed. (New York, 1903), vol. 4,
pp. 432–89.

1. That the proclamation was without authority.

2. That it was contrary to our treaties with France.

3. That it was contrary to the gratitude which is due from this to that country, for the succors afforded to us in our own revolution.

4. That it was out of time and unnecessary.

In order to judge of the solidity of the first of these objections, it is necessary to examine what is the nature and design of a proclamation of neutrality.

It is to *make known* to the Powers at war, and to the citizens of the country whose government does the act, that such country is in the condition of a nation at peace with the belligerent parties, and under no obligations of treaty to become an *associate in the war* with either, and that this being its situation, its intention is to observe a corresponding conduct by performing towards each the duties of neutrality; to warn all persons within the jurisdiction of that country to abstain from acts that shall contravene those duties, under the penalties which the laws of the land, of which the *jus gentium* is part, will inflict.

This, and no more, is conceived to be the true import of a proclamation of neutrality.

. . .

In stating that the proclamation of neutrality does not imply the non-performance of any stipulations of treaties which are not of a nature to make the nation an associate in the war, it is conceded that an execution of the clause of guaranty, contained in the eleventh article of our treaty of alliance with France, would be contrary to the sense and spirit of the proclamation because it would engage us with our whole force as an *auxiliary* in the war; it would be much more than the case of a definite succor, previously ascertained.

It follows that the proclamation is virtually a manifestation of the sense of the government, that the United States are, *under the circumstances of the case, not bound* to execute the clause of guaranty.

If this be a just view of the force and import of the proclamation, it will remain to see whether the President, in issuing it, acted within his proper sphere, or stepped beyond the bounds of his constitutional authority and duty.

It will not be disputed that the management of the affairs of this country with foreign nations is confided to the Government of the United States.

It can as little be disputed that a proclamation of neutrality, when a nation is at liberty to decline or avoid a war in which other nations are engaged, and means to do so, is a *usual* and a *proper* measure. *Its main object is to prevent the nation's being responsible for acts done by its citizens, without the privity or connivance of the government, in contravention of the principles of neutrality;* an object of the greatest moment to a country whose true interest lies in the preservation of peace.

The inquiry, then, is what department of our government is the proper one to make a declaration of neutrality, when the engagements of the nation permit, and its interests require that it should be done?

A correct mind will discern at once, that it can belong neither to the legislative nor judicial department, and therefore of course must belong to the executive.

The legislative department is not the *organ* of intercourse between the United States and foreign nations. It is charged neither with *making* nor *interpreting* treaties. It is therefore not naturally that member of the government which is to pronounce on the existing condition of the nation with regard to foreign powers, or to admonish the citizens of their obligations and duties in consequence; still less is it charged with enforcing the observance of those obligations and duties.

. . .

Those who object to the proclamation will readily admit that it is the right and duty of the executive to interpret those articles of our treaties which give to France particular privileges, in order to the enforcement of them: but the necessary consequence of this is, that the executive must judge what are their proper limits; what rights are given to other nations, by our contracts with them; what rights the law of nature and nations gives, and our treaties permit, in respect to those countries with which we have none; in fine, what are the reciprocal rights and obligations of the United States, and of all and each of the powers at war.

. . .

The President is the Constitutional EXECUTOR of the laws. Our treaties, and the laws of nations, form a part of the law of the land. He who is to execute the laws must first judge for himself of their meaning. In order to the observance of that conduct which the laws of nations, combined with our treaties, prescribed to this country, in reference to the present war in Europe, it was necessary for the President to judge for himself, whether there was any thing in our treaties incompatible with an adherence to neutrality. Having decided that there was not, he had a right, and if in his opinion the interest of the nation required it, it was his duty as executor of the laws, to proclaim the neutrality of the nation, to exhort all persons to observe it, and to warn them of the penalties which would attend its non-observance.

The proclamation has been represented as enacting some new law. This is a view of it entirely erroneous. It only proclaims a *fact*, with regard to the *existing state* of the nation; informs the citizens of what the laws previously established require of them in that state, and notifies them that these laws will be put in execution against the infractors of them.

NO. II

July 3, 1793

The second and principal objection to the proclamation, namely, that it is inconsistent with the treaties between the United States and France, will now be examined.

It has been already shown that it does not militate against the performance of any of the stipulations in those treaties, which would not make us an associate or party in the war, and especially that it does not interfere with the privileges secured to France by the seventeenth and twenty-second articles of the treaty of commerce, which, except the clause of guaranty, constitute the most material discriminations to be found in our treaties in favor of that country.

Official documents have likewise appeared in the public papers, which serve as a comment upon the sense of the proclamation in this particular, proving that it was not deemed by the executive incompatible with the performance of the stipulations in those articles, and that in practice they are intended to be observed.

It has, however, been admitted that the declaration of neutrality excludes the idea of an execution of the clause of guaranty.

It becomes necessary, therefore, to examine whether the United States would have a valid justification for not complying with it, in case of their being called upon for that purpose by France.

Without knowing how far the reasons which have occurred to me may have influenced the President, there appear to me to exist very good and substantial grounds for a refusal.

The alliance between the United States and France is of the defensive kind. In the caption it is denominated a "treaty of alliance eventual and defensive." In the body (article the second) it is called a defensive alliance. The words of that article are as follows: "The essential and direct end of the present defensive alliance is to maintain effectually the liberty, sovereignty, and independence, absolute and unlimited, of the United States, as well in matters of government as of commerce."

The leading character, then, of our alliance with France being defensive, it will follow that the meaning, obligation, and force of every stipulation in the treaty must be tested by the principles of such an alliance, unless in any instance terms have been used which clearly and unequivocally denoted a different intent.

The principle question consequently is: What is the nature and effect of a defensive alliance? When does the *casus foederis* take place in relation to it?

Reason, the concurring opinions of writers, and the practice of nations will answer: "When either of the allies is *attacked*," when "war is *made upon him*, not when he *makes war upon another*": in other words, the stipulated assistance is to be given "when our ally is engaged in a defensive, not when he is engaged in an offensive, war." This obligation to assist only in a defensive war constitutes the essential difference between an alliance which is merely defensive and one which is both offensive and defensive. In the latter case there is an obligation to co-operate as well when the war, on the part of our ally, is of the latter, as when it is of the former, description. To affirm, therefore, that the United States are bound to assist France in the war in which she is at present engaged, will be to convert our treaty with her into an alliance offensive and defensive, contrary to the express and reiterated declarations of the instrument itself.

This assertion implies that the war in question is an offensive war on the part of France.

And so undoubtedly it is, with regard to all the Powers with whom she was at war, at the time of issuing the proclamation.

No position is better established than that the nation which first declares or actually begins a war, whatever may have been the causes leading to it, is that which makes an offensive war. Nor is there any doubt that France first declared and began the war against Austria, Prussia, Savoy, Holland, England, and Spain. . . .

July 6, 1793

France, at the time of issuing the proclamation, was engaged in a war with a considerable part of Europe, and likely to be embroiled with almost all the rest, without a single ally in that quarter of the globe.

· · ·

Our guaranty does not look to France herself. It does not relate to her immediate defence, but to the defence and preservation of her American colonies; objects of which she might be deprived, and yet remain a great, a powerful, and a happy nation.

· · ·

As in the present instance, good faith does not require that the United States should put in jeopardy their essential interests, perhaps their very existence, in one of the most unequal contests in which a nation could be engaged, to secure France — what? Her West Indian islands and other less important possessions in America. For it is always to be remembered, that the stipulations of the United States do, in no event, reach beyond this point. If they were, upon the strength of their guaranty, to engage in the war, and could make any arrangement with the belligerent Powers, for securing to France those islands and those possessions, they would be at perfect liberty instantly to withdraw. They would not be bound to prosecute the war one moment longer.

They are under no obligation in any event, as far as the faith of treaties is concerned, to assist France in defence of her liberty; a topic on which so much has been said, so very little to the purpose, as it regards the present question.

· · ·

On these grounds, also, as well as that of the present war being offensive on the side of France, the United States have the valid and honorable pleas to offer against the execution of the guaranty if it should be claimed by France; and the President was in every view fully justified in pronouncing that the duty and interest of the United States dictated a neutrality in the war.

NO. IV

A third objection to the proclamation is, that it is inconsistent with the gratitude due to France for the services rendered to us in our revolution.

Those who make this objection disavow, at the same time, all intentions to maintain the position that the United States ought to take part in the war. They profess to be friends to our remaining at peace. What then do they mean by the objection?

If it be no breach of gratitude to refrain from joining France in the war, how can it be a breach of gratitude to declare that such is our disposition and intention?

The two positions are at variance with each other; and the true inference is, either that those who make the objection really wish to engage this country in the war, or that they seek a pretext for censuring the conduct of the Chief Magistrate, for some purpose very different from the public good.

They endeavor in vain to elude this inference by saying that the proclamation places France upon an equal footing with her enemies, while our treaties require distinctions in her favor, and our relative situation would dictate kind offices to her, which ought not to be granted to her adversaries.

They are not ignorant that the proclamation is reconcilable with both these objects, as far as they have any foundation in truth or propriety.

It has been shown that the promise of "a friendly and impartial conduct" toward all the belligerent Powers is not incompatible with the performance of any stipulations in our treaties, which would not include our becoming an associate in the war; and it has been observed that the conduct of the executive, in regard to the seventeenth and twenty-second articles of the treaty of commerce, is an unequivocal comment upon the terms. They were, indeed, naturally to be understood, with the exception of those matters of positive compact, which would not amount to taking part in the war; for a nation then observes a friendly and impartial conduct toward two contending Powers, when it only performs to one of them what it is obliged to do by stipulations in antecedent treaties, which do not constitute a participation in the war.

Neither do those expressions imply that the United States will not exercise their discretion in doing kind offices to some of the parties, without extending them to others, so long as they have no relation to war; for kind offices of that description may, consistently with neutrality, be shown to one party and refused to another.

If the objections mean that the United States ought to favor France, in things relating to war, and where they are not bound to do it by treaty, they must in this case also abandon their pretensions of being friends to peace. For such a conduct would be a violation of neutrality, which would not fail to produce war.

It follows then, that the proclamation is reconcilable with all that those who censure it contend for: taking them upon their own ground, that nothing is to be done incompatible with the preservation of peace.

But though this would be a sufficient answer to the objection under consideration, yet it may not be without use to indulge some reflections on this very favorite topic of gratitude to France, since it is at this shrine that we are continually invited to sacrifice the true interests of the country; as if "all for love, and the world well lost," were a fundamental maxim in politics.

Faith and justice between nations are virtues of a nature the most necessary and sacred. They cannot to be too strongly inculcated, nor too highly respected. Their obligations are absolute, their utility unquestionable; they relate to objects which, with probity and sincerity, generally admit of being brought within clear and intelligible rules.

But the same cannot be said of gratitude. It is not very often that between nations it can be pronounced with certainty that there exists a solid foundation for the sentiment; and how far it can justifiably be permitted to operate, is always a question of still greater difficulty.

The basis of gratitude is a benefit received or intended, which there was no right of claim, originating in a regard to the interest or advantage of the party on whom the benefit is, or is meant to be, conferred. If a service is rendered from views relative to the immediate interest of the party who performs it, and is productive of reciprocal advantages, there seems scarcely, in such a case, to be an adequate basis for a sentiment like that of gratitude. The effect at least would be wholly disproportioned to the cause, if such a service ought to beget more than a disposition to render in turn a correspondent good office, founded on mutual interest and reciprocal advantage. But gratitude would require much more than this: it would exact to a certain extent even a sacrifice of the interest of the party obliged to the service or benefit of the one by whom the obligation had been conferred.

Between individuals, occasion is not unfrequently given for the exercise of gratitude. Instances of conferring benefits from kind and benevolent dispositions or feelings toward the person benefited, without any other interest on the part of the person who renders the service, than the pleasure of doing a good action, occur every day among individuals. But among nations they perhaps never occur. It may be affirmed as a general principle, that the predominant motive of good offices from one nation to another, is the interest or advantage of the nation which performs them.

Indeed, the rule of morality in this respect is not precisely the same between nations as between individuals. The duty of making its own welfare the guide of its actions, is much stronger upon the former than upon the latter: in proportion to the greater magnitude and importance of national compared with individual happiness, and to the greater permanency of the effects of national than of individual happiness, and to the greater permanency of the effects of national than of individual conduct. Existing millions, and for the most part future generations, are concerned in the present measures of a government; while the consequences of the private actions of an individual ordinarily terminate with himself, or are circumscribed within a narrow compass.

Whence it follows that an individual may, on numerous occasions, meritoriously indulge the emotions of generosity and benevolence, not only without an eye to, but even at the expense of, his own interest. But a government can rarely, if at all, be justifiable in pursuing a similar course; and, if it does so, ought to confine itself within much stricter bounds.* Good offices which are indifferent to the interest of a nation performing them, or which are compensated by the existence or expectation of some reasonable equivalent, or which produce an essential good to the nation to which they are rendered without real detriment to the affairs of the benefactors, prescribe perhaps the limits of national generosity or benevolence.

It is not here meant to recommend a policy absolutely selfish or interested in nations; but to show, that a policy regulated by their own interest, as far as justice and good faith permit, is, and ought to be, their prevailing one; and that either to ascribe to them a different principle of action, or to deduce, from the supposition of it, arguments for a self-denying and self-sacrificing gratitude on the part of a nation which may have received from another good offices, is to misrepresent or misconceive what usually are, and ought to be, the springs of national conduct. . . .

---

* This conclusion derives confirmation from the reflection, that under every form of government rulers are only trustees for the happiness of their nation, and cannot, consistently with their trust, follow the suggestions of kindness or humanity toward others, to the prejudice of their constituents.

July 20, 1793

The remaining objection to the proclamation of neutrality still to be discussed is, that it was out of time and unnecessary.

To give color to this objection it is asked, why did not the proclamation appear when the war commenced with Austria and Prussia? Why was it forborne till Great Britain, Holland, and Spain became engaged? Why did not the government wait till the arrival at Philadelphia of the minister of the French Republic? Why did it volunteer a declaration not required of it by any of the belligerent parties?

To most of these questions solid answers have already appeared in the public prints; little more can be done than to repeat and enforce them.

Austria and Prussia are not maritime powers. Contraventions of neutrality as against them were not likely to take place to any extent, or in a shape that would attract their notice. It would, therefore, have been useless, if not ridiculous, to have made a formal declaration on the subject, while they were the only parties opposed to France.

But the reverse of this was the case with regard to Spain, Holland, and England. These are all commercial and maritime nations. It was to be expected that their attention would be immediately drawn toward the United States with sensibility, and even with jealousy. It was to be feared that some of our citizens might be tempted by the prospect of gain to go into measures which would injure them, and hazard the peace of the country. Attacks by some of these Powers upon the possessions of France in America were to be looked for as a matter of course. While the views of the United States as to that particular were problematical, they would naturally consider us as a Power that might become their enemy. This they would have been more apt to do on account of these public demonstrations of attachment to the cause of France, of which there has been so prodigal a display. Jealousy, everybody knows, especially if sharpened by resentment, is apt to lead to ill treatment; ill treatment, to hostility.

In proportion to the probability of our being regarded with a suspicious, and consequently an unfriendly, eye by the Powers at war with France; in proportion to the danger of imprudences being committed by any of our citizens, which might occasion a rupture with them, the policy on the part of the government, of removing all doubt as to its own disposition, and of deciding the condition of the United States, in view of the parties concerned, became obvious and urgent.

Were the United States now, what, if we do not rashly throw away the advantages we possess, they may expect to be in fifteen or twenty years, there would have been more room for an insinuation which has been thrown out, namely, that they ought to have secured to themselves some advantages as the consideration of their neutrality, — an idea, however, the justice and magnanimity of which cannot be commended. But in their present situation, with their present strength and resources, an attempt of that kind could have only served to display pretensions at once excessive and unprincipled. The chance of obtaining any collateral advantage, if such a chance there was, by leaving doubt of their intentions as to peace or war, could not wisely have been put, for a single instant, in competition with the tendency of a contrary conduct to secure our peace.

The conduciveness of the declaration of neutrality to that end was not the only recommendation to the adoption of the measure. It was of great importance that our own citizens should understand, as soon as possible, the opinion which the government entertained of the nature of our relations to the warring parties, and of the propriety or expediency of our taking a side or remaining neuter. The arrangements of our merchants could not but be very differently affected by the one hypothesis or the other; and it would necessarily have been very detrimental and perplexing to them to have been left in uncertainty.

. . .

But there has been a criticism several times repeated, which may deserve a moment's attention. It has been urged that the proclamation ought to have contained some reference to our treaties; and that the generality of the promise to observe a conduct *friendly* and *impartial* towards the belligerent Powers, ought to have been qualified with expressions equivalent to these, *"as far as may consist with the treaties of the United States."*

The insertion of such a clause would have entirely defeated the object of the proclamation, by rendering the intention of the government equivocal. That object was to assure the Powers at war, and our own citizens, that in the opinion of the executive it was consistent with the duty and interest of the nation to observe neutrality, and that it was intended to pursue a conduct corresponding with that opinion. Words equivalent to those contended for would have rendered the other part of the declaration nugatory, *by leaving it uncertain whether the executive did or did not believe a state of neutrality to be consistent with our treaties.* Neither foreign Powers nor our own citizens would have been able to have drawn any conclusion from the proclamation, and both would have had a right to consider it as a mere equivocation.

By not inserting any such ambiguous expressions, the proclamation was susceptible of an intelligible and proper construction. While it denoted on the one hand that, in the judgment of the executive, there was nothing in our treaties obliging us *to become a party in the war*, it left it to be expected, on the other, that all stipulations compatible with neutrality, according to the laws and usages of nations, would be enforced. It follows that the proclamation was, in this particular, exactly what it ought to have been.

The words, "make known the disposition of the United States," have also given a pretext for cavil. It has been asked, how could the President undertake to declare the disposition of the United States? The people, for ought he knew, may have a very different sentiment. Thus, a conformity with a republican propriety and modesty is turned into a topic of accusation.

Had the President announced his own disposition, he would have been chargeable with egotism, if not presumption. The constitutional organ of intercourse between the United States and foreign nations, whenever he speaks to them, it is in that capacity; it is in the name and on the behalf of the United States. It must, therefore, be with greater propriety that he speaks of their disposition than of his own.

It is easy to imagine that occasions frequently occur in the communications to foreign governments and foreign agents, which render it necessary to speak of the friendship or *friendly disposition* of the United States, of *their disposition* to cultivate harmony and good understanding, to reciprocate neighborly offices, and the like. It is usual, for example, when public ministers are received, for some complimentary expressions to be interchanged. It is presumable that the late reception of the French minister did not pass without some assurance on the part of the President of the friendly disposition of the United States towards France. Admitting it to have happened, would it be deemed an improper arrogation? If not, why was it more so, to declare the disposition of the United States to observe a neutrality in the existing war?

. . .

Kings and princes speak of their own dispositions, the magistrates of republics of the dispositions of their nations. The President, therefore, has evidently used the style adapted to his situation, and the criticism upon it is plainly a cavil.

OPINION ON FRENCH TREATIES

Thomas Jefferson

April 28, 1793

I proceed, in compliance with the requisition of the President, to give an opinion in writing on the general Question, Whether the U.S. have a right to renounce their treaties with France, or to hold them suspended till the government of that country shall be established?

In the Consultation at the President's on the 19th inst. the Secretary of the Treasury took the following positions & consequences. "France was a monarchy when we entered into treaties with it: but it has now declared itself a Republic, & is preparing a Republican form of government. As it may issue in a Republic, or a Military despotism, or in something else which may possibly render our alliance with it dangerous to ourselves, we have a right of election to renounce the treaty altogether, or to declare it suspended till their government shall be settled in the form it is ultimately to take; and then we may judge whether we will call the treaties into operation again, or declare them forever null. Having that right of election now, if we receive their minister without any qualifications, it will amount to an act of election to continue the treaties; & if the change they are undergoing should issue in a form which should bring danger on us, we shall not be then free to renounce them. To elect to continue them is equivalent to the making a new treaty at this time in the same form, that is to say, with a clause of guarantee; but to make a treaty with a clause of guarantee, during a war, is a departure from neutrality, and would make us associates in the war. To renounce or suspend the treaties therefore is a necessary act of neutrality."

If I do not subscribe to the soundness of this reasoning, I do most fully to its ingenuity. — I shall now lay down the principles which according to my understanding govern the case.

I consider the people who constitute a society or nation as the source of all authority in that nation, as free to transact their common concerns by any agents they think proper, to change these agents individually, or the organisation of them in form or function whenever they please: that all the acts done by those agents under the

FROM *The Works of Thomas Jefferson*, Paul L. Ford, ed. (New York, 1914), vol. 7, pp. 283-301.

authority of the nation, are the acts of the nation, are obligatory on them, & enure to their use, & can in no wise be annulled or affected by any change in the form of the government, or of the persons administering it. Consequently the Treaties between the U.S. and France, were not treaties between the U.S. & Louis Capet, but between the two nations of America & France, and the nations remaining in existance, tho' both of them have since changed their forms of government, the treaties are not annulled by these changes.

The Law of nations, by which this question is to be determined, is composed of three branches. 1. The Moral law of our nature. 2. The Usages of nations. 3. Their special Conventions. The first of these only, concerns this question, that is to say the Moral law to which Man has been subjected by his creator, & of which his feelings, or Conscience as it is sometimes called, are the evidence with which his creator has furnished him. The Moral duties which exist between individual and individual in a state of nature, accompany them into a state of society & the aggregate of the duties of all the individuals composing the society constitutes the duties of that society towards any other; so that between society & society the same moral duties exist as did between the individuals composing them while in an unassociated state, their maker not having released them from those duties on their forming themselves into a nation. Compacts then between nation & nation are obligatory on them by the same moral law which obliges individuals to observe their compacts. There are circumstances however which sometimes excuse the non-performance of contracts between man & man: so are there also between nation & nation. When performance, for instance, becomes *impossible,* non-performance is not immoral. So if performance becomes *self-destructive* to the party, the law of self-preservation overrules the laws of obligation to others. For the reality of these principles I appeal to the true fountains of evidence, the head & heart of every rational & honest man. It is there Nature has written her moral laws, & where every man may read them for himself. He will never read there the permission to annul his obligations for a time, or for ever, whenever they become "dangerous, useless, or disagreeable." Certainly not when merely *useless* or *disagreeable,* as seems to be said in an authority which has been quoted, Vattel, 2. 197, and tho he may under certain degrees of *danger,* yet the danger must be imminent, & the degree great. Of these, it is true, that nations are to be judges for themselves, since no one nation has a right to sit in judgment over another. But the tribunal of our consciences remains, & that also of the opinion of the world. These will revise the sentence we pass in our own case, & as we respect these, we must see that in judging ourselves we have honestly done the part of impartial & vigorous judges.

But Reason, which gives this right of self-liberation from a contract in certain cases, has subjected it to certain just limitations.

I.   The danger which absolves us must be great, inevitable & imminent. Is such the character of that now apprehended from our treaties with France? What is that danger.

1. Is it that if their government issues in a military despotism, an alliance with them may taint us with despotic principles? But their government, when we allied ourselves to it, was a perfect despotism, civil & military, yet the treaties were made in that very state of things, & therefore that danger can furnish no just cause.
2. Is it that their government may issue in a republic, and too much strengthen our republican principles? But this is the hope of the great mass of our constituents, & not their dread. They do not look with longing to the happy mean of a limited monarchy.
3. But says the doctrine I am combating, the change the French are undergoing may possibly end in something we know not what, and bring on us danger we know not whence. In short it may end in a Rawhead & bloody-bones in the dark. Very well. Let Rawhead & bloody bones come, & then we shall be justified in making our peace with him, by renouncing our antient friends & his enemies. For observe, it is not the *possibility of danger*, which absolves a party from his contract: for that possibility always exists, & in every case. It existed in the present one at the moment of making the contract. If *possibilities* would avoid contracts, there never could be a valid contract. For possibilities hang over everything. Obligation is not suspended, till the danger is become real, & the moment of it so imminent, that we can no longer avoid decision without forever losing the opportunity to do it. But can a danger which has not yet taken it's shape, which does not yet exist, & never may exist, which cannot therefore be defined, can such a danger I ask, be so imminent that if we fail to pronounce on it in this moment we can never have another opportunity of doing it?
4. The danger apprehended, is it that, the treaties remaining valid, the clause guarantying their West India islands will

engage us in the war? But Does the Guarantee engage us to enter into the war in any event?

Are we to enter into it before we are called on by our allies? Have we been called on by them? — shall we ever be called on? Is it their interest to call on us?

Can they call on us before their islands are invaded, or imminently threatened?

If they can save them themselves, have they a right to call on us?

Are we obliged to go to war at once, without trying peaceable negociations with their enemy?

If all these questions be against us, there are still others behind.

Are we in a condition to go to war?

Can we be expected to begin before we are in condition?

Will the islands be lost if we do not save them? Have we the means of saving them?

If we cannot save them are we bound to go to war for a desperate object?

Will not a 10. years forbearance in us to call them into the guarantee of our posts, entitle us to some indulgence?

Many, if not most of these questions offer grounds of doubt whether the clause of guarantee will draw us into the war. Consequently if this be the danger apprehended, it is not yet certain enough to authorize us in sound morality to declare, at this moment, the treaties null.

5. Is the danger apprehended from the 17th article of the treaty of Commerce, which admits French ships of war & privateers to come and go freely, with prizes made on their enemies, while their enemies are not to have the same privilege with prizes made on the French? But Holland & Prussia have approved of this article in our treaty with France, by subscribing to an express Salvo of it in our treaties with them. (Dutch treaty 22. Convention 6. Prussian treaty 19.) And England in her last treaty with France (art. 40) has entered into the same stiuplation verbatim, & placed us in her ports on the same footing on which she is in ours, in case of a war of either of us with France. If we are engaged in such a war, England must receive prizes made on us by the French, & exclude those made on the French by us. Nay further, in this very article of her treaty with France, is a salvo of any similar article in any anterior treaty of either party, and ours with France being anterior, this salvo confirms it ex-

pressly. Neither of these three powers then have a right to complain of this article in our treaty.

6. Is the danger apprehended from the 22d. Art. of our treaty of commerce, which prohibits the enemies of France from fitting out privateers in our ports, or selling their prizes here. But we are free to refuse the same thing to France, there being no stipulation to the contrary, and we ought to refuse it on principles of fair neutrality.

7. But the reception of a Minister from the Republic of France, without qualifications, it is thought will bring us into danger: because this, it is said, will determine the continuance of the treaty, and take from us the right of self-liberation when at any time hereafter our safety would require us to use it. The reception of the Minister at all (in favor of which Col. Hamilton has given his opinion, tho reluctantly as he confessed) is an acknolegement [sic] of the legitimacy of their government: and if the qualifications meditated are to deny that legitimacy, it will be a curious compound which is to admit & deny the same thing. But I deny that the reception of a Minister has any thing to do with the treaties. There is not a word, in either of them, about sending ministers. This has been done between us under the common usage of nations, & can have no effect either to continue or annul the treaties.

But how can any act of election have the effect to continue a treaty which is acknoleged to be going on still? For it was not pretended the treaty was void, but only void-able if we chuse to declare it so. To make it void would require an act of election, but to let it go on requires only that we should do nothing, and doing nothing can hardly be an infraction of peace or neutrality.

But I go further & deny that the most explicit declaration made at this moment that we acknolege the obligation of the treatys could take from us the right of non-compliance at any future time when compliance would involve us in great & inevitable danger.

I conclude then that few of these sources threaten any danger at all; and from none of them is it inevitable: & consequently none of them give us the right at this moment of releasing ourselves from our treaties,

II.   A second limitation on our right of releasing ourselves is that we are to do it from so much of the treaties only as is bringing great & inevitable danger on us, & not from the residue, allowing to the other party a right at the same time to determine whether on our non-compliance with the part they will declare the whole void. This right they would have, but we should not. Vattel. 2. 202. The only part of the treaties which can really lead us into danger is the clause of guarantee. That clause is all then we could suspend in any case, and the residue will remain or not at the will of the other party.

III. A third limitation is that where a party from necessity or danger withholds compliance with part of a treaty, it is bound to make compensation where the nature of the case admits & does not dispense with it. 2. Vattel 324. Wolf. 270, 443. If actual circumstances excuse us from entering into the war under the clause of guarantee, it will be a question whether they excuse us from compensation. Our weight in the war admits of an estimate; & that estimate would form the measure of compensation.

If in withholding a compliance with any part of the treaties, we do it without just cause or compensation, we give to France a cause of war, and so become associated in it on the other side. An injured friend is the bitterest of foes, & France had not discovered either timidity, or over-much forbearance on the late occasions. Is this the position we wish to take for our constituents? It is certainly not the one they would take for themselves.

. . .

Upon the whole I conclude

That the treaties are still binding, notwithstanding the change of government in France: that no part of them, but the clause of guarantee, holds up *danger*, even at a distance.

And consequently that a liberation from no other part could be proposed in any case: that if that clause may ever bring *danger*, it is neither extreme, nor imminent, nor even probable: that the authority for renouncing a treaty, when *useless* or *disagreeable*, is either misunderstood, or in opposition to itself, to all their writers, & to every moral feeling: that were it not so, these treaties are in fact neither useless nor disagreeable.

That the receiving a Minister from France at this time is an act of no significance with respect to the treaties, amounting neither to an admission nor a denial of them, forasmuch as he comes not under any stipulation in them:

That were it an explicit admission, or were an express declaration of this obligation now to be made, it would not take from us that right which exists at all times of liberating ourselves when an adherence to the treaties would be *ruinous* or *destructive* to the society: and that the not renouncing the treaties now is so far from being a breach of neutrality, that the doing it would be the breach, by giving just cause of war to France.

2
JAY'S TREATY

The expansion of the French Revolutionary wars after 1793 brought on — as President Washington feared it might — the involvement of the United States in the affairs of Europe. The intensification of the war on the high seas, arising from the determination of Britain to use her naval power to punish and defeat France, raised the question of America's neutral rights. The United States was faced with a challenge to her right to trade with belligerent powers as custom, if not international law, allowed. Equally serious, she faced for the first time the British exercise of the right of impressment — a right which England deemed essential to her physical survival, but which the United States found a direct and potent threat to her sovereignty as a newly independent nation.

Unfortunately, these dangerous problems were complicated by other equally volatile issues. First, there was the matter of debts to English creditors. The legitimacy of many of these had been recognized in the peace treaty, but their collection had been impeded by the action of certain states. Second, there was a dispute over the drawing of the boundary in the northeast. The Treaty of 1783 had stipulated where the line should be, but because of inadequately drawn maps it was difficult, and in some instances impossible, to find accurately the rivers and heights of land named by the peace commissioners. And finally there was the case of the northwest posts. It had been stipulated in the treaty that these would be evacuated with "all deliberate speed." But for reasons which she found sufficient for herself, but not persuasive to the United States, Britain had not done so. The President chose John Jay to seek a resolution of these contentious and explosive disputes.

It is probably fair to say that Jay secured as favorable a settlement as either the power of the United States permitted or the strenuous circumstances admitted. But Jay's Treaty was violently criticized in the United States, for although it secured the withdrawal of British troops from the posts, established commissions to settle boundary disputes with Canada, and opened up a limited trade with British possessions, it failed to secure any relief from the maritime practices which so outraged American opinion.

Alexander Hamilton, writing in 1795 under the name of *Camillus*, defended the settlement and refuted the virulent criticism of it. He had, of course, a particular interest in doing so, for he had been a powerful advocate of reaching a peaceful settlement with Britain. The opposing view was put by James Madison who felt that the treaty betrayed America's interests and who believed that more skillful and less conciliatory negotiations would have secured more favorable terms.

CAMILLUS

NO. II

Alexander Hamilton

1795

Previous to a more particular discussion of the merits of the treaty, it may be useful to advert to a suggestion which has been thrown out, namely: that it was forseen by many that the mission to Great Britain would produce no good result, and that the event has corresponded with the anticipation.

The reverse of this position is manifestly true.

All must remember the very critical posture of this country at the time that mission was resolved upon. A recent violation of our rights, too flagrant and too injurious to be submitted to, had filled every American breast with indignation, and every prudent man with alarm and disquietude. A few hoped, and the great body of the community feared, that war was inevitable.

In this crisis two sets of opinion prevailed: one looked to measures which were to have a compulsory effect upon Great Britain, the sequestration of British debts, and the cutting off intercourse wholly or partially between the two countries; the other to *vigorous*

FROM *The Works of Alexander Hamilton,* Henry Cabot Lodge, ed. (New York, 1903), vol. 5, pp. 199-209.

preparations for war, and *one more effort* of negotiation, under the solemnity of an extraordinary mission, to avert it.

That the latter was the best opinion, no truly sensible man can doubt; and it may be boldly affirmed that the event has entirely justified it.

If measures of coercion and reprisal had taken place, war, in all human probability, would have followed.

National pride is generally a very untractable thing. In the councils of no country does it act with greater force than in those of Great Britain. Whatever it might have been in her power to yield to negotiation, she could have yielded nothing to compulsion, without self-degradation, and without the sacrifice of that political consequence which, at all times very important to a nation, was peculiarly so to her at the juncture in question. It should be remembered, too, that from the relations in which the two countries have stood to each other, it must have cost more to the pride of Great Britain to have received the law from us than from any other power.

When one nation has cause of complaint against another, the course marked out by practice, the opinion of writers, and the principles of humanity, the object being to avoid war, is to precede reprisals of any kind by a demand of reparation. To begin with reprisals is to meet on the ground of war, and put the other party in a condition not to be able to recede without humiliation.

Had this course been pursued by us, it would not only have rendered war morally certain, but it would have united the British nation in a vigorous support of their government in the prosecution of it; while, on our part, we should have been quickly distracted and divided. The calamities of war would have brought the most ardent to their senses, and placed them among the first in reproaching the government with precipitation, rashness, and folly for not having taken every chance, by pacific means, to avoid so great an evil.

The example of Denmark and Sweden is cited in support of the coercive plan. Those powers, it is asserted, by arming and acting with vigor, brought Great Britain to terms.

But who is able to tell us the precise course of this transaction, or the terms gained by it? Has it appeared that either Denmark or Sweden has obtained as much as we have done — a stipulation of reparation for the violation of our property, contrary to the laws of war?

Besides, what did Denmark and Sweden do? They armed, and they negotiated. They did not begin by retaliations and reprisals. The United States also armed and negotiated, and, like Denmark and Sweden, prudently forbore reprisals. The conduct of the three countries agreed in principle, equally steering clear of a precipitate resort to reprisals, and contradicting the doctrines and advice of our war party.

The course pursued by our government was, then, in coincidence with the example of Denmark and Sweden — and, it may be added, was in every view the wisest.

Few nations can have stronger inducements than the United States to cultivate peace. Their infant state in general, their want of a marine in particular, to protect their commerce, would render war, in an extreme degree, a calamity. It would not only arrest our present rapid progress to strength and prosperity, but would probably throw us back into a state of debility and impoverishment, from which it would require years to emerge.

Our trade, navigation, and mercantile capital would be essentially destroyed. Spain being an associate of Great Britain, a general Indian war might be expected to desolate the whole extent of our frontier; our exports obstructed, agriculture would of course languish; all other branches of industry would proportionately suffer; our public debt, instead of a gradual diminution, would sustain a great augmentation, and draw with it a large increase of taxes and burthens on the people.

But these evils, however great, were, perhaps, not the worst to be apprehended. It was to be feared that the war would be conducted in a spirit which would render it more than ordinarily calamitous. There are too many proofs that a considerable party among us is deeply infected with those horrid principles of Jacobinism which, proceeding from one excess to another, have made France a theatre of blood, and which, notwithstanding the most vigorous efforts of the national representation to suppress it, keeps the destinies of France, to this moment, suspended by a thread. It was too probable, that the direction of the war, if commenced, would have fallen into the hands of men of this description. The consequences of this, even in imagination, are such as to make any virtuous man shudder.

It was, therefore, in a peculiar manner, the duty of the government to take all possible chances for avoiding war. The plan adopted was the only one which could claim this advantage.

To precipitate nothing, to gain time by negotiations, was to leave the country in a situation to profit by any events which might turn up, tending to restrain a spirit of hostility to Great Britain, and to dispose her to reasonable accommodation.

The successes of France, which opportunely occurred, allowing them to have had an influence upon the issue, so far from disparaging the merit of the plan that was pursued, serve to illustrate its wisdom.

This was one of the chances which procrastination gave, and one which it was natural to take into the calculation.

Had the reverse been the case, the posture of negotiation was still preferable to that of retaliation and reprisal; for in this case, the triumphs of Great Britain, the gauntlet having been thrown by us, would have stimulated her to take it up without hesitation.

By taking the ground of negotiation in the attitude of preparation for war, we at the same time carried the appeal to the prudence of the British Cabinet, without wounding its pride, and to the justice and interest of the British nation, without exciting feelings of resentment.

This conduct was calculated to range the public opinion of that country on our side, to oppose it to the indulgence of hostile views in the Cabinet, and, in case of war, to lay the foundation of schism and dissatisfaction.

But one of the most important advantages to be expected from the course pursued, was the securing of unanimity among ourselves, if, after all the pain taken to avoid the war, it had been forced upon us.

As, on the one hand, it was certain that dissension and discontent would have embarrassed and enfeebled our exertions, in a war produced by any circumstances of intemperance in our public councils, or not endeavored to be prevented by all the milder expedients usual in similar cases; so, on the other, it was equally certain that our having effectually exhausted those expedients would cement us in a firm mass, keep us steady and persevering amidst whatever vicissitudes might happen, and nerve our efforts to the utmost extent of our resources.

This union among ourselves and disunion among our enemies were inestimable effects of the moderate plan, if it had promised no other advantage.

But to gain the time was of vast moment to us in other senses. Not a seaport of the United States was fortified, so as to be protected against the insults of a single frigate. Our magazines were, in every respect, too scantily supplied. It was highly desirable to obviate these deficiencies before matters came to extremity.

Moreover, the longer we kept out of war, if obliged to go into it at last, the shorter would be the duration of the calamities incident to it.

The circumstances of the injury of which we more immediately complain afforded an additional reason for preceding reprisals by negotiation. The order of the 6th of November directed neutral vessels to be brought in for *adjudication.* This was an equivocal phrase;

and though there was too much cause to suspect that it was intended to operate as it did, yet there was a possibility of misconstruction; and that possibility was a reason, in the nature of the thing, for giving the English Government an opportunity of explaining before retaliations took place.

To all this it may be added, that one of the substitutes for the plan pursued, the sequestration of debts, was a measure no less dishonest than impolitic; as will be shown in the remarks which will be applied to the 10th article of the treaty.

But is it unimportant to the real friends of republican government, that the plan pursued was congenial to the public character which is ascribed to it? Would it have been more desirable that the government of our nation, outstripping the war maxims of Europe, should, without a previous demand of reparation, have rushed into reprisals, and consequently into a war?

However this may be, it is a well-ascertained fact, that our country never appeared so august and respectable as in the position which it assumed upon this occasion. Europe was struck with the dignified moderation of our conduct; and the character of our government and nation acquired a new elevation.

It cannot escape an attentive observer, that the language which, in the first instance, condemned the mission of an Envoy Extraordinary to Great Britain, and which now condemns the treaty negotiated by him, seems to consider the United States as among the first-rate powers of the world in point of strength and resources, and proposes to them a conduct predicated upon that condition.

To underrate our just importance would be a degrading error. To overrate it may lead to dangerous mistakes.

A very powerful state may frequently hazard a high and haughty tone with good policy; but a weak state can scarcely ever do it without imprudence. The last is yet our character; though we are the embryo of a great empire. It is, therefore, better suited to our situation to measure each step with the utmost caution; to hazard as little as possible, in the cases in which we are injured; to blend moderation with firmness; and to brandish the weapons of hostility only when it is apparent that the use of them is unavoidable.

It is not to be inferred from this, that we are to crouch to any power on earth, or tamely to suffer our rights to be violated. A nation which is capable of this meanness will quickly have no rights to protect, or honor to defend.

But the true inference is, that we ought not lightly to seek or provoke a resort to arms; that, in the differences between us and other nations, we ought carefully to avoid measures which tend to widen the breach; and that we should scrupulously abstain from whatever may be construed into reprisals, till after the employment of all amicable means has reduced it to a certainty that there is no alternative.

If we can avoid a war for ten or twelve years more, we shall then have acquired a maturity, which will make it no more than a common calamity, and will authorize us, in our national discussions, to take a higher and more imposing tone.

This is a consideration of the greatest weight to determine us to exert all our prudence and address to keep out of war as long as it shall be possible; to defer, to a state of manhood, a struggle to which infancy is ill adapted. This is the most effectual way to disappoint the enemies of our welfare; to pursue a contrary conduct may be to play into their hands, and to gratify their wishes. If there be a foreign power which sees with envy or ill-will our growing prosperity, that power must discern that our infancy is the time for clipping our wings. We ought to be wise enough to see that this is not a time for trying our strength.

Should we be able to escape the storm which at this juncture agitates Europe, our disputes with Great Britain terminated, we may hope to postpone war to a distant period. This, at least, will greatly diminish the chances of it. For then there will remain only one power with whom we have any embarrassing discussions. I allude to Spain, and the question of the Mississippi; and there is reason to hope that this question, by the natural progress of things, and perseverance in an amicable course, will finally be arranged to our satisfaction without the necessity of the *dernier ressort.*

The allusion to this case suggests one or two important reflections. How unwise would it have been to invite or facilitate a quarrel with Great Britain at a moment when she and Spain were engaged in a common cause, both of them having, besides, controverted points with the United States! How wise will it be to adjust our differences with the most formidable of these two powers, and to have only to contest with one of them!

This policy is so obvious, that it requires an extraordinary degree of infatuation not to be sensible of it, and not to view with favor any measure which tends to so important a result.

This cursory view of the motives which may be supposed to have governed our public councils in the mission to Great Britain, serves not only to vindicate the measures then pursued, but warns us against a prejudiced judgment of the result, which may, in the end, defeat the salutary purposes of those measures.

I proceed now to observe summarily that the objects of the

mission, contrary to what has been asserted have been substantially obtained. What were these? They were principally:

1. To adjust the matters of controversy concerning the inexecution of the treaty of peace, and especially to obtain restitution of our Western posts.

2. To obtain reparation for the captures and spoilations of our property in the course of the existing war.

Both these objects have been provided for, and it will be shown, when we come to comment upon the articles which make the provisions in each case, that it is a reasonable one, as good a one as ought to have been expected; as good a one as there is any prospect of obtaining hereafter; one which it is consistent with our honor to accept, and which our interest bids us to close with.

The provisions with regard to commerce were incidental and auxiliary. The reasons which may be conceived to have led to the including of the subject in the mission will be discussed in some proper place.

ON JAY'S TREATY

MADISON TO – –

James
Madison

Orange, August 23, 1795

Dear Sir,

— Your favor of the 3d instant did not come to hand till a few days ago, having been probably retarded by the difficulty the post met with in passing the water-courses, which have been much swelled of late by excessive rains. It gives me much pleasure to learn that your health has been so much improved, as well as that you are taking advantage of it to co-operate in elucidating the great subject before the public. We see here few of the publications relating to it, except those which issue from meetings of the people, and which are of course republished everywhere. The only Philadelphia paper that comes to me is the Aurora, which, besides frequent miscarriages, is not, I find, the vehicle used by the regular champions

FROM *The Writings of James Madison,* Gaillard Hunt, ed. (New York, 1906), vol. 6, pp. 238-57.

on either side. I have occasionally seen Dunlap's, and in that some
specimens of the Display of the "Features, etc." I wish much to see the whole of it. Your obliging promise to forward it, along with any other things of the kind, will have a good opportunity by the return of Mr. Wilson Nicholas, who is on his way to Philadelphia, and will call on me on his way home. I requested the favour of him to apprize you of the opportunity. I am glad to find that the author of the "Features, etc." meditates a similar operation on "The Defence of the Treaty, by Camillus," who, if I mistake not, will be betrayed by his Anglomany into arguments as vicious and as vulnerable as the Treaty itself. The Resolutions of the Chamber of Commerce in New York justify this anticipation. What can be more absurd than to talk of the advantage of securing the *privileges* of sending raw materials to a manufacturing nation, and of buying merchandizes which are hawked over the four quarters of the globe for customers? To say that we must take the Treaty or be punished with hostilities, is something still worse. By the way, it is curious to compare the language of the author and abettors of the Treaty with that held on the subject of our commercial importance, when the Constitution was depending. Jay himself could then view its adoption as the only thing necessary to extort the Posts, etc., and *open the West India Ports.* (See his address to the people of New York in the Museum). The Federalist (No. XI) will exhibit a still more striking contrast on this point in another quarter. You intimate a wish that I would suggest any ideas in relation to the Treaty that may occur to my reflections. In my present sequestered situation, I am too little possessed of the particular turns of the controversy to be able to adapt remarks to them. In general, I think it of importance to avoid laying too much stress on minute or doubtful objections, which may give an occasion to the other party to divert the public attention from the palpable and decisive ones, and to involve the question in uncertainty, if not to claim an apparent victory. The characteristics of the Treaty which I have wished to see more fully laid open to the public view are:

1. Its ruinous tendency with respect to the carrying trade. The increase of our shipping under the new Government has, in most Legislative discussions, been chiefly ascribed to the advantage given to American vessels by the difference of 10 per cent. on the impost in their favor. This, in the valuable cargoes from Great Britain, has been sufficient to check the preference of British Merchants for British bottoms; and it has not been deemed safe hitherto by Great Britain to force on a contest with us in

this particular by any countervailing regulations. In consequence of the Treaty, she will no doubt establish such regulations, and thereby leave the British capital free to prefer British vessels. This will not fail to banish our tonnage from the trade with that country. And there seems to have been no disposition in the negociator to do better for our navigation in the West India trade; especially if the exclusion of our vessels from the re-exportation of the enumerated articles, Sugar, Coffee, etc., be taken into account. The nature of our exports and imports, compared with that of the British, is a sufficient, but at the same time our only defence against the superiority of her capital. The advantage they give us in fostering our navigation ought never to have been abandoned. If this view of the subject be just, and were presented to the public with mercantile skill, it could not fail to make a deep impression on New England. In fact, the whole Treaty appears to me to assassinate the interest of that part of the Union.

2. The insidious hostility of the Treaty to France, in general; but particularly the operation of the 15th article, which, as far as I have seen, has been but faintly touched on, though it be, in fact, pregnant with more mischief than any of them. According to all our other Treaties, as well as those of all other nations, the footing of the most favored nations is so qualified that those entitled to it must pay the price of any particular privilege that may be granted in a new Treaty. The Treaty of Jay makes every new privilege result to Great Britain, without her paying any price at all. Should France, Spain, Portugal, or any other nation, offer the most precious privileges in their trade, as the price of some particular favor in ours, no bargain could be made unless they would agree not only to let the same favor be extended to Great Britain, but extended gratuitously. They could not purchase for themselves without at the same time purchasing for their rival. In this point of view, the 15th article may be considered as a direct bar to our treating with other nations, and particularly with the French Republic. Much has been said of a suspected backwardness to improve our commercial arrangements with France, and a predilection for arrangements with Great Britain, who had less to give, as well as less inclination to give what she had. It was hardly imagined that we were so soon to grant every thing to Great Britain for nothing in return; and to make it a part of this bad bargain with her, that we should not be able to make a good one with any other nation.

3. The spirit in which every point of the law of nations is regulated. It is the interest of the United States to enlarge the rights of neutral nations. It is the general interest of humanity that this should be done. In all our other Treaties this policy has prevailed. The same policy has pervaded most of the modern Treaties of other nations. Great Britain herself has been forced into it in several of her Treaties. In the Treaty of Jay, every principle of liberality, every consideration of interest, has been sacrificed to the arbitrary maxims which govern the policy of Great Britain. Nay, a new principle has been created, in the face of former complaints of our Executive, as well as against the fundamental rights of nations and duties of humanity, for the purpose of aiding the horrible scheme of starving a whole people out of their liberties.

I. Even waiving the merits of the respective complaints and pretensions of the two parties, as to the inexecution of the Treaty of peace, the waiver implies that the two parties were to be viewed either as equally culpable or equally blameless; and that the execution of the Treaty of peace equally by both ought now to be provided for. Yet, whilst the United States are to comply in the most ample manner with the article unfulfilled by them, and to make compensation for whatever losses may have accrued from the delay, Great Britain is released altogether from one of the articles unfulfilled by her, and is not to make the smallest compensation for the damages which have accrued from her delay to execute the other.

The inequality of these terms is still further increased by concessions on the part of the United States, which, besides adding to the Constitutional difficulties unnecessarily scattered through the Treaty, may, in a great measure, defeat the good consequences of a surrender of the Western posts.

The British settlers and traders, within an undefined Tract of Country, are allowed to retain both their lands and their allegiance at the same time; and, consequently, to keep up a foreign and unfriendly influence over the Indians within the limits of the United States.

The Indians within those limits are encouraged to continue their trade with the British by the permission to bring their goods duty free from Canada, where the goods, being charged with no such impost as is payable on the goods of the United States, will be offered for sale with that tempting preference; a regulation but too likely, also, to cloak the frauds of smuggling traders in a country favorable to them. The reciprocity in this case is ostensible only, and fallacious.

Under another ostensible and fallacious reciprocity, the advantage secured to the United States, in the fur trade, by their possession of the carrying places, is abandoned to the superiority of British capital, and the inferiority of the Canada duties on imports.

A part only of the Ports, harbours, and bays, of a single British Province, is made free to the United States, in consideration of a freedom of all the ports, harbors, and bays, of the whole United States. The goods and merchandize of the United States, not entirely prohibited by Canada, (but which, in fact, are always entirely prohibited, when partial and temporary admissions are not dictated by necessity,) may be carried there, in consideration of a free admission of all goods and merchandize from Canada, not entirely prohibited by the U. States, (where, in fact, there never is this entire prohibition.) A like stipulation, liable to the like observations, is extended to the exports of the United States and the Province of Canada. These are further instances of a nominal and delusive reciprocity.

In the case of the Mississippi, there is not even an ostensible or nominal, reciprocity. The ports and places on its Eastern side are to be equally free to both the parties; although the Treaty itself supposes that the course of the Northern Boundary of the United States will throw the British beyond the very source of that river. This item of the Treaty is the more to be noticed, as a repetition and extension of the stipulated privileges of Great Britain on the Mississippi will probably be construed into a partiality in the United States to the interests and views of that nation on the American Continent, not likely to conciliate those from whom an amicable adjustment of the navigation of the Mississippi is to be expected; and were no doubt intended by Great Britain as a snare to our good understanding with the nations most jealous of her encroachments and her aggrandizement.

II. Without remarking on the explicit provision for redressing past spoliations and vexations, no sufficient precautions are taken against them in future. On the contrary,

By omitting to provide for the respect due to sea letters, passports, and certificates, and for other customary safeguards to neutral vessels, "a general search-warrant, (in the strong but just language of our fellow Citizens of Charlestown) is granted against the American navigation." Examples of such provisions were to be found in our other Treaties, as well as in the Treaties of other nations. And it is matter of just surprise that they should have no place in a Treaty with Great Britain, whose conduct on the seas so particularly suggested and enforced every guard to our rights that could reasonably be insisted on.

By omitting to provide against the arbitrary seizure and impressment of American seamen, that valuable class of Citizens remains exposed to all the outrages, and our commerce to all the interruptions, hitherto suffered from that cause.

By expressly admitting that provisions are to be held contraband in cases other than when bound to an invested place, and impliedly admitting that such cases exist at present, not only a retrospective sanction may be given to proceedings against which indemnification is claimed, but an apparent license is granted to fresh and more rapacious depredations on our lawful commerce. And facts seem to show that such is to be the fruit of the impolitic concession. It is conceived that the pretext set up by Great Britain, of besieging and starving whole nations, and the doctrine grounded thereon, of a right to intercept the customary trade of neutral nations in articles not contraband, ought never to have been admitted into a Treaty of the United States; because —

1. It is a general outrage on humanity, and an attack on the useful intercourse of nations.
2. It appears that the doctrine was denied by the Executive in the discussions with Mr. Hammond, the British Minister, and demands of compensation founded on that denial are now depending.
3. As provisions constitute not less than __% of our exports, and as Great Britain is nearly half her time at war, an admission of the doctrine sacrifices a correspondent proportion of the value of our commerce.
4. After a public denial of the doctrine, to admit it, in the midst of the present war, by a formal Treaty, would have but too much of the effect, as well as the appearance, of voluntarily concurring in the scheme of distressing a nation in friendship with this Country, and whose relations to it, as well as the struggles for freedom in which they are engaged, give them a title to every good office not strictly forbidden by the duties of neutrality.
5. It is no plea for the measure to hold it up as an alternative to the disgrace of being involuntarily treated in the same manner, without a faculty to redress ourselves; the disgrace of being plundered with impunity against our consent being, under no circumstances, greater than the disgrace of consenting to be plundered with impunity; more especially as the calamity in the former case might not happen in another

war; whereas, in the latter case, it is bound upon us for as much as twelve years as there may be of war within that period.

By annexing to the implements of war, enumerated as contraband, the articles of ship-timber, tar, or rosin, copper in sheets, sails, hemp, and cordage, our neutral rights and national interests are still further narrowed. These articles were excluded by the United States from the contraband list when they were themselves in a state of war.* Their other Treaties expressly declare them not to be contraband. British Treaties have done the same. Nor, as is believed, do the Treaties of any nation in Europe, producing these articles for exportation, allow them to be subjects of confiscation. The stipulation was the less to be admitted, as the reciprocity assumed by it is a mere cover for the violation of that principle; most of the articles in question being among the exports of the United States, whilst all of them are among the imports of Great Britain.

By expressly stipulating with Great Britain against the freedom of enemy's property in neutral bottoms, the progress towards a compleat and formal establishment of a principle in the law of nations so favorable to the general interest and security of commerce receives all the check the United States could give to it. Reason and experience have long taught the propriety of considering free ships as giving freedom to their cargoes. The several great maritime nations of Europe have not only established it at different times by their Treaties with each other, but on a solemn occasion (the armed neutrality) jointly declared it to be the law of nations by a specific compact, of which the United States entered their entire approbation. Great Britain alone dissented. But she herself, in a variety of prior Treaties, and in a Treaty with France since, (1786), has acceded to the principle. Under these circumstances, the United States, of all nations, ought to be the last to unite in a retrograde effort on this subject, as being more than any other interested in extending and establishing the commercial rights of neutral nations. Their situation particularly fits them to be carriers for the great nations of Europe during their wars. And both their situation and the genius of their Government and people promise them a greater share of peace and neutrality than can be expected by any other nation. The relation of the United States by Treaty on this point to the enemies of Great Britain was another reason for avoiding the stipulation. Whilst British goods in American vessels are pro-

* See Ordinance regulating captures in 1781.

tected against French and Dutch capture, it was enough to leave French and Dutch goods in American vessels to the ordinary course of Judicial determinations, without a voluntary, a positive, and an invidious provision for condemning them. It has not been overlooked, that a clause in the Treaty proposes to renew, at some future period, the discussion of the principle it now settles; but the question is then to be, not only in what, but whether in any cases, neutral vessels shall protect enemy's property; and it is to be discussed at the same time, not whether in any, but in what cases, provisions and other articles, not bound to invested places, may be treated as contraband. So that when the principle is in favor of the United States, the principle itself is to be the subject of discussion; when the principle is in favor of Great Britain, the application of it only is to be the subject discussion.

III.   Whenever the law of nations comes into question, the result of the Treaty accommodates Great Britain in relation to one or both of the Republics at war with her, as well as in diminution of the rights and interests of the United States.

Thus, American vessels bound to Great Britain are protected by sea papers against French or Dutch searches; bound to France or Holland, are left exposed to British searches, without regard to such papers.

British property in American vessels is not subject to French or Dutch confiscation. French or Dutch property in American vessels is subjected to British confiscation.

American provisions in American vessels, bound to the enemies of Great Britain, are left by Treaty to the seizure and use of Great Britain; provisions, whether American or not, in American vessels, cannot be touched by the enemies of Great Britain.

Timber for ship-building, tar, or rosin, copper in sheets, sails, hemp, and cordage, bound to the enemies of Great Britain, for the equipment of vessels of trade only, are contraband; bound to Great Britain for the equipment of vessels of war, are not contraband.

American citizens, entering, as volunteers, the service of France or Holland against Great Britain, are to be punished. American volunteers joining the arms of Great Britain against France or Holland are not punishable.

British ships of war and privateers, with their prizes made on Citizens of Holland, may freely enter and depart the ports of the United States. Dutch ships of war and privateers, with their prizes made on subjects of Great Britain, are to receive no shelter or refuge in the ports of the United States. And this advantage in war is given to Great Britain, not by a Treaty prior, and having no relation, to an existing war, but by a Treaty made in the midst of war, and prohibiting a like article of Treaty with Holland for equalizing the advantage.

The article prohibiting confiscations and sequestrations is unequal between the United States and Great Britain. American Citizens have little, if any, interest in public or bank Stock, or in private debts within Great Britain. British subjects have a great interest in all within the United States. Vessels and merchandize belonging to individuals, governed by the same "confidence in each other, and in regard to their respective Governments for their municipal laws, and for the laws of nations allowed to be part thereof as consecrates private debts," are not exempted from such proceedings. So that, where much would be in the power of the United States, and little in the power of Great Britain, the power is interdicted. Where more is in the power of Great Britain than of the United States, the power is left unconfined. Another remark is applicable. When the modern usage of nations is in favor of Great Britain, the modern usage is the rule of the Treaty. When the modern usage was in favor of the United States, the modern usage was rejected as a rule for the Treaty.

IV. The footing on which the Treaty places the subject of Commerce is liable to insuperable objections.

1. The nature of our exports and imports, compared with those of other Countries, and particularly of Great Britain, has been thought by the Legislature of the United States to justify certain differences in the tonnage and other duties in favor of American bottoms; and the advantage possessed by Great Britain in her superior capital was thought at the same time to require such countervailing encouragements. Experience has shown the solidity of both these considerations. The American navigation has, in a degree, been protected against the advantage on the side of British capital, and has increased in proportion; whilst the nature of our exports, being generally necessaries or raw materials, and of our imports, consisting mostly of British manufactures, has restrained Great Britain from any attempt to counteract the protecting duties afforded to our navigation. Should the Treaty go into effect, this protection is relinquished; Congress are prohibited from substituting any other; and the British capital, having no

longer the present inducement to make use of American bottoms, may be expected, *through whatever hands operating,* to give the preference to British bottoms.

2. The provisions of the Treaty which relate to the West Indies, where the nature of our exports and imports gives a commanding energy to our just pretensions, instead of alleviating the general evil, are a detail of peculiar humiliations and sacrifices. Nor is a remedy by any means to be found in the proposed suspension of that part of the Treaty. On the contrary,

If Great Britain should accede to the proposition, and the Treaty be finally established without the twelfth article, she will, in that event, be able to exclude American bottoms altogether from that channel of intercourse, and to regulate the whole trade with the West Indies in the manner hitherto complained of; whilst, by another article of the Treaty, the United States are completely dispossessed of the right and the means hitherto enjoyed of counteracting the monopoly, unless they submit to a universal infraction of their trade, not excepting with nations whose regulations may be reciprocal and satisfactory.

3. The Treaty, not content with these injuries to the United States in their commerce with Great Britain, provides, in the XV article, against the improvement or preservation of their commerce with other nations, by any beneficial Treaties that may be attainable. The general rule of the United States in their Treaties, founded on the example of other nations, has been, that where a nation is to have the privileges that may be granted to the most favored nations, it should be admitted gratuitously to such privileges only as are gratuitously granted; but should pay for privileges not gratuitously granted the compensations paid for them by others. This prudent and equitable qualification of the footing of the most favored nation was particularly requisite in a Treaty with Great Britain, whose commercial system, being matured and settled, is not likely to be materially varied by grants of new privileges that might result to the United States. It was particularly requisite at the present juncture, also, when an advantageous revision of the Treaty with France is said to be favored by that Republic, when a Treaty with Spain is actually in negotiation, and Treaties with other nations whose commerce is important to the United States cannot be out

of contemplation. The proposed Treaty, nevertheless, puts Great Britain in all respects, *gratuitously*, on the footing of the most favored nation; even as to future privileges, for which the most valuable considerations may be given. So that it is not only out of the power of the United States to grant any peculiar privilege to any other nation, as an equivalent for peculiar advantages in commerce or navigation to be granted to the United States; but every nation desiring to treat on this subject with the United States is reduced to the alternative, either of declining the Treaty altogether, or of including Great Britain *gratuitously*, in all the privileges it purchases for itself. An article of this import is the greatest obstacle, next to an absolute prohibition, that could have been thrown in the way of other Treaties; and that it was insidiously meant by Great Britain to be such is rendered the less doubtful by the other kindred features visible in the Treaty.

It can be no apology for these commerical disadvantages that better terms could not be obtained at the crisis when the Treaty was settled. If proper terms could not be obtained at that time, commercial stipulations, which were no wise essentially connected with the objects of the Envoyship, ought to have waited for a more favorable season. Nor is a better apology to be drawn from our other Treaties. The chief of these were the auxiliaries or the guaranties of our independence, and would have been an equivalent for greater commerical concessions than were insisted on. (Under other circumstances, there is no ground to suppose that the same treaties, though more favorable in several material articles than the Treaty in question, would have been embraced by the United States.)

V.   A Treaty thus unequal in its conditions, thus derogatory to our national rights, thus insidious in some of its objects, and thus alarming in its operation to the dearest interests of the United States in their commerce and navigation, is, in its present form, unworthy the voluntary acceptance of an Independent people, and is not dictated to them by the circumstances in which Providence has kindly placed them. It is sincerely believed that such a Treaty would not have been listened to at any former period when Great Britain was most at her ease, and the United States without the respectability they now enjoy. To pretend that, however injurious the Treaty may be, it ought to be submitted to in order to avoid the hostile resentment of Great Britain, which would evidently be as impolitic as it would be unjust on her part, is an artifice too contemptible to answer its purpose. It will not easily be supposed that a refusal to part with our rights without an equivalent will be made the pretext of a war on us; much less that such a pretext will be founded on our refusal to mingle a sacrifice of our commerce and navigation with an adjustment of political differences. Nor is any evidence to be found, either in History or Human nature, that nations are to be bribed out of a spirit of encroachment and aggressions by humiliations which nourish their pride, or by concessions which extend their resources and power.

To do justice to all nations; to seek it from them by peaceable means in preference to war; and to confide in this policy for avoiding that extremity, or securing the blessing of Heaven when forced upon us, is the only course of which the United States can never have reason to repent.

3

A PLEA FOR NEUTRALITY

The pressures which Washington found himself under as President were unending and exacting. While Jay's Treaty had removed some of the disputes which were dividing Britain and the United States, it did not settle all of them. And it had served to anger France which too often assumed that the United States should act in accordance with the views of Paris rather than the interests of Washington. The intolerable conduct of Genêt, the French minister to the United States, had exceeded all the bounds of diplomatic behavior. After his depature from the scene his immediate successor, Joseph Fauchet, behaved in a manner less offensive, but equally calculated to damage the United States, for he did his best to ensure that Jay's Treaty would be rejected by the United States. Pierre Adet, the next French minister, was as assiduous in his interference in American affairs as those who had gone before him for he tried not only to arouse the general public against the treaty, but he also intrigued with members of the House of Representatives to deny the government the funds necessary to implement certain articles of Jay's Treaty.

It was in this atmosphere of tension and turbulence that President Washington drew up his Farewell Address. It was not delivered as a speech, but rather first appeared on September 17, 1796 in a newspaper. In it the President warned against the growth of violent partisan spirit and cautioned the nation against entering into permanent foreign alliances. He did not call for the isolation of the United States from all foreign affairs, for that would have been as unattainable as it would have been foolish. He did want a policy of noninvolvement so that the United States could enjoy the fruits of its independence and the joys of its liberty.

49

FAREWELL ADDRESS

George
Washington

FRIENDS AND FELLOW CITIZENS

The period for a new election of a citizen to administer the Executive Government of the United States being not far distant, and the time actually arrived when your thoughts must be employed in designating the person who is to be clothed with that important trust, it appears to me proper, especially as it may conduce to a more distinct expression of the public voice, that I should now apprise you of the resolution I have formed, to decline being considered among the number of those out of whom a choice is to be made.

I beg you, at the same time, to do me the justice to be assured, that this resolution has not been taken without a strict regard to all the considerations appertaining to the relation which binds a dutiful citizen to his country; and that, in withdrawing the tender of service, which silence, in my situation, might imply, I am influenced by no diminution of zeal for your future interest; no deficiency of grateful respect for your past kindness; but am supported by a full conviction that the step is compatible with both.

The acceptance of, and continuance hitherto in, the office to which your sufferages have twice called me, have been a uniform sacrifice of inclination to the opinion of duty, and to a deference for what appeared to be your desire. I constantly hoped, that it would have been much earlier in my power, consistently with motives which I was not at liberty to disregard, to return to that retirement from which I had been reluctantly drawn. The strength of my inclination to do this, previous to the last election, had led to the preparation of an address to declare it to you; but mature reflection on the then perplexed and critical posture of our affairs with foreign nations, and the unanimous advice of persons entitled to my confidence, impelled me to abandon the idea.

I rejoice that the state of your concerns, external as well as internal, no longer renders the pursuit of inclination incompatible with the sentiment of duty or propriety; and am persuaded, whatever partiality may be retained for my services, that, in the present circumstances of our country, you will not disapprove my determination to retire.

The impressions with which I first undertook the arduous trust, were explained on the proper occasion. In the discharge of this trust,

FROM *American State Papers,* Foreign Relations, vol. 1, pp. 34–8.

I will only say, that I have with good intentions contributed toward the organization and administration of the Government the best exertions of which a very fallible judgment was capable. Not unconscious, in the outset, of the inferiority of my qualifications, experience in my own eyes, perhaps still more in the eyes of others, has strengthened the motives to diffidence of myself; and every day the increasing weight of years admonishes me more and more that the shades of retirement is as necessary to me as it will be welcome. Satisfied that, if any circumstances have given peculiar value to my services, they were temporary, I have the consolation to believe, that, while choice and prudence invite me to quit the political scene, patriotism does not forbid it.

In looking forward to the moment which is intended to terminate the career of my public life, my feelings do not permit me to suspend the deep acknowledgement of that debt of gratitude which I owe to my beloved country, for the many honors it has conferred upon me; still more for the steadfast confidence with which it has supported me; and for the opportunities I have thence enjoyed of manifesting my inviolable attachment, by services faithful and persevering, though in usefulness unequal to my zeal. If benefits have resulted to our country from these services, let it always be remembered to your praise, and as an instructive example in our annals, that, under circumstances in which the passions, agitated in every direction, were liable to mislead; amidst appearances sometimes dubious; vicissitudes of fortune often discouraging; in situations in which not unfrequently want of success has countenanced the spirit of criticism; the constancy of your support was the essential prop of the efforts and a guarantee of the plans by which they were effected. Profoundly penetrated with this idea, I shall carry it with me to my grave, as a strong incitement to unceasing vows, that Heaven may continue to you the choicest token of its beneficence; that your union and brotherly affection may be perpetual; that the free constitution, which is the work of your hands, may be sacredly maintained; that its administration, in every department, may be stamped with wisdom and virtue; that in fine the happiness of the People of these States, under the auspices of liberty, may be made complete, by so careful a preservation, and so prudent a use of this blessing, as will acquire to them the glory of recommending it to the applause, the affection, and the adoption, of every nation which is yet a stranger to it.

Here, perhaps, I ought to stop: but a solicitude for your welfare, which cannot end with my life, and the apprehension of danger, natural to that solicitude, urge me, on an occasion like the present, to offer to your solemn contemplation, and to recommend to your frequent review, some sentiments, which are the result of much reflection, of no inconsiderable observation, and which appear to me all important to the permanency of your felicity as a people. These will be afforded to you with the more freedom, as you can only see in them the disinterested warnings of a parting friend, who can possibly have no personal motive to bias his counsel: nor can I forget, as an encouragement to it, your indulgent reception of my sentiments on a former and not dissimilar occasion.

Interwoven as is the love of liberty with every ligament of your hearts, no recommendation of mine is necessary to fortify or confirm the attachment.

The unity of government, which constitutes you one people, is also now dear to you. It is justly so: for it is a main pillar in the edifice of your real independence; the support of your tranquillity at home; your peace abroad; of your safety; of your prosperity; of that very liberty which you so highly prize. But as it is easy to forsee, that, from different causes and from different quarters, much pains will be taken, many artifices employed, to weaken, in your minds, the conviction of this truth; as this is the point in your political fortress against which the batteries of internal and external enemies will be most constantly and actively (though often covertly and insidiously) directed, it is of infinite moment, that you should properly estimate the immense value of your national union to your collective and individual happiness; that you should cherish a cordial, habitual, and immoveable attachment to it; accustoming yourselves to think and speak of it as of the palladium of your political safety and prosperity; watching for its preservation with jealous anxiety; discountenancing whatever may suggest even a suspicion that it can in any event be abandoned; and indignantly frowning upon the first dawning of every attempt to alienate any portion of our country from the rest, or to enfeeble the sacred ties which now link together the various parts.

．　．　．

Observe good faith and justice towards all nations; cultivate peace and harmony with all. Religion and morality enjoin this conduct: and can it be that good policy does not equally enjoin it? It will be a worthy of a free, enlightened, and, at no distant period, a great nation, to give to mankind the magnanimous and too novel example of a people always guided by an exalted justice and benevolence. Who can doubt that, in the course of time and things, the fruits of such a plan would richly repay any temporary advantages which might be lost by a steady adherence to it? Can it be, that Providence has not connected the permanent felicity of a nation with its virtue? The experiment, at least, is recommended by every sentiment which enobles human nature. Alas! is it rendered impossible by its vices?

In the execution of such a plan, nothing is more essential than that permanent inveterate antipathies against particular nations, and passionate attachment for others, should be excluded; and that, in place of them, just and amicable feelings towards all should be cultivated. The nation which indulges towards another an habitual hatred, or an habitual fondness, is, in some degree, a slave. It is a slave to its animosity or to its affection, either of which is sufficient to lead it astray from its duty and its interest. Antipathy in one nation against another, disposes each more readily to offer insult and injury, to lay hold of slight causes of umbrage, and to be haughty and intractable, when accidental or trifling occasions of dispute occur. Hence frequent collisions; obstinate, envenomed, and bloody contests. The nation, prompted by ill-will and resentment, sometimes impels to war the government, and bloody the best calculations of policy. The government sometimes participates in the national prosperity, and adopts, through passion, what reason would reject; at other times, it makes the animosity of the nation subservient to projects of hostility, instigated by pride, ambition, and other sinister and pernicious motives. The peace, often, sometimes, perhaps, the liberty of nations has been the victim.

So, likewise, a passionate attachment of one nation to another produces a variety of evils. Sympathy for the favorite nation, facilitating the illusion of an imaginary common interest, in cases where no real common interest exists, and infusing into one the enmities of the other, betrays the former into a participation in the quarrels and wars of the latter, without adequate inducement or justification. It leads also to concessions to the favorite nation of privileges denied to others, which is apt doubly to injure the nation making the concessions; by unnecessarily parting with what ought to have been retained, and by exciting jealousy, ill-will, and a disposition to retaliate, in the parties from whom equal privileges are withheld: and it gives to ambitious, corrupted, or deluded citizens (who devote themselves to the favorite nation) facility to betray or sacrifice the interest of their own country, without odium, sometimes even with popularity; gilding with the appearances of a virtuous sense of obligation, a commendable deference for public opinion, or a laudable zeal for public good, the base or foolish compliance of ambition, corruption, or infatuation.

As avenues to foreign influence in innumerable ways, such attachments are particularly alarming to the truly enlightened and independent patriot. How many opportunities do they afford to tamper with domestic factions, to practice the art of seduction, to mislead public opinion, to influence or awe the public councils! Such an attachment of a small or weak, towards a great and powerful nation, dooms the former to be the satellite of the latter.

Against the insidious wiles of foreign influence (I conjure you to believe me fellow-citizens) the jealousy of a free people ought to be *constantly* awake; since history and experience prove that foreign influence is one of the most baneful foes of republican government. But that jealousy, to be useful, must be impartial; else it becomes the instrument of the very influence to be avoided, instead of a defence against it. Excessive partiality for one foreign nation, and excessive dislike for another, cause those whom they actuate to see danger only on one side, and serve to veil and even second the arts of influence on the other. Real patriots, who may resist the intrigues of the favorite, are liable to become suspected and odious; while its tools and dupes usurp the applause and confidence of the people, to surrender their interests.

The great rule of conduct for us, in regard to foreign nations, is, in extending our commercial relations, to have with them as little political connexion as possible. So far as we have already formed engagements, let them be fulfilled with perfect good faith. Here let us stop.

Europe has a set of primary interests, which to us have none, or a very remote relation. Hence she must be engaged in frequent controversies, the cause of which are essentially foreign to our concern. Hence, therefore, it must be unwise in us to implicate ourselves, by artificial ties, in the ordinary vicissitudes of her politics, or the ordinary combinations and collisions of her friendships or enmities.

Our detached and distant situation invites, and enables us to pursue, a different course. If we remain one people, under an efficient government, the period is not far off when we may defy material injury from external annoyance; when we may take such an attitude as will cause the neutrality we may at any time resolve upon, to be scrupulously respected; when belligerent nations, under the impossibility of making acquisitions upon us, will not lightly hazard the giving us provocation; when we may choose peace or war, as our interest, guided by justice, shall counsel.

Why forego the advantages of so peculiar a situation? Why quit our own, to stand upon foreign ground? Why, by interweaving our destiny with that of any part of Europe, entangle our peace and prosperity in the toils of European ambition, rivalship, interest, humor, or caprice?

'Tis our true policy to steer clear of permanent alliances with any portion of the foreign world — so far, I mean, as we are now at liberty to do it: for let me not be understood as capable of patronising infidelity to existing engagements. I hold the maxim no less applicable to public than to private affairs, that honesty is always the best policy. I repeat it, therefore, let those engagements be observed in their genuine sense. But, in my opinion, it is unnecessary, and would be unwise, to extend them.

Taking care always to keep ourselves, by suitable establishments, on a respectable defensive posture, we may safely trust to temporary alliances for extraordinary emergencies.

Harmony, and a liberal intercourse with all nations, are recommended by policy, humanity, and interest. But even our commercial policy should hold an equal and impartial hand; neither seeking nor granting exclusive favors or preferences; consulting the natural course of things; diffusing and diversifying, by gentle means, the streams of commerce, but forcing nothing; establishing with Powers so disposed, in order to give trade a stable course, to define the rights of our merchants, and enable the Government to support them, conventional rules of intercourse, the best that present circumstances and mutual opinion will permit, but temporary, and liable to be, from time to time, abandoned or varied, as experience and circumstances shall dictate; constantly keeping in view, that 'tis folly in one nation to look for disinterested favors from another; that it must pay with a portion of its independence for whatever it may accept under that character; that by such acceptance it may place itself in the condition of having given equivalents for nominal favors, and yet with being reproached with ingratitude for not giving more. There can be no greater error than to expect or calculate upon real favors from nation to nation. 'Tis all illusion, which experience must cure — which a just pride ought to discard.

In offering to you, my countrymen, these counsels of an old and affectionate friend, I dare not hope they will make the strong and lasting impression I could wish; that they will control the usual current of the passions, or prevent our nation from running the course which has hitherto marked the destiny of nations: but if I may even flatter myself that they may be productive of some partial benefit, some occasional good; that they may now and then recur to moderate the fury of party spirit, to warn against the mischiefs of foreign intrigues, to guard against the impostures of pretended patriotism; this hope will be a full recompense for the solicitude for your welfare by which they have been dictated.

How far, in the discharge of my official duties, I have been guided by the principles which have been delineated, the public records and other evidences of my conduct must witness to you and to the world. To myself, the assurance of my own conscience is, that I have at least believed myself to be guided by them.

In relation to the still subsisting war in Europe, my proclamation of the 22d of April, 1793, is the index to my plan. Sanctioned by your approving voice, and by that of your Representatives in both Houses of Congress, the spirit of that measure has continually governed me, uninfluenced by any attempts to deter or divert me from it.

After deliberate examination, with the aid of the best lights I could obtain, I was well satisfied that our country, under all circumstances of the case, had a right to take, and was bound in duty and interest to take, a neutral position. Having taken it, I determined, as far as should depend upon me, to maintain it with moderation, perseverance, and firmness.

The consideration which respect the right to hold this conduct, it is not necessary on this occasion to detail. I will only observe, that, according to my understanding of the matter, that right, so far from being denied by any of the belligerent Powers, has been virtually admitted by all.

The duty of holding a neutral conduct may be inferred, without any thing more, from the obligation which justice and humanity imposes on every nation, in cases, in which it is free to act, to maintain inviolate the relations of peace and amity towards other nations.

The inducements of interest, for observing the conduct, will best be referred to your own reflections and experience. With me a predominant motive has been to endeavor to gain time to our country to settle and mature its yet recent institutions; and to progress, without interruption, to that degree of strength and consistency, which is necessary to give it, humanly speaking, the command of its own fortunes.

Though in reviewing the incidents of my administration, I am unconscious of intentional error, I am nevertheless too sensible of my defects, not to think it probable that I may have committed many errors. Whatever they may be, I fervently beseech the Almighty to avert or mitigate the evils to which they may tend. I shall also carry with me the hope that my country will never cease to view them with indulgence; and that, after forty-five years of my life dedicated to its service, with an upright zeal, the faults of incompetent abilities will be consigned to oblivion, as myself must soon be to the mansions of rest.

Relying on its kindness in this as in other things, and actuated by that fervent love towards it which is so natural to a man, who views in it the native soil of himself and his progenitors for several generations; I anticipate, with pleasing expectations, in that retreat, in which I promise myself to realize, without alloy, the sweet enjoyment of partaking, in the midst of my fellow-citizens, the benign influence of good laws under a free government — the ever favorite object of my heart; and the happy reward, as I trust, of our mutual cares, labors, and dangers.

GEO. WASHINGTON

United States, 17th September, 1796

4

THE UNDECLARED WAR WITH FRANCE

 The years from 1797 to 1801 have been called a period of "quasi-war" with France. Certainly the strains upon Franco-American relations in this short span of time have seldom been matched in the history of the two countries. The French reaction to the negotiating and ratification of Jay's Treaty was as intemperate as it was ill-judged, for it was based upon the assumption that the United States should support France in its disputes with other nations. James Monroe, the American minister to Paris, did little to ease tensions and his open advocacy of French interests led to his recall to America.

By 1797, too, the war had reached a new level of violence. In the period from July 1796 to June 1797, French privateers had seized over three hundred American merchant ships and generally treated the rights of the United States in a cavalier fashion.

For example, the XYZ affair had shown both a contempt for diplomatic usage and international custom. President Adams had appointed three commissioners to negotiate with France in order to avoid a disastrous war with that nation. However, the Americans were approached by three agents who clearly represented Talleyrand, the French Minister of Foreign Affairs, and informed them that before diplomatic discussions could take place the United States would have to apologize to France for her behavior and pay a substantial bribe. This impertinent demand was quite properly rejected out of hand, but news of the affair aroused deep and passionate resentment in the United States. Indeed, when John Adams published the correspondence surrounding this extraordinary incident, it appeared that the President was preparing the nation for war. However, like his predecessor in office, he soon realized the terrible consequences that could flow from such a course of action and so he chose to exercise restraint and defend America's interests by avoiding confrontations when possible and negotiating disputes firmly when feasible.

Robert Goodloe Harper (1765–1825), a Federalist member of the House of Representatives from South Carolina, published a lengthy address to his constituents in which he analyzed France's actions and motives and suggested the kind of policy which he felt the United States should pursue in the face of ever present danger. That policy should be one of firmness in the face of provocation, a refusal to be intimidated by threats, and a willingness to protect America's interests by force. It was only through the determination to risk war, he insisted, that peace could be secured. Thomas Jefferson, who shared his nation's strong distaste for France's conduct, urged moderation. He did not deny that war might come, but he urged that every effort should be made to delay its onslaught. The expression of these opinions was best illustrated in a number of letters he wrote to friends and associates at the height of the crisis.

OBSERVATIONS ON THE DISPUTE BETWEEN THE UNITED STATES AND FRANCE, 1797

Robert Goodloe Harper

FROM *Observations on the Dispute between the United States and France, 1797* (Philadelphia, 1797), pp. 9–10, 92–101.

In this situation France finding her schemes opposed only by the vast maritime power of England, and the unbroken courage and constancy of Austria, formed the resolution of destroying the commerce of England, thereby to cut off her pecuniary resources, and sap the foundation of her naval strength. This plan rendered the co-operation of the United States more important to her than ever; for she considers us one of England's best customers; and consequently as the nation which contributes most to the support of her commerce, her manufactures, and her wealth. Our situation too in the neighbourhood of the West Indies, our abundance of provisions and of warlike and naval stores, and the great number of our ships and seamen, would enable us to be very hurtful to England in war, as well as very useful in peace. By such a war indeed we should suffer greatly, but that is no part of the care of France.

Accordingly she has unceasingly renewed, and pressured with greater and greater eagerness, her indirect attempts to bring us into the war. Foreseeing that her hopes of success would be greatly lessened, if not wholly destroyed by the treaty [Jay's Treaty], she opposed it with all her might and in all its stages. Even the unconstitutional opposition to it in the House of Representatives, she aided by every mean in her power. Finding all her attempts finally frustrated, her vexation and ill humour no longer knew any bounds, and she resolved to try different means for effecting what she had in vain essayed to bring about by intrigue.

That this is the true spring of her conduct, that her anger at the British treaty does not arise from any of its particular provisions, but from its general tendency to preserve peace between this country and Great Britain, is proved in the most manifest manner by the conduct she pursues at this moment towards other neutral nations who have made no treaties with England. She has long threatened Portugal with invasion by the Spaniards, unless she would shut her ports against the English. She has lately required Hamburg and Bremen to break off all commerce with England, and on their refusal has recalled her minister from Hamburg. She has made the same demand on Denmark; and even required the Danes to block up the mouth of the Elbe, a river not in their territories, against the English. We have not heard the pretext for these demands, which Denmark has pointedly refused; but no doubt they were founded on the French construction of *the laws of neutrality*; the same laws whereby, according to France, the Swiss were bound to drive the emigrants from their territories, and we to permit her to raise armies, equip ships of war, and sell prizes in ours.

That such is the real project of France and the true source of her anger at the British treaty, is further proved by the testimony of General Pinckney, who having travelled through a great part of France, and continued near two months in Paris, had the best means of penetrating their views. In his letter from Paris of Feb. 1st. 1797 he says, "I most ardently wish that we would banish all party distinctions and foreign influence; and think and act only as Americans — for all parties in this country (France) unite in thinking that we ought to act *as if we were altogether their dependents*, and indebted to them solely, and not to our exertions, for our liberty and independence. *Hence*, our treaty with Great Britain is here generally execrated; and our having *any kind of commercial connections* with that country, *even if the treaty had not been made* would I believe, have been disliked. They wish to destroy the trade of England, and they look upon us as one of her best customers; *and to obtain their object they care not what we suffer.*"

This is the testimony of a man remarkable for the warmth of his good wishes towards France, and who, if he did not dislike the British treaty, certainly never said a word in its favour. From his testimony, as well as evidence of their own conduct, it manifestly appears that their dislike of the treaty does not proceed, as they pretend, from any stipulations in it injurious to them, but from its tendency to preserve an amicable intercourse between us and England.

The united force of all these considerations, drawn from the instructions to the ministers of France in this country and their conduct here, from the plain and direct tendency of the measures which she wished us to adopt, from the nature of her plans in Europe, and from her recent conduct towards the neighbouring powers, establish in the most incontrovertible manner the opinion, that her object always has been to draw us into the war. This point is still further confirmed by another event. It has been proposed through the Dutch, to our minister at Holland, as appears by his letter of Nov. 4th 1796, that we should make *common cause* with France and Holland against England, in order to compel her to relinquish the right of taking her enemies' goods on board of neutral ships, and "to restore peace to the two Hemispheres."

This leads us to enquire what are the motives of her present conduct; and gives us also the clue whereby they may be discovered.

It is impossible to suppose that the measures lately adopted by France can mean no more than retaliation for the injuries which she pretends to have received. Admitting these injuries to have taken place, and many of them she knows never did take place, admitting all her pretensions to be well founded, and many of them she knows not to be well founded, still those injuries and pretensions could never have authorized her present proceedings. The detention of a few privateers, and the restoration of a few prizes by our courts, even if illegal as she pretends; the privileges said to be ceded to Britain, even had they been ceded; the prohibition to arm vessels and sell prizes in our ports, had she possessed a right to do so; the suffering of a few British ships of war to violate our neutrality, even had we suffered it; more especially considering that all these pretended injuries were much more than counter-balanced by real ones from her; could never have occasioned, much less authorized, the universal capture and condemnation of our property, the imprisonment, and in many cases which may occur, the death of our citizens, and the expulsion from her territory of a minister sent to conciliate. Some other cause must be sought for aggressions such as these.

Still less can it be believed that mere anger and vexation at the disappointment of her views, could have given rise to them. They may and no doubt, have been much aggravated by this cause, but it could not have produced them.

Nor can it in my opinion, be supposed that a design to drive us into a serious quarrel with her, can have given birth to these measures. She too well knows the consequences of such a quarrel to herself, and its necessary effect in counteracting her most favourite scheme, to force it upon us. Her most favourite scheme is to undermine the naval power of England, by destroying the commerce whereby it is nourished and supported. Hence her requisitions to Denmark and the Hanse towns; hence the precipitation whereby she forced Holland and Spain into the war against England; hence her threats to Portugal; hence the violence wherewith in contempt of every right and every engagement she seized Leghorn, a neutral port in which England carried on an extensive trade; hence her oppressions at Genoa; and hence her unwearied efforts to work up the discontents between us and Britain into an open rupture. The direct and even the avowed object of all these measures has been to sap the very foundations of the English power, by excluding its commerce from every port. But France well knows that a quarrel between her and this country would of necessity bring us nearer to England. She knows that having then a common interest with England against her, this common interest would beget a union of means, and a co-operation of measures. She knows that our commerce armed for its own defence would float safely into the ports of England, under convoy of the British flag. She knows that Britain would gain our ports as stations for her ships, would be permitted to recruit her marine among our seamen, and to draw supplies of all sorts from our country, while she herself would be excluded from all these advantages. She knows that as a consequence of these united measures, her colonies and those of Spain and Holland, which she justly considers as her own, would be instantly deprived of all supplies, and must sink under the arms of the two countries. She knows that the American market, already so great, and increasing with a rapidity so incalculable, must in that case be secured almost exclusively to England, and wholly shut to herself and her associates. She knows that by a war with her we should be compelled to call forth our resources for the formation of a marine, which would place us in a situation to be still less in fear of her power or in need of her assistance. She knows, in fine, that a war against her, in which we must co-operate with England, would have a powerful tendency to restore that union of interest, of means, and of good will between the two countries, which for half a century past has been the object of her jealousy and dread, and which she has undertaken two wars to break. Her policy, as profound as it is atrocious, will not be confined to the present time only, but looks forward to the period, not a remote one, when the United States must, in the necessary course of nature, become the most numerous, the most opulent, and the most powerful nation on earth.

I cannot therefore be persuaded, that France intends to quarrel seriously with this country. To think so I must suppose that her counsels are guided by passion and not policy, of which I have perceived no appearance. I have observed much wickedness in her plans, but no folly. I have observed a determination in her to oppress where she thought it advantageous, and to deceive where she could not oppress; to drive or seduce every nation into her measures, in order to crush by their assistance those whose power she dreaded; and on whose vigilance she could not impose; in fine, to sacrifice without remorse to her ambition, all those whom she found weak enough to become her instruments under the name of allies; but I have not observed a neglect of the means whereby her schemes were to be promoted, much less a system of measures calculated to defeat them; and I firmly believe, that nothing could so obviously and strongly tend to defeat her schemes against England as that close union of measures and interests between the two countries, which a quarrel between us and herself must produce.

The very anxiety which she has discovered to place the vast weight of this country in her own scale, is a security that she does not intend to throw it into the scale of her adversary.

Her measures therefore, I believe, have a different and indeed an opposite object. Having failed to seduce, she now is attempting to drive us into her schemes. The means which she employs for effecting this purpose, though most unjust and atrocious, are wise according to the information on which she acts. By this information she has been wholly deceived: we know that she has been deceived, in what manner and to what extent, and this knowledge gives us the true key to her present conduct.

In the first place she has been deceived by the measures of our government. She has seen in them a moderation and forbearance, a desire for peace, and a patience under her numberless acts of insult and injury, which she has construed into a mean, spiritless, and submissive disposition. Having no idea herself of justice, good faith, or moderation, she cannot conceive of them in others; and the acts which they produce, she attributes to avarice, weakness or fear.

To the same motives has she imputed the spirit of peace and conciliation which our government has displayed towards England.

She has been deceived by the conduct of that party in our government, whereby the measures of which she complains, have been opposed. Observing that this party had always expressed very warm good will to her, and a strong attachment to her cause, and had advocated a system of measures much more conformable to her views, than that which was finally adopted, she took up an opinion that they were actuated, not by a desire to promote what they believed to be the good of their own country, but by a blind devotion to her interests. She believed, and still does believe, this to be a French party, ready to go all lengths in assisting her projects, and sufficiently powerful, if not to direct the government according to her will, at least to prevent it from taking effective measures against her. It must be confessed, and a painful confession it is, that there are some individuals whose conduct has given too much reason for this opinion; but it is also most certain that France has fallen into an utter mistake about the views and principles of this description of our fellow citizens in general. They, like the rest, advocated certain measures not because they were thought desirable to any foreign power, but from a belief that they were calculated to promote the good of this country: and France should she push her experiment, will find that however Americans may differ in opinion about the best method of conducting their own affairs, there will be but one mind and one spirit among them on the question of repelling foreign aggression and foreign interference.

France has also been deceived by the conduct of the people in this country. At the commencement of her revolution she saw them every where display the strongest proofs of attachment to her cause, and good wishes for her success. She saw her minister, on his arrival in the country, received with the warmest cordiality. She heard the whole American people exultingly hail the birth of a new republic, in a nation which they fondly called their ally and friend, and to which they were proud to acknowledge their obligations and their gratitude. Far from ascribing these generous effusions to their true source, she regarded them as proofs of a blind and slavish attachment to her interests; and when she saw the government repel her attempts, and steadily refuse to come into her measures, she supposed that it acted in opposition to the wishes of the people, by whom in case of a struggle, it would not be supported.

She had observed also a strong and universal resentment, excited throughout this country, by the aggressions of England; and this she construed into a deadly and lasting hatred to the British nation, which would at all times incline the people to war with it, and render any co-operation or union of measures between the two countries, difficult if not impossible.

In these two points, she mistakes as widely as in the former. We were delighted with the French revolution, because we thought that it would bestow liberty and happiness on a great people. We felt affection to France because we considered her as our ally and our friend. We felt grateful for her assistance, because it had been highly useful to us. But when these services are made the pretence for the most inadmissable demands, when, instead of an ally and a friend, we find her a proud and unjust assailant, we feel a resentment proportioned to the injury, and strengthened by the reflection, that this injury comes from a quarter, where we had given friendship and expected to receive it.

So, with respect to England, when her injuries ceased and an honorable reparation was agreed to, we thought our resentment ought also to cease.

In these mistakes there can be no doubt that France has been greatly fortified by her emissaries in this country, and by some of our citizens both here and in Europe. They have confirmed her in the idea, to adopt the expression of General Pinckney, in his letter of Dec. 20th, 1796, "that our government acts upon principles opposed to the sentiments of a large majority of our people; that we are a people divided by party, the mere creatures of foreign influence, and regardless of our national character, honour and interest."

Believing therefore, that the government, torn by party, is too feeble to resist her; that thwarted in its operations by the affections, the sentiments, and the wishes of the people, it will be unable to oppose any effectual exertions against her attacks; that a powerful party in the government, and a great majority of the people, will take part with her against the government itself, or at least will withhold from it all effectual support; that the people, wholly immersed in the pursuits of gain, have lost that martial spirit whereby they were distinguished in the late war, and will submit to any indignities or injuries, rather than risk their persons and wealth in a contest; she has come to a resolution to attack and pillage us, to mal-treat us in every manner, and to refuse all intercourse with us, in the firm persuasion that the government, however unwillingly, will be obliged to yield, and that we shall submit to her terms, as the price of her forbearance.

These terms, in substance and necessary effect, are a rupture with Britain and the exclusion of her commerce from our ports; and such a construction of the treaty with France, as shall permit her to arm vessels, inlist [sic] crews, and sell prizes in our country, free from the interference of our courts of justice.

Should she even fail in this, still she has no doubt that we, from our desire of peace, will always be ready to make an accommodation, and to relinquish our claim to indemnity as the price of deliverance from further aggression. In the meantime she will accomplish, she thinks, two very important objects; she will wound the commerce of England through our sides; and by plundering us, she will not only acquire some aid to her treasury, but also give employment and support to great numbers of her people. A third object and of no small importance, will be the destruction, in part, of our resources; whereby we should be rendered more dependent on her as allies, and less formidable as enemies.

Such in my opinion, my fellow citizens, are the objects of France in her present measures towards this country, and I am firmly persuaded that the only method of inducing her to abandon those measures, is to convince her by our conduct that they will not be effectual; to convince her by firm united and vigorous measures that her opinions respecting us are erroneous; and that we are determined, at all hazards and under any possible sacrifice, to maintain our rights, repel unjust attacks, and seek reparation for injuries wantonly committed: that we are not a feeble, pusillanimous or divided people, opposed to our own government, and ready to acquiesce in or aid the interference of foreigners in our affairs. We ought to show them at the same time, that while we are resolved to repel injury, we are willing to make every reasonable advance towards a just accommodation: that while we prepare firmly and vigorously for war, we are desirous of cultivating peace, as long as any hope of preserving it remains: that although we mean to appeal firmly to the sword if driven to that extremity, we shall make the appeal with reluctance and regret.

This is the system recommended by the President in his speech to both Houses at the opening of Congress. He declares his resolution to make another attempt to negotiate and recommend that this attempt should be fortified and seconded by serious preparations at home. This will give weight to our complaints, and should redress be refused, will place us in a situation to meet the unfavorable event with energy and success. I perfectly concur in these sentiments and shall give my voice for supporting them in the House in the most efficacious manner. The subject is now under discussion, and I have reason to believe, that the system recommended by the President will be adopted.

This system is exactly conformable to that which was formerly adopted respecting Britain. When Britain, after repeated remonstrances on our part, continued her depredations on our commerce, though in so doing broke no Treaty, though she did not recal [sic] her minister or drive away ours, we resolved to prepare for resistance, but in the meantime to make another attempt by negotiation; and fortunately the attempt was successful. Britain gave up her measures, and agreed to make restitution for the past. Should France be induced to act in the same manner, we shall once more have the satisfaction of seeing our rights vindicated by that union of moderation and firmness which has heretofore redounded so much to the honour and advantage of our country. Should she refuse and war proves necessary, the recollection that we have done all in our power to avoid it, will enable us to support the struggle with unanimity and fortitude.

Should the system recommended by the President be adopted, it is impossible to foresee what particular measures of preparation will be preferred. As to the person to be sent to France, there can be no doubt that it will be General Pinckney. The firmness, good sense, and moderation which he displayed while in Paris, reflect honour on himself and the country, and have received universal approbation here. It is agreed by all parties that our honour and interests can be no where safer than in his hands.

Such, my fellow citizens, is the system of measures towards France, which in my opinion, ought to be adopted. I am persuaded that they intend not to make war upon us, but to scourge and frighten us into submission: and that the only possible method of making them desist from the attempt, is to convince them, not merely by declarations, but by effectual preparations for war, that we are not frightened, and will not submit to be scourged. When they understand this, I am fully persuaded that they will abandon their project. Our negotiation I believe will be successful, but the foundations of its success must be laid in the House of Representatives; and these foundations must be vigorous and effectual preparations for war. We must consider ourselves as in the presence of a bully, who can be prevented from striking us in no manner but by shewing him that we are able and resolved to return the blow.

Should I however mistake in all this, still the same system will be right. Should the views of France be different from what I have supposed; should the plan of French aggrandizement, to borrow the words of an eloquent speaker in the House of Representatives, require America to be driven into the war, war we shall have in spite of all our peaceable endeavours to avert it: and in that case the sooner we set about serious preparations, the better we shall be able to repel and retort the attack.

Thus, in either case, our course must be the same. Whether France intends to make war upon us, to bully us, or under pretence of "just displeasure" to continue her depredations on us for the purpose of injuring England, as long as we will submit to them, still our wisdom lies in speedy and effectual preparation.

Should any ask, what are the sacrifices we must incur by a war, and what are our means of becoming formidable to France? I would answer that as to sacrifices the greatest we can make is that of our rights and our independence; that war is an evil always to be avoided, but infinitely less than national degradation, and submission to the will of a foreign power; that every possible loss of property and lives may be repaired by time and industry, if we preserve our honour and our government, but that these, once lost, can never be restored; in fine that a nation that weighs its purse against its rights, never fails in the end to lose both one and the other.

To shew that we will submit to injuries, for fear of loss, amounts to bribing foreign nations with our own money, to insult and attack us.

I would answer that we magnanimously resolved to resist the power of Britain more than twenty years ago, when our resources were infinitely less than at present, and our situation for employing them far more disadvantageous, and that this resolution created the means of resistance. I would answer that we possess a population probably little short of six millions; a country abounding with every thing necessary for the subsistance and arming of troops; more ships and sailors than any nation on earth except England; an extensive revenue not felt by the people, and capable of very great increase without oppression; a union among ourselves, cemented by habit, mutual interest, and affection; a martial spirit and enterprize, which so gloriously displayed itself in the war for our independence; experienced officers formed in that war, and still ready to bleed for their country; a wise government possessing our confidence, and capable of uniting and directing our exertions in a word, that steady persevering courage, that lofty unconquerable spirit of independence, wherein the true strength of nations consists, more than in population, in wealth, in fleets, in armies, or in generals; and which, wherever it exists, finds all other means or makes them.

I would answer that we still possess WASHINGTON, the Hero and Patriot, who conducted us with so much glory through our former struggle, and whose martial figure, which age has rendered more venerable without impairing its strength, would again be seen at the head of our armies.

I would answer that with not half our numbers, few of our other advantages, and in a situation far more contiguous and more exposed, the Swiss have courageously and successfully maintained their rights, and preserved their tranquility, by those measures which we now recommend, by proving to all parties: that though desirous of peace they were prepared for war; were prepared to place their houses, their families, and the bones of their fathers, under the protection of their swords, and to stake the last drop of their blood on the success of the contest.

I would answer that if driven into a war we can buy at a price cheap to ourselves, the full co-operation of the British navy: that our numerous merchant ships can speedily be converted into ships of war: that by withholding supplies from France and her allies in the West Indies, we can most effectually aid the operations of her enemies: that Britain being thus enabled to call home a great part of her present force in the West Indies, will increase still more her internal safety, and the superiority of her navy in Europe: and that New Orleans and the Floridas must fall into our hands, whereby we shall secure the navigation of the Mississippi, free ourselves from a troublesome neighbour, and obtain complete controul [sic] over the southern Indians.

I would answer, in fine, in the words of a celebrated writer, that when courage is not wanting, all other means will be found or created.

I might conclude this long address my fellow citizens, by an exhortation to summon up your fortitude, and prepare bravely to meet the attacks which may be made on our country. The subject supplies ample materials for an appeal to all the feelings which distinguish the Patriot and the Hero. But I know it is not necessary. The men who fought at King's Mountain and the Cowpens, do not need an exhortation, to bleed for their country should she be forced to call for their assistance: and I know that, in case of that awful event which we so anxiously desire to avert, America will again find the sons of ninety-six district among the bravest of her defenders.

Philadelphia, May 25th, 1797

THOMAS JEFFERSON TO EDMUND PENDLETON

Philadelphia, April 2, 1798

DEAR SIR,

— The late war message of the president has added new alarm. Town meetings have begun in Massachusetts, and are sending on their petitions & remonstrances by great majorities, against war-measures, and these meetings are likely to spread. The present debate, as it gets abroad, will further show them, that it is their members who are for war measures. It happens, fortunately, that these gentlemen are obliged to bring themselves forward exactly in time for the Eastern elections to Congress, which come on in the course of the ensuing summer. We have, therefore, great reason to expect some favorable changes in the representatives from that quarter. The same is counted on with confidence from Jersey, Pennsylvania, & Maryland; perhaps one or two also in Virginia; so that, after the next election, the whigs think themselves certain of a very strong majority in the H of Representatives; and tho' against the other branches they can do nothing good, yet they can hinder them from doing ill. The only source of anxiety, therefore, is to avoid war for the present moment. If we can defeat the measures leading to that during this session, so as to gain this summer, time will be given, as well for the public mind to make itself felt, as for the operations of France to have their effect in England as well as here. If, on the contrary war is forced on, the tory interest continues dominant, and to them alone must be left, as they alone desire to ride on the whirlwind, & direct the storm. The present period, therefore, of two or three weeks, is the most eventful ever known since that of 1775 and will decide whether the principles established by that contest are to prevail, or give way to those they subverted. Accept the friendly salutations & prayers for your health & happiness, of, dear Sir, your sincere and affectionate friend.

  P.S. Compliments to Mr. Taylor. I shall write to him in a few days.

FROM *The Works of Thomas Jefferson*, Paul L. Ford, ed. (New York, 1904), vol. 8, pp. 394–7.

THOMAS JEFFERSON TO ARCHIBALD STUART

Philadelphia, June 8, 1798

DEAR SIR,

— I inclose you some further communications from our envoys at Paris. To the information contained in these I can add that by the latest accounts Mr. Pinckney was gone into the south of France for the health of his family, Mr. Marshall to Amsterdam, and Mr. Gerry remained at Paris. It appears that neither themselves nor the French government dreamt of war between the two countries. It seems also fairly presumable that the douceur of 50,000 Guineas mentioned in the former dispatches was merely from X. and Y. as not a word is ever said by Talleyrand to our envoys, nor by them to him on the subject. It is now thought possible that Gerry may be pursuing the treaty for he was always viewed with more favor by the French government than his collegues whom they considered as personally hostile to them. It seems they offered to pay in time for unjustifiable spoliations, and insist on a present loan (and it would be much more than an equivalent). There seems nothing to prevent a conclusion, unless indeed the brig *Sophia* should arrive too soon and bring him away. She sailed from hence the 1st of April with positive orders to the envoys to come away. In the meantime, besides accumulating irritations we are proceeding to actual hostilities. You will have seen in the papers the bills already passed, and the measures now proposed. Every thing will be carried which is proposed. Nobody denies but that France has given just cause of war, but so has Gr. Britain and she is now capturing our vessels as much as France, but the question was one merely of prudence, whether seeing that both powers in order to injure one another, bear down every thing in their way, without regard to the rights of others, spoliating equally Danes, Swedes & Americans, it would not be more prudent in us to bear with it as the Danes and Swedes do, curtailing our commerce, and waiting for the moment of peace, when it is probable both nations would for their own interest and honour retribute for their wrongs. However the public mind has been artfully inflamed by publications well calculated to deceive them and them only and especially in the towns, and irritations have been multiplied so as

FROM *The Works of Thomas Jefferson*, Paul L. Ford, ed. (New York, 1904), vol. 8, pp. 436-9.

to shut the door of accomodation, and war is now inevitable. I imagine that France will do little with us till she has made her peace with England, which, whether her invasion succeeds or fails, must be made this summer and autumn. The game on both sides is too heavy to be continued. When she shall turn her arms on us, I imagine it will be chiefly against our commerce and fisheries. If any thing is attempted by land it will probably be to the westward. Our great expence will be in equipping a navy to be lost as fast as equipped, or to be maintained at an expence which will sink us with itself, as the like course is sinking Great Britain. Of the two millions of Dollars now to be raised by a tax on lands, houses & slaves, Virginia is to furnish between 3 and 400,000 but this is not more than half of the actual expence if the provisional army be raised, nor one tenth of what must be the annual expences. I see no way in which we can injure France so as to advance to negotiation (as we must do in the end) on better ground than at present and I believe it will thus appear to our citizens generally as soon as the present fervor cools down and there will be many sedatives to effect this. For the present however, nothing can be done. Silence and patience are necessary for a while; and I must pray you, as to what I now write, to take care it does not get out of your own hand, nor a breath of it in a newspaper. . . .

PART II

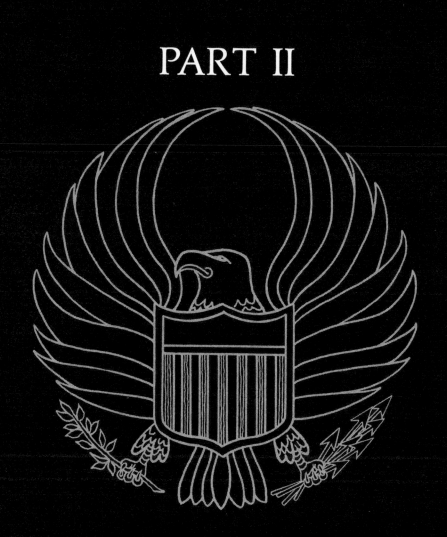

THE SEARCH
FOR
SECURITY

5

THE LOUISIANA PURCHASE

There are few occasions in history when a single decision may assure the future greatness of a nation. In the course of American events the Louisiana Purchase must be ranked as one of these. By the acquisition of this enormous territory the United States added an incalculable measure to her wealth and resources and opened the way to a rapid and unexpected expansion to the Pacific Ocean.

It is one of the nice touches of history that the President responsible for all this should have been Jefferson, who had long believed in a strict interpretation of the Constitution, and who had long argued that the Federal government lacked the authority to enlarge the union by purchase or conquest. But necessity often makes pragmatists of us all, and Jefferson recognized that a continued French presence in New Orleans posed a somber threat to American security. We would, he wrote, from the moment France took New Orelans, have to "marry ourselves to the British fleet and nation." Rather than become dependent upon the bounty of a nation which he distrusted, Jefferson authorized Livingstone and Monroe to purchase New Orleans. To their surprise, Napoleon offered them the whole of the Louisiana territory. He did so not because of a love for the United States, but rather because his losses in Santo Domingo had been so terrible and his involvement in Europe so extensive that he had decided to rid himself of his American possessions.

While all westerners and a majority in the remainder of the country rejoiced in the Louisiana Purchase, some Federalists denounced it. In a series of articles in *The National Intelligencer* Franklin (a pseudonym), carefully examined their opposition and cogently argued in favor of the President's actions.

"THE LOUISIANA PURCHASE"

NATIONAL INTELLIGENCER
Wednesday, September 28, 1803

Franklin
[pseud.]

Of this important event it is proposed to take some concise and plain views; such as naturally arise from it, and such as may tend to give correct information to the people of their states. The correspondence between the Secretary of State and our ministers in France, and between the latter and the French government not being published, it is impossible for us to form a judgement *absolutely correct.* Deciding alone on facts within our knowledge if other facts shall be found to exist, it is possible that our judgement may be unfounded. It is further possible, not only that the arguments urged against the measure, but likewise those adduced in favor of it, may be inconclusive, and such as neither its friends or enemies would advance, if acquainted with all the circumstances connected with the transaction. This should inspire our minds with diffidence, and should moderate the ardor of our approbation or disapprobation. We should realize that we may be in the wrong. Still as the subject is deeply interesting, and as attempts are made to impress the people with sentiments of hostility to the measures of the government, it is expedient, perhaps necessary, to frustrate the effects of ignorance or misrepresentation, to take the best view of the subject that known fact admit of.

In the *first* place, then, let us consider whether there could be any improper motive in the Executive to accept of the cession, and make the purchase.

Secondly. Is there any good reason for considering the Executive uninformed of the true interests of the country.

If these two enquiries shall be satisfactorily solved, let us, enquire, *thirdly,* whether there was not a necessity imposed upon the Executive to act.

Fourthly. Whether a purchase of territory was not the most eligible and just step that could be taken.

Fifthly. Whether it was not best to extend the purchase to Louisiana, instead of confining it to New Orleans.

Sixthly. Whether war with England or France would not have been the inevitable effect of any other measures pursued either for the attainment of New Orleans or Louisiana.

Seventhly. Whether the sum paid is too great.

Eighthly. Whether the cession will depress the value of our western lands; and

Ninthly. Whether it will indanger the union.

A plain view of these points will, it is believed, embrace, all the information and discussion necessary for the forming a correct judgement of the wisdom of the measure.

Let us then, in the *first* place, consider, whether there could be any improper motives in the Executive to accept of the cession, and to make the purchase.

As none have been directly alleged, it might be fair to infer, without further remark, that none exists. As, however, there has been a wantonness of insinuation by the opposition prints, it may be proper to notice the most prominent reproaches.

The President is charged with an undue attachment to France. He is charged almost in the same breath with a dread of the First Consul. It will not escape notice that there is a strong incompatibility between these two sentiments. If he feels the one, he possess the other. It is a strong evidence of the weakness of the arguments, of an adversary, when they conflict with each other. But is either true? We can only judge of what we do not know from that which we do know. Now we know that the President is a warm friend of liberty and of republican government; we know that the government of France entertains the most deadly hostility to republicanism. Is it then likely that he feels any extraordinary partiality to that government? It is likely that he feels in his character of chief magistrate of the country a due respect for the chief magistrate of France; but it is also likely that he feels the same respect for the king of England or the emperor of Russia. It is likely that he considers it his duty to cultivate the good will of that government as the best preservative of peace, and therefore manifests himself a good will to France; but it does not follow that his good will arises from any sinister motive, especially as we find the same cordiality subsisting between him and the government of Great Britain. If there be a fact capable of proving the impartial and enlightened deportment of our government to foreign powers, and particularily to France, it is the good understanding that subsists between it and England. This proves to demonstrate that we are not partial to France.

Is there any ground for the reproach that the President is afraid of the First Consul? Has he offered incense to this distinguished character? Has he ever dwelt with rapture on the splendour of his exploits? Has he ever courted his favour? Has he ever crouched to his power? If not one of these charges can be made with justice, whence but from malice springs this audacious calumny?

Is it pretended that the executive has made a bargain with France by which they will put in their pockets a part of the sum paid for the cession? No. This is not even surmised. The integrity of the president and the secretary of state has never been questioned. There is not a man in America that doubts either.

But one other impure motive can be ascribed, and that is a dread to go to war, not from a conviction of its impolicy, but from a fear of its destroying his popularity. But why this fear? If the *President* expected such a war would be unpopular, would it not be his duty, as the representative of the people, as the organ of their will, to avoid it? Would it not have been criminal, under such circumstances, to have hurried the nation into it? Surely it would; and this very reproach constitutes his best defence.

Thus it appears that every impure motive that can be ascribed is far fetched, distorted, unjust. On the contrary there are the most obvious reasons for it. This will appear in the sequel of these enquiries.

NATIONAL INTELLIGENCER
Monday, October 3, 1803

The third enquiry is, whether there was not a necessity imposed upon the executive to act.

In the month of December last the president officially informed Congress of the suspension of the right of deposit at New-Orleans. In consequence of this information the House of Representatives after mature deliberation came to the following resolution.

Resolved that this house receive with great sensibility the information of a disposition in certain officers of the Spanish government at New-Orleans to obstruct the navigation of the river Mississippi, as secured to the United States by the most solemn stipulation: That, adhering to that humane and wise policy which ought ever to characterize a free people, and by which the United States have always professed to be governed; willingly, at the same time, to ascribe this breach of compact to the unauthorized misconduct of certain individuals, rather than to a want of good faith on the part of his Catholic majesty; and relying with perfect confidence on the vigilance and wisdom of the executive, they will wait the issue of such measures as that department of the government shall have pursued for asserting the rights and vindicating the injuries of the United States: — holding it to be their duty at the same time, to express their unalterable determination to maintain the boundaries, and the rights of navigation and commerce thro' the river Mississippi, as established by existing treaties.

About the same time that these resolves were passed, resolutions were offered in the two houses, the avowed object of which was to obtain the possession of New-Orleans by force. After mature deliberation these resolutions were rejected by great majorities. The Senate, on their part, came to the following resolution:

> Resolved, That the president of the United States be, and he is thereby authorized, whenever he shall judge it expedient, to require of the executives of the several states, to take effectual measures to organize, arm, and equip, according to law, and hold in readiness to march at a moments warning, 80,000 effective militia, officers included.
> Resolved, That the president may, if he judges expedient, authorize the executives of the several states to accept, as part of the detachment aforesaid, any corps of volunteers; who shall continue in service for such time, not exceeding___months, and perform such services as shall be prescribed by law.
> Resolved, that___dollars be appropriated for erecting, at such place or places on the western waters, as the president may judge most proper, one or more arsenals.

In the spirit of these resolutions an act passed the two houses by an unanimous vote authorizing the expenditure of two millions of dollars, and actually placing that sum under the immediate control of the president.

From these facts it is evident that the legislature must have come to three decisions; — first, to decline, under existing circumstances, going to war, secondly, to wait the issue of executive negotiation under the pledge of its support, and thirdly to sanction the purchase of New-Orleans, or some other place of deposit, or of Louisiana. The two first appear from the above resolutions, and the last appears from the appropriation of two millions.

Under these circumstances there can remain no doubt of its being the duty of the executive to act. Having announced to Congress, that he had taken certain steps, Congress sanction them by their expression of confidence, and authorise their further prosecution by furnishing the means of effecting them.

So far as relates to a declaration of war the powers of Congress are full and preclusive of those of the president, with them alone it rests to say whether war shall be declared or peace maintained. So long as they do not do the first they produce a necessity in the executive, as far as depends upon him, to preserve the last. Had then, the president taken any step which should have led to war when he had within his power the lawful means of averting it, he would have infringed upon the powers of the legislature; he would have been guilty of usurpation; he might have been impeached and punished.

Being forbidden a resort to war, and being compelled to proceed in effectuating the object of the government, his only remaining resource was negociation. We have already seen that the legislature, in manner the most intelligible, by the appropriation of two millions, either sanctioned a purchase as the original suggestion of the president, or as the fruits of their own reflection — For, on no other ground than the contemplation of purchase, could such an appropriation have been made.

The fourth enquiry is whether a purchase of territory was not the most eligible and just step that could be taken.

It is a strong argument in favour of purchase, that the public from the earliest periods of the negociation, looked to it in the event of a favorable issue. That this was the case, there is, at this period, no necessity of shewing, when all the circumstances attending this affair are fresh in every man's memory. However dangerous or delusive it may be to be guided by public opinion in nations that are extremely depressed and ignorant, it will in general be both safe and desirable to be governed by it, when the people are well informed.

The negociation had two objects: one, the restoration of our rights of deposit, violated by the Spanish Intendant: the other, security that such violation would not be repeated. The first object might, perhaps, have been obtained without purchase. But would the nation have been satisfied with this? If there be any truth in the declarations of the opponents of the administration *they* would not. What should we, indeed, have gained by the accomplishment of this object? No other than a right, acknowledged by France, to deposit our goods at New-Orleans, subject to undefined conditions, and revocable, as by Spain, at any moment. Would there have been any safety in this? Would the nation have asserted its dignity by obtaining merely a *nominal* recognition of a previous right? . . .

If then it be ascertained, that neither the public feeling, nor the security of our rights, would have been satisfied by a mere restitution of the deposit, it only remains to consider whether any thing short of purchase would have been effectual.

We might have obtained New-Orleans by force, of this there can be no doubt. But would this have given us the secure and indisturbed [sic] possession of our right? Is there a man in the nation who does not believe that the use of force on our part would have produced it on the part of France? . . .

The absurdity of France giving us New-Orleans for nothing, need not be considered. Nations are too seldom just and never generous. She would have had an equivalent; and that could only be found in money, or partial commercial stipulations in her favor. Against the latter every voice among us is united.

They, therefore, who object to a purchase, and who still insist upon the necessity of obtaining the secure possessions of our rights, have no other alternative than war. . . .

NATIONAL INTELLIGENCER
Wednesday, October 5, 1803

The fifth enquiry is, whether it was not best to extend the purchase to Louisiana, instead of confining it to New-Orleans.

Had the purchase been confined to New-Orleans, the whole western bank of the Mississippi would have been occupied by France or some other power into the whole hands of Louisiana might have fallen.

To insure the safety of New-Orleans would have required a strong military force, the extent of which would have depended entirely on the quantus [sic] of force kept up by the proprietors of Louisiana. This of itself would have been a great evil, even supposing that we preserved peace with the neighbouring nation. This however, is more than can rationally be expected. Adjoining powers, who are competitors for the same object, are in constant danger of being embroiled. Nor is it probable that peace would permanently have continued between the United States and the power possessed of Louisiana. Without any such sources of difference our short experience as a nation has convinced us that we are to expect occasional injuries from both France and England. Under the infliction of these injuries on the Mississippi, it would have been absolutely impossible to repress a resistance or retaliation on the part of our citizens, who, feeling their power, would not scruple to exert it in the vindication of their rights. The effect would have been frequent war. . . .

NATIONAL INTELLIGENCER
Friday, October 14, 1803

The last enquiry is whether the cession of Louisiana will endanger the union.

If it is calculated to produce this effect, there is not a good citizen that will not deprecate it as the most mournful event, that has befallen America. On the union of these states depend the power of the empire and the happiness of our citizens. Divided into separate confederacies, it is too probable that all the evils that have attended other contiguous and rival states will await us.

But it is confidently affirmed that the cession of Louisiana will not endanger the union. It will on the contrary eminently conduce to cement and strengthen it.

The idea that the cession will endanger the union arises from the prevalent opinion that our empire is already sufficiently if not too extensive, for a republican government; and that an extension of it will terminate in dismemberment or despotism. Into the truth of this position we shall soon enquire.

In the mean time acquiescing in it for arguments sake, does it follow that the cession will *endanger* the union, that is, will make that union less secure than it would otherwise be? This can only be affirmed on the supposition that if the cession of Louisiana had not been made, it would have remained in the possession of, and under the government of a foreign power to that period when, from its extended population, it would have endangered the union — for it is not contended that, in its present condition, it can have any such effect.

Now, is there a man in the nation, who does not know that this region, independent of cession, would be ours before the arrival of that period. Let any one who questions that result, consider the relative strength of these states compared with the feebleness of Louisiana; let him consider that the future progress, in wealth, in enterprise, and in numbers, of our present western country, would vastly exceed that of Louisiana under a foreign government; let him consider the unavoidable jealousy and rivalry of contiguous states; let him consider the powerful temptations offered to cupidity, and the ease with which conquest could be effected, from a large, if not the larger portion of population being American; let him consider the late spirit that animated the inhabitants of our western waters, and their fixed purpose to acquire the rights to which they viewed themselves entitled by God and nature; — let all these things be considered, and let it be answered whether the possession of Louisiana by the United States had not become a matter of inevitable necessity. It was doubtless this consideration, more than all the others, that induced a government, whose views were not limited to the present moment, to direct its attention to the peaceable possession of what otherwise would have involved a sacrifice of the blood of our citizens. If then the addition of Louisiana to our present limits shall ultimately endanger the union, it is a danger, not the effect of choice but of necessity; and not ascribable to the measures of government, but to the will of God. Even if this shall be the *ultimate* effect, it was no less the duty of a wise administration to adopt those measures, which were most calculated to protract this gloomy period, and in the *intermediate* space of time to avert the evils that were likely to flow from disputes between our citizens and those of the power owning Louisiana, and the wars between the two nations consequent thereon. That the possession of Louisiana by a foreign nation would have had these effects cannot admit of a doubt. In the very infancy of such relations, such disputes have already arisen, and wars threatened as their natural offspring. The results of these collisions would have been either the *unauthorized* seizure of Louisiana by our western citizens, or declared war. The first would have been an evil of awful magnitude. It would have been an act of extreme usurpation, not to say rebellion; and might have claimed the forcible interference of the government, but for its inability to suppress it. In such event the government would have interfered, or it would not. If it had interfered, beside the gloomy spectacle of citizens embruing his hand in the blood of citizen, it might have exposed the present states to early dismemberment; for what circumstances would have been so likely to produce this effect as the general government carrying its arms into the western country to repress measures on which they were resolutely bent? How easy, perhaps unavoidable the transition from such a state of things, to an assertion of independent authority, an union with the country west of the Mississippi, and an alliance with a formidable European nation? Then, indeed, the sun of our glory would have soon set; the western states on *this side of that river* would have been *our enemies,* and their power would have soon equalled that of the states on the Atlantic.

But it is not true that the cession of Louisiana will ultimately endanger the union. It is not true that a republican government, such as ours, is unsuited to an extensive territory. On the contrary, I boldly affirm that a confederated government is the only government that can, with a promise of Perpetuity, unite the remote parts of a great empire. I am not ignorant of the maxims of writers on government, nor insensible to the weight of authority. — But granting their maxims to be perfectly correct, they do not apply to our system of government. It is certainly true that a democracy, strictly speaking, must be limited in extent to a small territory; it may possibly be true that no single government, not despotic, can hold together an extensive territory: — but it does not thence follow that a government in all its parts representative, and composed of a federal head depriving its powers equally from every portion of the union, will be inadequate to hold in indissoluble ties the greatest empire. The difficulties that arise under the first governments will not exist under the last. Of the first inequality of power and wealth is the unavoidable effect: in the latter the same equality will pervade the whole community. So far from endangering the union by the increase of the states, its highest security will flow from this source. At present, it is possible, perhaps, for one great state successfully to frustrate the execution of the laws of the general government, and to maintain its independence of the federal head; but when the states shall be increased, in proportion to that increase the power of the great states will decline, and come under subjection to that of the smaller states rendered more powerful from a union of their strength. The larger too the surface of the country, and the more varied the pursuits and interests of its citizens, the greater will be the difficulty to inflame the passions of a part, so as to hazard the tranquility or welfare of the whole.

This view is deeply interesting to Americans. I shall not now stop to fill up its details; trusting at present to the reflections of my countrymen, and reserving a full discussion of the great question of the compatibility of a republican government and an extensive empire for a separate enquiry.

By the cession of Louisiana to the United States at this time, they become in a great measure the arbiters of their own fate. With them it will rest to guide with a judicious hand what accident or misdirection might have led in many a devious course. On them it will devolve to encourage or repress, as the general welfare shall require, the population of the region west of the Mississippi. Instead of finding centuries, hereafter, powerful enemies, it will depend on their wisdom, their justice, their magnanimity, to raise ardent friends. The object is equal to the boldest conceptions, and worthy of the most expanded talents. On us it depends to give existence to countless millions of freemen. The task is god like! May it inspire us with a virtue whose purity, and spirit whose resolution shall overcome all obstacles, and issue in the happiness of the western world!

6

THE UNITED STATES AND NEUTRAL RIGHTS

 International law is a difficult and contentious subject. Custom and usage are useful but not infallible guides for understanding it, for the law is changed by the great powers as they bend and alter it to suit their own interests. During the Revolutionary and Napoleonic Wars the United States found herself in a continuous dispute over the interpretation of neutral and maritime rights with both Britain and France. These disputes ranged over a wide variety of subjects which included the definition of blockades and contraband and the legitimacy of the British Orders in Council and the French Berlin and Milan decrees. But even more fundamental than these to the United States was the argument over impressment and search on the high seas. Britain argued that she had the right to the services of all her subjects in times of crises and that this obligation could not be avoided by becoming a naturalized citizen of another nation. Indeed, Britain rejected the very principle of naturalization. In doing so she challenged the sovereignty of the United States, which felt that if recent citizens of that new country could not claim the protection of the flag how could it survive.

Charles Jared Ingersoll (1782–1862), a Democrat and supporter of Jefferson, published in 1808 an extensive critique of the American position on these issues. It was a defense and justification of the American posture which was presented with skill and effectiveness.

A VIEW OF THE RIGHTS AND WRONGS, POWER AND POLICY OF THE UNITED STATES OF AMERICA

Charles Jared Ingersoll

FROM *The United States and Neutral Rights: A View of the Rights and Wrongs, Power and Policy of the United States of America* (Philadelphia, 1808).

The injurious and unjust impositions by foreign powers on the commerce of the United States are numerous, flagrant, and increasing. Frauds and illegal traffic have been taken for granted from the sudden and unexampled magnitude; and, without any proof whatever of its unfairness or duplicity, the great maritime powers have presumed, from their unfounded suspicions, to harrass and oppress it with multiplied restraints, vexations, and prohibitions, which, if they had not the irresistible means, they never would have ventured to impose. Suspicions and jealousies have instigated, directed, and enforced their blows: after their infliction, and all the harm is done, we are left at our leisure to remonstrate, and negative their propriety. A calculation of the losses thus sustained is unattainable: but it will not be exaggerating their amount, including what we have been robbed of, and what we have been prevented from making, to state them, notwithstanding the prodigious and seemingly unnatural augmentation of American commerce, at full one-third of its fair and lawful profits. Of this third, at least two-thirds have gone into the treasures of England; for her subjects take care to convert what they get to their own use, and seldom burn or sink it, as has been done by the French. These wrongs are inflicted in various ways, and under several pretexts. England, who has the dominion of the ocean, boldly asserts her right to examine, seize, capture, and condemn in a number of cases, by virtue of the law of nations, or by virtue of such of her own orders and acts as she maintains to be issued and executed conformably to that law. France and Spain do not seem to place their piracies on an appeal to the law of nations, but rather refer them to a necessary retaliation and reaction of the extensions and interpolations of England, and of our submission to them. The principle is the same on which England acts, when she searches our vessels, sends them in on suspicion, or turns them away from blockaded places, and that on which France acts, when she burns and sinks them: a principle of self-preservation and belligerent annoyance, without regard to the effects on neutrals. Its operation is more pernicious in one case than the other; but its essence and justice are the same in both.

From other maritime nations of Europe, from Russia, Denmark, Holland, Prussia, and Portugal, all of whom have enjoyed the means of annoying it, and with whose rights and emoluments it has clashed as much as with those of France and England, American commerce has met with no molestation. I shall, therefore, in this inquiry, consider chiefly the conduct of England, because she pretends to justify her piracies, and because I think that to their extension on her part, and sufferance on ours, all our maritime embarrassments are ascribable. Palpable or mere retaliating violations of our flag may be provided against, and, in process of time, prevented; but it is impossible to foresee, and successfully resist, as they occur, unfounded and sophisticated positions of pretended rights, insinuating themselves as expositions of an unwritten but binding system, with which England seems determined gradually to overspread, deface, and obliterate the usages of foreign intercourse, and the natural immunities of neutrality.

The English government is seldom satisfied with a bare exercise of its power. All their public acts are accompanied with public explanations of their conformity to the laws of nations, to the institutions of which inscrutable system the English lay claim to a rigorous adherence. It will therefore be proper, in the first place, to examine briefly what that system is, whence it derives any authority it may have, and how far that authority is binding.

$$\cdot \quad \cdot \quad \cdot$$

. . . It is always understood in America, and appears lately to have suggested itself even in England, that whatever belligerent rights accrue to nations on the interruption of wars, they are not to be exercised against neutrals, otherwise the situation of the neutral is changed by the war, and neutrality is in effect no national attitude at all. If a neutral, in time of peace, may trade with all the world, no two or half a dozen powers going to a war have a right to curtail or abridge the pre-existing rights of his neutrality. It is a monstrous position for a belligerent to take, when he announces to neutrals, as England does to the United States, after hostilities commence, you cannot now be permitted to carry on commerce, in which you were extensively engaged before the war begun on our part, because, if you do, you succour our enemies, whose trade we mean to cut off, and that will injure us, and, therefore, we cannot suffer it. What had the neutral to do in occasioning the war, that he should be made a collateral party to its privations? The regulations of blockade and contraband are on a different footing. If what was free to neutrality before the war, be closed by what the English term a belligerent right, during the war's continuance, the neutral right, though pre-existing, is sacrificed to a belligerent demand, though of subsequent date, and of the belligerent's own creation, without having in any way consulted the neutral previously. A nation going to war should deliberately envisage and provide for its effects; and if one of these effects must necessarily be the extension of neutral commerce, by throwing open channels theretofore shut, this should form part of the previous consideration, as a natural consequence of the war, which the belligerent must expect, and has no right to contest. The case is vastly strengthened, when, instead of a trade extending itself by the pressure of war, we consider a trade flourishing during peace, and arrested by war.

• • •

1. It will never, I trust, be too late to maintain the principle, that free ships make free goods. Maritime tyranny has, it is true, notwithstanding several hard struggles, almost driven it from political inquiry. It is useless to dwell upon it here, because, while we must submit, it would be impolitic by ill-timed and improbable efforts to endanger the rights we have. If a concert with Russia, France, Holland, and Spain, all of whom, with Denmark, must desire it, could be effectuated for freeing the ocean of privateers and search ships, and directing, by common agreement, the operations of war against ships of war, leaving the merchant-man to the peaceable pursuit of his traffic; and if such a system could be secured without our being drawn into hostilities, it certainly were a consummation devoutly to be wished. But peace and neutrality are the vital sparks of America, and whatever we may hope to see one day achieved, provided this belligerent pretension can be restricted to the least onerous executions, it is better we bear those ills we have, than fly to others that we know not of. If American vessels are to be stopped and examined in every latitude, forced to exhibit their papers and letters on board the examining ship, and, on the slightest suspicion, be sent to distant ports for interrogation and trial, the least alleviation to be expected should be, in the first instance, a candid and decent examination in their own cabins; and, if sent in, a speedy and cheap trial, according to the law of nations.

What is their treatment? Compelled, at the peril of being fired upon, no matter what the weather may be, to put out their boat, and go on board the examining vessel, where in general they experience an arrogant overhauling, and the most indecent reception. This is not only on the high seas, the highway of nations; but English squadrons hover, like birds of prey, round our estuaries, and harbours, and cover the whole extent of American coast, stopping and ransacking every sail that appears, from the rich Indiaman or London trader, down to the wood shallop, that plies between the counties and the capitals, or the pleasure boat with ladies, that makes an hour's excursion without the port. This is a state of dependence and blockade on our part, and of outrage and investment on theirs, which the catastrophe of Pierce for an interval suspended. But unless permanent and strong ground be taken by the American government for preventing the recurrence of such ignominious and inhuman scenes, no doubt they will be re-acted with more ranting, insolence, and bloodshed than ever.

It is a heavy injury to the American flag, that free ships do not make free goods, for the right to search is a great impediment to fair trade; it is a cruel aggravation of that injury, that its infliction is so wantonly harsh and opprobrious. . . .

2. Of all the acts of injustice committed on American commerce, by foreign powers, the most crying is the impressment of our seamen from our vessels. This is a grievance proceeding from England alone, which in the nature of things will never be inflicted by other nations. France and Spain will never want American seamen; and, if they should, they will never have it to say, as the English allege that it is almost impossible to distinguish ours from theirs. This is a pretension not to be varnished with excuses, nor justified by necessity. It is arbitrary, unjust, and tyrannical; and, as England has made all Americans feel, has been so exacerbated by the unmanly and brutal manner in which it has been exercised in many, but particularly one fatal instance, [the Chesapeake] that the dispute, from being one of right and policy, now involves the dearer considerations of national honour and sensibility.

When we are robbed of our property by foreign captors, and courts, and barred of all indemnity by the sanctity of their adjudications, it is natural that our complaints should be loud and deep, though it cannot be said our patience has not been long suffering, and silent. But when our persons, our liberties, our lives are to be sacrificed to the phrenzy of aggrandizement, humanity dispenses with the calculations of policy, and a generous and enthusiastic indignation supersedes all discussion. . . .

3. While it cannot be denied that what is styled the universal law of nations, contains no restriction whatever on the indiscriminate transportations of all articles of commerce, it must be conceded that treaties for the last three centuries stipulate against the legality of certain articles denominated contraband of war. There is therefore, in effect, as much of a law on this subject as on any other: though jurists have chosen to distinguish it from most others, by a declaration, in which (*mirabile dictu*) they agree, that contraband is a creation of treaties, and not within the scope of the law of nations. Unless to besieged or blockaded places, there would seem to be no reason for the prohibition of supplies, in time of war more than in time of peace: otherwise the subsequent belligerent pretension destroys the pre-existent neutral right; and if the voice of humanity is to have any authority, in most cases its calls are much louder in war than in peace, for the commercial assistance of neutrals. As the law of nations never did, and does not, specify a single article of contraband, it follows that the rights of parties must be referred to their treaties, and to them alone, for accommodation, when they clash in respect to what is or is not contraband. A treaty, creating certain regulations in this particular between any two countries, is no criterion in disputes between one of them and any other country. And when no treaty exists between two countries, one of them has no right to molest the other in the transportation of any supplies, munitions, or other articles of whatsoever species to any other country, which may happen to be at war with the first: for the law of nations does not include such a case; and it is offending all propriety to apply by force the assertion of any principle not established by law. Thus Russia, with whom the United States have no treaty, would have no right to intercept warlike stores on their voyage from a port of the United States to a port in England, though Russia is at war with England; nor has England any right to intercept the exportation of instruments of war by vessels of the United States to any port in Russia, or any other country with which England is at war; provided always that port be not blockaded, which gives a right we shall consider presently. According to the laws of nations, it is, therefore, the right of the United States to ship the several materials for hostilities, which come under the specification of

contraband in the British treaty, to any and every part of the world, without let or hindrance from England, because having now no treaty with England, there exists no prohibition or understanding which can justify their seizure or condemnation. . . .

But the mischief did not stop here. In order that our rights might be completely prostrated, and our mouths hermetically sealed, one of those diplomatic ambiguities, which are framed to cause confusion worse confounded, was thrown over this whole article, in the shape of a declaration, in effect, that England should seize and condemn, as contraband, any provision *or other articles* which should be obnoxious to her future necessities. With the sanction of such a devouring clause as this, it cannot be surprising that England should, whenever it was convenient, direct the capture of any thing whatever, and its condemnation, as contraband. . . .

Though contraband has no footing in the law of nations, blockade has perhaps a firmer foundation in that law than any other belligerent right. I do not mean by this acknowledgement to concede the rights of neutrality to those of war; or to admit that the latter, in point of first principles, may, under any circumstances, supersede the former. But if there is any case, when the belligerent may so enforce his hostilities as to injure neutrals, it is when they attempt to break a line of circumvallation, which he has been at the expense and peril of drawing by his fleets or armies round a port or place of his enemy, for the purpose of distressing or reducing it. When an army or a squadron actually invest a town or harbour, by seige or blockade, war gives the right (if war can give any right) of preventing the approach of friends or succour; and reducing it to submission by famine, bombardment, storm, mining, or any other process of destruction. Neutrals cannot intervene with assistance, without futilizing the labours and designs of the blockading belligerent: wherefore, though it may be of much greater moment to the place blockaded that it should be saved from starvation or surrender, than it is to the blockading power to possess it, and therefore the neutral cannot be passive or active, without offending the wants of one party or the rights of the other, yet it seems agreed by all nations, which entitle themselves civilized, that the neutral shall remain passive, though a great loser by that situation, rather than be active. But this belligerent right is as defined as it is undeniable: nor was its definition or limitation ever doubtful in the smallest degree, till the excesses of England, in the present and last wars, transcended and overthrew them.

A blockade by sea is analogous at all points to a seige by land.

Certain principles are equally applicable to them both. There must be actual and sufficient investing force; and to legalize the enforcement of their privations on neutrals, there must be timely notice to them of their existence and extent. Proclamation blockades, without investing obsidiary fleets, are, in fact and in law, visionary and of no effect. No neutral is bound to pay any regard to them: for to deprive the neutral of his pre-existent right, it is a *sine qua non* that the place be surrounded with a sufficient squadron. Whenever the blockade surceases, partially, accidently, or for a time, by the blowing off of the blockading squadron, by its leaving the station in pursuit of an enemy, or by any other cause, the restoration of neutral rights is instantaneous and consummate. . . . All these principles have been, at different times, assailed and unhinged by the British admiralty courts. The decisions of Sir Wm. Scott on this subject during the last ten years, predicating themselves on the most abominable fallacies, have, in a course of successive invasions, destroyed them one after another. His decisions on blockade are at open war with each other, and with all law, common sense, and common decency. It is unnecessary here to explore their crooked course, because the fearful stage, at which this belligerent pretension has at last arrived, renders the review of all minor aberrations of little interest. I shall therefore pass at once from every anterior abuse, to concentrate attention on the late orders and decrees: those absurd and savage violations of neutrality and the laws of nature. In these, as in their other retaliating measures, the French do not pretend to assert abstract essential justice, or propriety. Even the English have here abandoned their usual policy, and boldly take their stand upon retaliation and necessity. American rights and American wrongs are equally disregarded in this ferocious contest, in which the colossal gladiators, become, the one intoxicated with success, and the other desperate with disaster, level their weapons at random, without considering whom they may destroy, and without even the appearance of regard for those refinements of civilization and comity which presided over their former battles. It is humiliating to the United States that they should be thus buffeted by both parties, without any further atonement than the reiterated asseverations of an inevitable retaliation, which itself tramples in the earth our most unquestional [sic] immunities. But as the question is stated on this issue by both belligerents, let us inquire for the source of these bitter waters of retaliation; and if we succeed in ascertaining it, the next step will be toward measures calculated to prevent their recurrence. . . .

7
THE EMBARGO

The inability of the United States either to secure a swift settlement of the *Chesapeake* affair or to gain relief from the oppressive maritime practices of Britain and France drove her to search for new initiatives and new measures. She had already tried nonimportation and nonintercourse acts and these had proved to be singularly ineffective. And since war was still an unthinkable alternative, Jefferson turned to an embargo — a measure which uniquely combined the advantages of punishing Europe for its transgressions and protecting American commerce from continued depredations.

The measure received quick Cabinet approval and rapid passage through Congress, but its results fell far short of the goals which its supporters had anticipated. Instead of coercing Britain and France it left them unmoved. And its effects upon the United States were nearly disastrous. Hardly any portion of the nation was left untouched. New England's commerce collapsed and southern and western states lost their export markets.

The most savage attacks upon the embargo came from the Federalists who felt that the embargo was chiefly aimed against Britain — the last hope of ordered and good government in Europe. Timothy Pickering, a New England Federalist, wrote a harsh denunciation of the measure. It was answered by John Quincy Adams (1767–1848), a member of the Senate from 1803 to 1808, who later served as minister to Russia and Great Britain, as well as President of the United States. Adams had voted for the embargo and held to the view that while it had failed in its main purpose, it was the only peaceful solution to the problems of 1807.

JOHN QUINCY ADAMS TO HARRISON GRAY OTIS

March 31, 1808

DEAR SIR:

I have received from one of my friends in Boston a copy of a printed pamphlet, containing a letter from Mr. Pickering to the Governor of the Commonwealth, intended for communication to the legislature of the State, during their session, recently concluded. But this object not having been accomplished, it appears to have been published by some friend of the writer, whose inducement is stated, no doubt truly, to have been the importance of the matter discussed in it, and the high respectability of the author.

The subjects of this letter are the embargo, and the differences in controversy between our country and Great Britain — subjects upon which it is my misfortune, in the discharge of my duties as a Senator of the United States, to differ from the opinions of my Colleague. The place where the question upon the first of them, in common with others of great national concern, was between him and me, in our official capacities a proper object of discussion, was the Senate of the Union. There it was discussed, and, as far as the constitutional authority of that body extended, there it was decided. Having obtained alike the concurrence of the other branch of the national legislature, and the approbation of the President, it became the law of the land, and as such I have considered it entitled to the respect and obedience of every virtuous citizen.

From these decisions, however, the letter in question is to be considered in the nature of an appeal; in the first instance, to our common constituents, the legislature of the state; and in the second, by the publication, to the people.

. . .

The first remark which obtrudes itself upon the perusal of Mr. Pickering's letter is, that in enumerating all the *pretences* (for he thinks there are no causes) for the embargo, and for a war with Great Britain, he has totally omitted the British Orders in Council of November 11, 1807, those orders under which millions of the property of our fellow citizens, are now detained in British hands, or

FROM *The Writings of John Quincy Adams*, W. C. Ford, ed. (New York, 1914), vol. 3, pp. 189-223.

confiscated to British captors, those orders, under which tenfold as many millions of the same property would have been at this moment in the same predicament, had they not been saved from exposure to it by the embargo, those orders which if once submitted to and carried to the extent of their principles, would not have left an inch of American canvas upon the ocean, but under British license and British taxation. An attentive reader of the letter, without other information, would not even suspect their existence. They are indeed in one or two passages, faintly, and darkly alluded to under the justifying description of "the orders of the British government, *retaliating* the French imperial decree:" but as causes for the embargo, or as possible causes or even *pretences* of war with Great Britain, they are not only unnoticed, but their very existence is by direct implication denied.

It is indeed true, that these orders were not officially communicated with the President's message recommending the embargo. They had not been officially received. But they were announced in several paragraphs from London and Liverpool newspapers of the 10th, 11th and 12th of November, which appeared in the *National Intelligencer* of 18th December, the day upon which the embargo message was sent to Congress. The British government had taken care that they should not be authentically known before their time — for the very same newspapers which gave this inofficial [sic] notice of these orders, announced also the departure of Mr. Rose, upon a special mission to the United States. And we know that of these all-devouring instruments of rapine Mr. Rose was not even informed. His mission was professedly a mission of conciliation and reparation for a flagrant, enormous, acknowledged outrage. But he was not sent with these Orders of Council in his hands. His text was the disavowal of Admiral Berkeley's conduct. The commentary was to be discovered on another page of the British ministerial policy. On the face of Mr. Rose's instructions, these Orders in Council were as invisible, as they are on that of Mr. Pickering's letter.

They were not merely without official authenticity. Rumors had for several weeks been in circulation derived from English prints, and from private correspondence, that such orders were to issue; and no inconsiderable pains were taken here to discredit the fact. Assurances were given that there was reason to believe no such orders to be contemplated. Suspicion was lulled by declarations equivalent nearly to a positive denial: and these opiates were continued for weeks after the embargo was laid, until Mr. Erskine received instructions to make the official communication of the orders themselves, in their proper shape, to our government.

Yet, although thus unauthenticated, and even although thus in some sort denied, the probability of the circumstances under which they were announced, and the sweeping tendency of their effects, formed to my understanding a powerful motive, and together with the papers sent by the President, and his express recommendation, a decisive one, for assenting to the embargo. As a precautionary measure, I believed it would rescue an immense property from depredation, if the orders should prove authentic. If the alarm was groundless, it must very soon be disproved, and the embargo might be removed with the danger.

The omission of all notice of these facts in the pressing enquiries "why the Embargo was laid?" is the more surprising, because they are of all the facts, the most material, upon a fair and impartial examination of the expediency of that Act, when it passed. And because these orders, together with the subsequent "retaliating decrees" of France and Spain, have furnished the only reasons upon which I have acquiesced in its continuance to this day. If duly weighed, they will save us the trouble of resorting to jealousies of secret corruption, and the imaginary terrors of Napoleon for the real cause of the embargo. These are fictions of foreign invention. The French Emperor had *not* declared that he would have no neutrals. He had *not* required that our ports should be shut against British commerce — but the Orders of Council if submitted to would have degraded us to the condition of colonies. If resisted would have fattened the wolves of plunder with our spoils. The embargo was the only shelter from the Tempest — the last refuge of our violated peace.

I have indeed been myself of opinion that the embargo, must in its nature be a temporary expedient, and that preparations manifesting a determination of resistance against these outrageous violations of our neutral rights ought at least to have been made a subject of serious deliberation in Congress. I have believed and do still believe that our internal resources are competent to the establishment and maintenance of a naval force, public and private, if not fully adequate to the protection and defence of our commerce, at least sufficient to induce a retreat from these hostilities and to deter from a renewal of them, by either of the warring parties; and that a system to that effect might be formed, ultimately far more economical, and certainly more energetic than a three years embargo. Very soon after the closure of our ports, I did submit to the consideration of the Senate, a proposition for the appointment of a committee to institute an enquiry to this end. But my resolution met no encouragement. Attempts of a similar nature have been made in the House of Representatives, but have been equally discountenanced, and from these determinations by decided majorities of both houses, I am not sufficiently confident in the superiority of my own wisdom to appeal, by a topical application to the congenial feelings of any one — not even of my own native section of the Union.

The embargo, however, is a restriction always under our own control. It was a measure altogether of defence and of experiment. If it was injudiciously or over-hastily laid, it has been every day since its adoption open to repeal: if it should prove ineffectual for the purposes which it was meant to secure, a single day will suffice to unbar the doors. Still believing it a measure justified by the circumstances of the time, I am ready to admit that those who thought otherwise may have had a wiser foresight of events, and a sounder judgment of the then existing state of things than the majority of the national legislature, and the President. It has been approved by several of the State legislatures, and among the rest by our own. Yet of all its effects we are still unable to judge with certainty. It must still abide the test of futurity. I shall add that there were other motives which had their operation in contributing to the passage of the act, unnoticed by Mr. Pickering, and which having now ceased will also be left unnoticed by me. The Orders of Council of 11th November still subsist in all their force; and are now confirmed, with the addition of taxation, by act of Parliament.

As they stand in front of the real causes for the embargo, so they are entitled to the same pre-eminence in enumerating the causes of hostility, which the British ministers are accumulating upon our forbearance. They strike at the root of our independence. They assume the principle that we shall have no commerce in time of war, but with her dominions, and as tributaries to her. The exclusive confinement of commerce to the mother country, is the great principle of the modern colonial system; and should we by a dereliction of our rights at this momentous stride of encroachment surrender our commercial freedom without a struggle, Britain has but a single step more to take, and she brings us back to the stamp act and the tea tax.

Yet these orders — thus fatal to the liberties for which the sages and heroes of our revolution toiled and bled — thus studiously concealed until the moment when they burst upon our heads — thus issued at the very instant when a mission of atonement was professedly sent — in these orders we are to see nothing but a "retaliating order upon France" — in these orders, we must not find so much as a cause — nay not so much as a pretence, for complaint against Britain.

To my mind, sir, in comparison with those orders, the three causes to which Mr. Pickering explicitly limits our grounds for a rupture with England, might indeed be justly denominated *pretences;* in comparison with them, former aggressions sink into insignificance. To argue upon the subject of our disputes with Britain, or upon the motives for the embargo, and keep them out of sight, is like laying your finger over the *unit* before a series of noughts, and then arithmetically proving that they all amount to nothing.

It is not however in a mere omission, nor yet in the history of the embargo, that the inaccuracies of the statement I am examining have given me the most serious concern — it is in the view taken of the questions in controversy between us and Britain. The wisdom of the embargo is a question of great, but transient magnitude, and omission sacrifices no national right. Mr. Pickering's object was to dissuade the nation from a war with England, into which he suspected the administration was plunging us, under French compulsion. But the tendency of his pamphlet is to reconcile the nation, or at least the commercial states, to the servitude of British protection, and war with all the rest of Europe. Hence England is represented as contending for the common liberties of mankind, and our only safe-guard against the ambition and injustice of France. Hence all our sensibilities are invoked in her favor, and all our antipathies against her antagonist. Hence, too, all the subjects of difference between us and Britain are alleged to be on our part mere *pretences,* of which the *right* is unequivocally pronounced to be *on her side.* Proceeding from a Senator of the United States, specially charged as a member of the executive with the maintenance of the nation's rights, against foreign powers, at a moment extremely critical of pending negotiation upon all the points thus delineated, this formal *abandonment* of the American cause, this summons of unconditional surrender to the pretensions of our antagonist, is in my mind highly alarming. It becomes therefore a duty to which every other consideration must yield to point out the errors of this representation. Before we strike the standard of the nation, let us at least examine the purport of the summons.

And first, with respect to the impressment of our seamen. We are told that "the taking of British seamen found on board our merchant vessels, by British ships of war, is agreeably to a *right,* claimed and exercised for ages." It is obvious that this claim and exercise of ages, could not apply to us, as an independent people. If the right was claimed and exercised while our vessels were navigating under the British flag, it could not authorize the same claim when their owners have become the citizens of a sovereign state.

As a relict of colonial servitude, whatever may be the claim of Great Britain, it surely can be no ground for contending that it is entitled to our submission.

If it be meant that the right has been claimed and exercised for ages over the merchant vessels of other nations, I apprehend it is a mistake. The case never occurred with sufficient frequency to constitute even a practice, much less a right. If it had been either, it would have been noticed by some of the writers on the laws of nations. The truth is, the question arose out of American independence — from the severance of one nation into two. It was never made a question between any other nation. There is therefore no right of prescription.

But, it seems, it has also been *claimed* and *exercised*, during the whole of three administrations of our national government. And is it meant to be asserted that this claim and exercise constitutes a right? If it is, I appeal to the uniform, unceasing and urgent remonstrances of the three administrations — I appeal not only to the warm feelings, but cool justice of the American people — nay, I appeal to the sound sense and honorable sentiment of the British nation itself, which, however, it may have submitted at home to this practice, never would tolerate its sanction by law, against the assertion. If it is not, how can it be affirmed that it is on our part a mere pretense?

But the first merchant of the United States, in answer to Mr. Pickering's late enquiries has informed him that since the affair of the *Chesapeake* there has been no cause of complaint — that he could not find a single instance where they had taken one man out of a merchant vessel. Who it is, that enjoys the dignity of the first merchant of the United States we are not informed. But if he had applied to many merchants in Boston as respectable as any in the United States, they could have told him of a valuable vessel and cargo, totally lost upon the coast of England, last [lost?] in August last, and solely in consequence of having had two of her men, native Americans taken from her by impressment, two months after the affair of the *Chesapeake.*

On the 15th of October, the king of England issued his proclamation, *commanding* his naval officers, to impress his subjects from neutral vessels. This proclamation is represented as merely "requiring the return of his subjects, the seamen especially, from foreign countries," and then "it is an acknowledged principle that every nation has a right to the service of its subjects in time of war." Is this, sir, a correct statement either of the proclamation, or of the question it involves in which *our* right is concerned? The king of England's right to the service of his subjects in time of war is nothing to us. The question is, whether he has a right to seize them forcibly on board of our vessels while under contract of service to our citizens, within our jurisdiction upon the high seas? And whether he has the right expressly to command his naval officers so to seize them. Is this an acknowledged principle? Certainly not. Why then is this proclamation described as founded upon uncontested principle? and why is the command, so justly offensive to us, and so mischievous as it might then have been made in execution, altogether omitted?

But it is not the taking of British subjects from our vessels, it is the taking under that color of that pretence of our own, native American citizens, which constitute the most galling aggravation of this merciless practice. Yet even this, we are told is but a pretence — for three reasons.

1. Because the number of citizens thus taken is *small.*

2. Because it arises *only* from the impossibility of distinguishing Englishmen from Americans.

3. Because, such impressed American citizens are delivered up, on duly authenticated proof.

. . .

Enough, of this disgusting subject. I cannot stop to calculate how many of these wretched victims are natives of Massachusetts, and how many natives of Virginia. I cannot stop to solve the knotty question of national jurisprudence whether some of them might not possible be slaves, and therefore not citizens of the United States. I cannot stay to account for the wonder, why, poor, and ignorant and friendless as most of them are, the voice of their complaints is so seldom *heard* in the great navigating states. I admit that we have endured this cruel indignity, through all the administrations of the General Government. I acknowledge that Britain claims the right of seizing her subjects in our merchant vessels, and that even if we could acknowledge it, the line of discrimination would be difficult to draw. We are not in a condition to maintain this right by war; and as the British government have been more than once on the point of giving it up of their own accord, I would still hope for the day when returning justice shall induce them to abandon it, without compulsion. Her subjects we do not want. The degree of protection which we are bound to extend them, cannot equal the claim of our own citizens. I would subscribe to any compromise of this contest, consistent with the rights of sovereignty, the duties of humanity, and the principles of reciprocity: but to the right of forcing even her own subjects out of our merchant vessels on the high seas I never can assent.

The second point upon which Mr. Pickering defends the pretensions of Great Britain, is her denial to neutral nations of the right of prosecuting with her enemies and their colonies, any commerce from which they are excluded in time of peace. His statement of this case adopts the British doctrine as sound. The *right*, as on the question of impressment, so on this, it surrenders at discretion — and it is equally defective in point of fact.

In the first place, the claim of Great Britain is not to "a right of imposing on this neutral commerce *some limits and restraints*," but of interdicting it altogether, at her pleasure; of interdicting it without a moment's notice to neutrals, after solemn decisions of her courts of admiralty, and formal acknowledgments of her ministers, that it is a lawful trade. And, on such a sudden, unnotified interdiction, of pouncing upon all neutral commerce navigating upon the faith of her decisions and acknowledgments, and of gorging with confiscation the greediness of her cruisers. This is the right claimed by Britain. This is the power she has exercised. What Mr. Pickering calls "limits and restraints," she calls relaxations of her right.

It is but little more than two years, since this question was agitated both in England and America, with as much zeal, energy and ability, as ever was displayed upon any question of national law. The British side was supported by Sir William Scott, Mrs. Ward, and the author of *War in Disguise*. But even in Britain their doctrine was refuted to demonstration by the Edinburg reviewers. In America, the rights of our country were maintained by numerous writers profoundly skilled in the science of national and maritime law. The *Answer to War in Disguise* was ascribed to a gentleman whose talents are universally acknowledged, and who by his official situations had been required thoroughly to investigate every question of conflict between neutral and belligerent rights which has occurred in the history of modern war. Mr. Gore and Mr. Pinckney, our two commissioners in London, under Mr. Jay's treaty, the former, in a train of cool and conclusive argument addressed to Mr. Madison, the latter in memorial of splendid eloquence from the merchants of Baltimore, supported the same cause; memorials, drawn by lawyers of distinguished eminence, by merchants of the highest character, and by statesmen of long experience in our national councils from Salem, from Boston, from New Haven, from New York, and from Philadelphia, together with remonstrances to the same effect from

Newburyport, Newport, Norfolk and Charleston. This accumulated mass of legal learning, of commercial information and of national sentiment from almost every inhabited spot upon our shores, and from one extremity of the Union to the other, confirmed by the unanswered and unanswerable memorial of Mr. Monroe to the British minister, and by the elaborate research and irresistible reasoning of the *examination* of the British doctrine, was also made a subject of full, and deliberate discussion in the Senate of the United States. A committee of seven members of that body, after three weeks of arduous investigation, reported three resolutions, the first of which was in these words:

> RESOLVED, that the capture and condemnation, under the orders of the British government, and adjudications of their courts of admiralty of American vessels, and their cargoes, on the pretext of their being employed in a trade with the enemies of Great Britain, prohibited in time of peace, is an unprovoked aggression upon the property of the citizens of these United States, a violation of their neutral rights, and *an encroachment upon their national independence.*

On the 13th of February, 1806 the question upon the adoption of this resolution, was taken in the Senate. The yeas and nays were required; but not a solitary *nay* was heard in answer. It was adopted by unanimous voice of all the senators present. They were twenty-eight in number, and among them stands recorded the name of Mr. Pickering.

Let us remember that this was a question most peculiarly and immediately of *commercial,* and not *agricultural* interest; that it arose from a call, loud, energetic and unanimous from all the merchants of the United States upon Congress, for the national interposition; that, many of the memorials invoked all the energy of the legislature, and pledged the lives and properties of the memorialists in support of any measures which Congress might deem necessary to vindicate those rights. Negotiation was particularly recommended from Boston, and elsewhere — negotiation was adopted — negotiation has failed — and now Mr. Pickering tells us that Great Britain has claimed and maintained her *right.* He argues that her claim is just — and is not sparing of censure upon those who still consider it as a serious cause of complaint.

But there was one point of view in which the British doctrine on this question was then only considered incidentally in the United States — because it was not deemed material for the discussion of our rights. We examined it chiefly as affecting the principles as between a belligerent and a neutral power. But in fact it was an infringement of the rights of war, as well as of the rights of peace. It was an unjustifiable enlargement of the sphere of hostile operations. The *enemies* of Great Britain had by the universal law of nations a right to the benefits of neutral commerce within their dominions (subject to the exception of *actual* blockade and contraband) as well as neutral nations had a right to trade with them. The exclusion from that commerce by this new principle of warfare which Britain, in defiance of all immemorial national usages, undertook by her single authority to establish, but too naturally led her enemies to resort to new and extraordinary principles, by which in their turn they might retaliate this injury upon her. The pretence upon which Britain in the first instance had attempted to color her injustice, was a miserable *fiction*. It was an argument against fact. Her reasoning was, that a neutral vessel by mere admission in time of war, into ports from which it would have been excluded in time of peace, became thereby deprived of its national character, and *ipso facto* was transformed into enemy's property.

Such was the basis upon which arose the far famed rule of the war of 1756. Such was the foundation upon which Britain *claimed* and *maintained* this supposed right of adding that new instrument of desolation to the horrors of war. It was distressing the enemy. Yes! Had she adopted the practice of dealing with them in poison; had Mr. Fox accepted the services of the man who offered to rid him of the French Emperor by assassination, and had the attempt succeeded, it would have been less distressing to France than this rule of the war of 1756; and not more unjustifiable. Mr. Fox had too fair a mind for either, but his comprehensive and liberal spirit was discarded, with the cabinet which he had formed.

It has been the struggle of reason and humanity, and above all of christianity for two thousand years to mitigate the rigors of that scourge of human kind, war. It is now the struggle of Britain to aggravate them. Her rule of the war of 1756, in itself and in its effects, was one of the deadliest poisons, in which it was possible for her to tinge the weapons of her hostility.

In itself and in its effects, I say. For the French decrees of Berlin and Milan, the Spanish and Dutch decrees of the same or the like tenor, and her own orders of January and November — these alternations of licensed pillage, this eager competition between her and her enemies for the honor of giving the last stroke to the vitals of maritime neutrality, all are justly attributed to her assumption and exercise of this single principle. The rule of the war of 1756 was the root, from which all the rest but suckers, still at every shoot growing ranker in luxuriance.

In the last decrees of France and Spain, her own ingenious fiction is adopted; and under them, every neutral vessel that submits to English search, has been carried into an English port, or paid a tax to the English government, is declared *denationalized*, that is to have lost her national character, and to have become English property. This is cruel in execution; absurd in agreement. To refute it were folly, for to the understanding of a child it refutes itself. But it is the reasoning of British jurists. It is the simple application to the circumstances and powers of France, of the rule of the war of 1756.

I am not the apologist of France and Spain; I have no national partialities; no national attachments but to you my own country. I shall never undertake to justify or to palliate the insults or injuries of any foreign power to that country which is dearer to me than life. If the voice of reason and of justice could be heard by France and Spain, they would say, you have done wrong to make the injustice of your enemy towards neutrals the measure of your own. If she chastises with whips do not you chastise with scorpions. Whether France would listen to this language, I know not. The most enormous infractions of our rights hitherto committed by her, have been more in menace than in accomplishment. The alarm has been justly great; the anticipation threatening; but the amount of actual injury small. But to Britain, what can we say? If we attempt to raise our voices, her minister has declared to Mr. Pinckney that she will not hear. The only reason she assigns for her recent Orders of Council is, that France proceeds on the same principles. It is not by the light of blazing temples, and amid the groans of women and children perishing in the ruins of the sanctuaries of domestic habitations at Copenhagen, that we can expect our remonstrances against this course of proceeding will be heard.

Let us come to the third and the last causes of complaint, which are represented as so frivolous and so unfounded — "the unfortunate affair of the *Chesapeake*." The orders of Admiral Berkeley, under which this outrage was committed, have been disavowed by his government. General professions of a willingness to make reparation for it, have been lavished in profusion; and we are now instructed to take these professions for *endeavors*: to believe them sincere, because his Britannic Majesty sent us a special envoy; and to cast the odium of defeating these endeavours upon our own government.

I have already told you, that I am not one of those who deem suspicion and distrust, in the highest order of political virtues. Baseless suspicion is, in my estimation, a vice, as pernicious in the management of public affairs, as it is fatal to the happiness of domestic life. When, therefore, the British ministers have declared their disposition to make ample reparation for an injury of a most atrocious character, committed by an officer of high rank, and, as they say, utterly without authority, I should most readily believe them, were their professions not positively contradicted by facts of more powerful eloquence than words.

Have such facts occurred? I will not allude to the circumstances of Mr. Rose's departure upon his mission at such a precise point of time, that his commission and the Orders of Council of 11th November, might have been signed with the same penful of ink. The subjects were not immediately connected with each other, and his Majesty did not chose to associate distinct topics of negotiation. The attack upon the *Chesapeake* was disavowed; and ample reparation was withheld only, because with the demand for satisfaction upon that injury, the American government had coupled a demand for the cessation of others; alike in kind, but of minor aggravation. But had reparation really been intended, would it not have been offered, not in vague and general terms, but in precise and specific proposals? Were any such made? None. But it is said Mr. Monroe was restricted from negotiating upon this subject apart; and therefore Mr. Rose was to be sent to Washington; charged with this single object; and without authority to treat upon or even to discuss any other. Mr. Rose arrives. The American government readily determines to treat upon the *Chesapeake affair*, separately from all others; but before Mr. Rose sets his foot on shore, in pursuance of a pretension made before by Mr. Canning, he connects with the negotiation, a subject far more distinct from the butchery of the *Chesapeake*, than the general impressment of our seamen, I mean the proclamation, interdicting to British ships of war, the entrance of our harbours.

The great obstacle which has always interfered in the adjustment of our differences with Britain, has been that she would not acquiesce in th principle upon which fair negotiation between independent nations can be conducted, the principle of reciprocity, that she refuses the application to us of the claim which she asserts for herself. The forcible taking of men from an American vessel, was an essential part of the outrage upon the *Chesapeake*. It was the ostensible purpose for which an act of war unproclaimed, was committed. The President's proclamation was a subsequent act, and was avowedly founded upon many similar aggressions, of which that was only the most aggravated.

If then Britain could with any color of reason claim that the general question of impressment should be laid out of the case altogether, she ought upon the principle of reciprocity to have laid equally out of the case, the proclamation, a measure so easily separable from it, and in its nature merely defensive. When therefore she made the repeal of the proclamation an indispensable preliminary to all discussion upon the nature and extent of that reparation which she had offered, she refused to treat with us upon the footing of an independent power. She insisted upon an act of self-degradation on our part, before she would even tell us, what redress she would condescend to grant for a great and acknowledged wrong. This was a condition which she could not but know to be inadmissible, and is of itself proof nearly conclusive that her cabinet never intended to make for that wrong any reparation at all.

But this is not all. It cannot be forgotten that when that atrocious deed was committed, amidst the general burst of indignation which resounded from every part of the Union, there were among us a small number of persons, who upon the opinion that Berkeley's orders were authorized by his government, undertook to justify them in their fullest extent. These ideas probably first propagated by British official characters, in this country, were persisted in until the disavowal of the British government took away the necessity for persevering in them, and gave notice where the next position was to be taken. This patriotic reasoning however had been so satisfactory at Halifax, that complimentary letters were received from Admiral Berkeley himself highly approving the spirit in which they were inculcated, and remarking how easily *peace*, between the United States and Britain might be preserved, if *that* measure of our national rights could be made the prevailing standard of the country.

When the news arrived in England, although the general sentiment of the nation was not prepared for the formal avowal and justification of this unparalleled aggression, yet there were not wanting persons there, ready to *claim and maintain* the right of searching national ships for deserters. It was said at the time, but for this we must of course rest upon the credit of inofficial [sic] authority, to have been made a serious question in the Cabinet Council; nor was its determination there ascribed to the eloquence of the gentleman who became the official organ of its communication. Add to this a circumstance, which without claiming irrefragable credence of a diplomatic note, has yet its weight upon the common sense of mankind; that in all the daily newspapers known to be in the ministerial interest, Berkeley was justified and applauded in every variety of form that publication could assume, excepting only that of official proclamation. The only part of his orders there disapproved was the reciprocal offer which he made of submitting his own ships to be searched in return — that was very unequivocally disclaimed. The ruffian right of superior force, was the solid base upon which the claim was asserted, and so familiar was this argument grown to the casuists of British national jurisprudence, that the right of a British man-of-war to search an American frigate, was to them a self-evident proof against the right of the American frigate to search the British man-of-war. The same tone has been constantly kept up, until our accounts of latest date; and have been recently further invigorated by a very explicit call for war with the United States, which they contend could be of no possible injury to Britain, and which they urge upon the ministry as affording them an excellent opportunity to accomplish a *dismemberment of this Union*. These sentiments have even been avowed in Parliament, where the nobleman who moved the address of the house of Lords in answer to the king's speech, declared that the right of searching national ships, ought to be maintained against the Americans, and disclaimed only with respect to European sovereigns.

. . .

Under all these circumstances, without applying any of the maxims of a suspicious policy to the British professions, I may still be permitted to believe that their ministry never seriously intended to make us honorable reparation, or indeed any reparation at all for that "unfortunate affair."

It is impossible for any man to form an accurate idea of the British policy towards the United States, without taking into consideration the state of parties in that government, and the views, characters and opinions of the individuals at their helm of state. A liberal and a hostile policy towards America, are among the strongest marks of distinction between the political systems of the rival statesmen of that kingdom. The liberal party are reconciled to our independence; and though extremely tenacious of every right of their own country, are systematically disposed to preserve *peace* with the United States. Their opponents harbor sentiments of a very different description. Their system is coercion. Their object the recovery of their lost dominion in North America. This party now stands high in power. Although Admiral Berkeley may never have received written orders from them for his enterprise upon the *Chesapeake*, yet in giving his instructions to the squadron at Norfolk, he knew full well under what administration he was acting. Every measure of that administration towards us since that time has been directed to the same purpose — to break down the spirit of our national independence. Their purpose, as far as it can be collected from their acts, is to force us into war with them or with their enemies; to leave us only the bitter alternative of their vengeance or their protection.

Both these parties are no doubt willing, that we should join them in the war of their nation against France and her allies. The late administration would have drawn us into it by treaty, the present are attempting it by compulsion. The former would have admitted us as allies, the latter will have us no otherwise than as colonists. On the late debates in Parliament, the Lord Chancellor freely avowed that the Orders of Council of 11th November were intended to make America *at last* sensible of the policy of joining England against France.

This too, sir, is the substantial argument of Mr. Pickering's letter. The suspicions of a *design* in our own administration have every interest and every motive that can influence the conduct of man to deter them from any such purpose. Nor have I seen anything in their measures bearing the slightest indication of it. But between a design of war with England, and a surrender of our national freedom for the sake of war with the rest of Europe, there is a material difference. This is the policy now in substance recommended to us, and for which the interposition of the commercial States is called. For this, not only are all the outrages of Britain to be forgotten, but the very assertion of our rights is to be branded with odium. *Impressment. Neutral trade. British taxation.* Everything that can distinguish a state of national freedom from a state of national vassalage, is to be *surrendered at discretion.* In the face of every fact we are told to believe every profession. In the midst of every *indignity,* we are pointed to British protection as our only shield against the universal conqueror. Every phantom of jealousy and fear is evoked. The image of France with a scourge in her hand is impressed into the service, to lash us into the refuge of obedience to Britain. Insinuations are even made that if Britain "with her thousand ships of war," has not destroyed our commerce, it has been owing to her indulgence, and we are almost threatened in her name with the "destruction of our fairest cities."

Not one act of hostility to Britain has been committed by us, she has not a pretence of that kind to allege. But if she will wage war upon us, are we to do nothing in our own defense? If she issues orders of universal plunder upon our commerce, are we not to withold it from her grasp? Is American pillages one of those rights which she has claimed and exercised until we are foreclosed from any attempt to obstruct its collection. For what purpose are we required to make this sacrifice of every thing that can give value to the name of freemen, this abandonment of the very right of self-preservation? Is it to avoid a war? Alas! Sir, it does not offer even this plausible plea for pusillanimity. For, as submission would make us to all substantial purposes British colonies, her enemies would unquestionably treat us as such, and after degrading ourselves into voluntary servitude to escape a war with her we should incur inevitable war with all her enemies, and be doomed to share the destinies of her conflict with a world in conflict.

Between this unqualified submission, and offensive resistance against the war upon maritime neutrality waged by the concurring decrees of all the great belligerent powers, the embargo was adopted, and has been hitherto continued. So far was it from being dictated by France, that it was calculated to withdraw, and has withdrawn from within her reach all the means of compulsion which her subsequent decrees would have put in her possession. It has added to the motives both of France and England, for preserving peace with us, and has diminished their inducements to war. It has lessened their capacities of inflicting injury upon us, and given us some preparation for resistance to them. It has taken from their violence the lure of interest. It has dashed the philter of pillage from the lips of rapine. That it is distressing to ourselves — that it calls for the fortitude of a people, determined to maintain their rights, is not to be denied. But the only alternative was between that and war. Whether it will yet save us from that calamity, cannot be determined, but if not, it will prepare us for the further struggle to which we may be called. Its double tendency of promoting peace and preparing for war, in its operation upon the belligerent rivals, is the great advantage, which more than outweighs all its evils.

If any statesman can point out another alternative, I am ready to hear him, and for any practicable expedient to lend him every possible assistance. But let not that expedient be, submission to trade under British licenses, and British taxation. We are told that even under these restrictions we may yet trade to the British dominions, to Africa and China, and with the colonies of France, Spain, and Holland. I ask not, how much of this trade would be left, when our intercourse with the whole continent of Europe being cut off would leave us no means of purchase, and no market for sale? I ask not, what trade we could enjoy with the colonies of nations with which we should be at war? I ask not, how long Britain would leave open to us avenues of trade, which even in these very orders of Council, she boasts of leaving open as a special indulgence? If we yield the principle, we abandon all pretence to national sovereignty. To yearn for the fragments of trade which might be left, would be to pine for the crumbs of commercial servitude. The boon, which we should humiliate ourselves to accept from British bounty, would soon be withdrawn. Submission never yet set boundaries to encroachment. From pleading for half empire, we should sink into suppliants for life. We should supplicate in vain. If we must fall, let us fall, freemen. If we must perish, let it be in defence of our RIGHTS.

To conclude, sir, I am not sensible of any necessity for the extraordinary interference of the commercial States, to control the general councils of the nation. If any interference could at this critical extremity of our affairs have a kindly effect upon our common welfare, it would be an interference to promote union and not a division — to urge mutual confidence, and not universal distrust — to strengthen the arm and not to relax the sinews of the nation. Our suffering and our dangers, though differing perhaps in degree, are universal in extent. As their causes are justly chargeable, so their removal is dependent not upon ourselves, but upon others. But while the spirit of *independence* shall continue to beat in unison with the pulses of the nation, no danger will be truly formidable. Our duties are, to prepare with concerted energy, for those which threaten us, to meet them without dismay, and to rely for their issue upon heaven.

8

AN ALTERNATIVE TO WAR

The failure of the embargo to achieve its goals was driven home to Americans with increasing force as each month passed. Jefferson had exhausted every diplomatic device at his command and retired from office worn down by his labors and disheartened by his inability to protect his country's interests. His successor was Madison who brought both experience and new energy to the task. But he was to find, like Jefferson, that the problems America faced were terribly difficult of solution.

First, of course, the embargo had to be repealed and a substitute measure found for it. Macon's Bill No. 2 was all that a distracted Congress could agree upon. This measure opened trade again with both Britain and France, but provided that if one of these powers repealed its restrictive decrees the United States would, if the other did not follow suit within ninety days, reimpose an embargo upon the offending power. The bill was a wretched measure which exposed the weakness of the United States and, even worse, permitted France or Britain to determine the direction which American foreign policy would take. If the bill could be defended, it was only on the grounds that Madison was aware of its frailty, but hoped that it would give him room to maneuver and might entice his antagonists into meaningful concessions.

It was France that promptly took advantage of Macon's Bill, for she announced that after November 1, 1810, the Berlin and Milan Decrees would be lifted and that if Britain did not rescind her Orders in Council within the stipulated time the United States would be duty bound to impose an embargo upon her. The blunt fact was, of course, that France continued to enforce her decrees, and that Britain refused to accept a doubtful statement of intent when Napoleon's actions so clearly belied his word.

Rufus King (1755–1827), a distinguished Federalist who represented New York in the Senate from 1789 to 1796, served as minister to England from 1796 to 1803 and sat again in the Senate from 1813 to 1825, was highly critical of Macon's Bill and the President's swift acceptance of the Duke of Cadore's letter announcing the conditional repeal of the French decrees. King's criticism of Macon's Bill No. 2 first appeared in the New York *Evening Post,* January 16, 1810, while his discussion of the Presidential Proclamations were probably enclosed in a letter written in December, 1810.

MACON'S BILL NO. 2

Rufus King

MACON'S BILL — Are we never to see the end of measures, equally repugnant to the recorded professions of our rulers, and subversive of the public welfare? After running through all the changes of commercial restrictions, which have humbled the spirit, impaired the morals, and utterly deranged the commerce of the country, is there no prospect of our administration being yet weaned from that folly, that spirit of *faction,* which is fast annihilating the sources of our wealth, as it has already emasculated and disgraced the nation? Or are we to content ourselves with humiliation, poverty and dishonour, provided we receive the approbation and countenance of France? I had really hoped that there did exist among us, if not a sufficiency of elevated pride and sound understanding, at least, such a portion of common sense, and common discernment, as would restrain our rulers from further experiments in the downward course, which, at a period certainly near, must deliver us up to civil convulsions, dissensions and ruin. These rulers, whatever may be their views or their wishes, cannot now plunge the nation into war. The last attempt, by their maneuvre with Mr. Jackson, to inflame the country and to raise it to the war pulse, has entirely failed. Whatever may have been the publick sensibility upon the rupture, the bulletin, the message, and the first appearance of the documents, the debates that have taken place in Congress, joined to the discussions that have appeared in all the leading federal papers, so far destroyed the public confidence in the integrity of these people, that they cannot now, if they would, excite a desire for war. Their only expectations, their only remaining chance for this is to effect the adoption of

FROM *The Life and Correspondence of Rufus King,* Charles R. King, ed. (New York, 1898), vol. 5, pp. 194–8.

measures, which however mischievous to the country, may produce such retaliatory regulations on the part of England, as may be made the occasion of agitating and inflaming the country to such a pitch as will enable them to bring about their object, indirectly.

Mr. Macon's Bill, whatever may have been designed, is a measure of this tendency. There can be no doubt of the authority of Congress to pass a navigation Act. But its principles must be such as will secure us against those retaliatory regulations, which must either put an end to all navigation, or must defeat the professed object of acquiring the whole or a principal part of it for ourselves. As the British navigation Act is deemed to be an authority and a model, let us examine its provisions and compare them with those of Mr. Macon's Bill.

According to the British navigation act, the trade between Great-Britain and a foreign country can be carried on only by British ships, and the ships of such foreign country — and foreign productions can only be imported into England directly from the country of their growth or manufacture. The limitations of this famous act apply only to the articles imported into Great-Britain; it being free for any vessel to export and to carry whithersoever may be desired, the produce and manufacture of Great Britain. Thus by way of illustration, while British merchandize may be exported to Russia in Russian or British vessels, or in the vessels of any other country, which Russia permits to import them, the productions of Russia can be imported into Great-Britain only in British or Russian vessels, and such importations must be directly from Russia, and not from any third place. In time of war, the King in council has by occasional acts of Parliament, a power to dispense with this restraint, as to the direct importations, and to permit foreign merchandize to be imported from intermediate or third places, so that as far as respects the productions and manufactures of Great-Britain, they may be exported in the vessels of any country; as far as concerns the productions and manufactures of any foreign country, they are permitted to be imported into England, such importation is confined to British vessels, and vessels of such foreign country; the right of carriage being common to both.

Mr. Macon's bill proposes a very different regulation: namely, that the whole of the imports of the United States from certain foreign countries, as well as the whole of the exports to these countries, shall be confined to American bottoms. Great-Britain as well as the United States, are commercial nations, and rivals in the carrying trade. It is a maxim alike ancient and equitable, that the law which others apply to us, we may justly apply to them. G. Britain therefore, from those motives which influence all states, will, without doubt, enact a regulation concerning commercial intercourse with them, of the like import with the regulations of Mr. Macon's bill concerning their commercial intercourse with us. The consequence will be that our vessels, being excluded from their ports, & their vessels excluded from ours, they will meet in the Western Islands and other intermediate places, whither we shall carry our exports, and where they, in virtue of a relaxation of this navigation law will come to receive them, as almost every other market will by belligerent Decrees and Orders be closed against us. G. Britain will be the principal and almost the only market for our produce, which is more than sufficient for its supply; so that, to the reductions of price from the want of competitions in the markets, the proposed regulations by requiring the double freight, will reduce still lower the price of our productions. And as by the proposed law, our vessels cannot import into the United States, the manufactures or produce of Great Britain or her territories, except directly; as we shall be shut out from their ports, in the manner that they are shut out from ours – the consequence must be, that no article of British growth or manufacture will be lawfully imported into the U.S. But although ten men may divert the course of a river, a million can not stop it from running to the sea, so although our rulers may forbid the importation of articles which our habits and wants, require, they cannot prevent our obtaining them. We shall be supplied, and the country will not only pay the value of these goods, but an additional sum sufficient to compensate the risk of bringing them. Not only will the goods be supplied at an enhanced price, but the revenue will be defrauded; since being imported contrary to law, no duty will be collected. But even these are not the worse effects of the regulation.

No country on earth possessed a body of more honorable merchants than those of the United States. In none, was there ever so large a revenue collected with so few frauds. Those honorable men, victims of the incapacity of our rulers, will be restrained by the law, but their places will be supplied, as under the existing and former restrictions their places have been supplied, by an unknown yet numerous body of adventurers, who in combination with foreigners, disregarding republicanism, scoffing at patriotism and despising our laws, will fill our markets with smuggled goods. – Already business has shifted hands, and a new class of men appearing amongst us with capital and credit to do that business which more worthy men feel themselves compelled to decline.

If all the power of France has been unable to enforce her prohibition, can we persuade ourselves that the United States will be able to succeed in this impolitic and immoral system? — a system tried during the course of the war of the revolution, and then proved to be utterly defective. What valuable purpose will be accomplished by the continuation of these restrictive measures? Will they coerce foreign nations? Will they restore the public prosperity or replenish the public treasury? They will do neither — and the only motive which can be imagined for their adoption, are first, a compliance with the views of France, and secondly, the hope of thereby prolonging the powers of faction. To rescue the country from these ruinous schemes, to preserve what remains of national honor, and national resources, there is but one course that can save us from ruin, to undo all that has been done — to restore commerce to its freedom and its former channels; to put the country in a condition to meet war; and with a spirit of moderation, firmness, impartiality, and good faith, to attempt an adjustment of our misunderstanding and disagreement with foreign nations. This has not been done since the departure of the _____ Adams, but when done, there are the best grounds for expecting that the result will be honorable and advantageous.

THE PRESIDENT'S PROC-LAMATIONS, 1810

The President has committed the same fault in his late Proclamation concerning France, that he did in his former Proclamation respecting England. In both he departed from the plain Text of the Law and issued his Proclamation, not upon the Existence of a Fact, on which alone he had authority to do so, but upon the Engagement, or Promise, in the one case of an unauthorized Ambassador, and in the other of a disavowed Minister of State. For admitting, contrary to our opinion, that the Duke of Cadore's Letter of August may be construed to be an unconditional Promise, that the Berlin and Milan Decrees should be effectually repealed on the 1st of November; it is now officially ascertained that they were not so repealed on that day; of course the Promise, or which is the same thing, the minister is disavowed, and the Fact, asserted in the name of the President, turns out to be not true.

Rufus King

FROM *The Life and Correspondence of Rufus King*, Charles R. King, ed. (New York, 1898), vol. 5, pp. 227–34.

On the faith of the President's first Proclamation, Property of a very large amount was shipped from this Country to Ports, from which by the British orders in Council we were excluded; and had these Orders been enforced, as in strictness they might have been, (Erskine's arrangement being unauthorized) our losses would have been immense. This did not happen; for England at the same time that she disavowed Erskine's arrangement, suspended the Orders in Council in favour of all American Vessels, which before the knowledge of the disavowal should have sailed for the blockaded Ports. In consequence of this equitable determination, not only were our merchants saved from loss, but in some cases they made very advantageous Voyages. Compare this Conduct of England, of hated, execrated England, with the recent conduct of beloved and applauded France; upon the Faith of the Duke of Cadore's Letter (vouched even by our President) written under the Eye and direction of the Emperor and published in the French official Gazette, our ships with valuable Cargoes have entered the Ports of France. To the astonishment of their owners they find that the Berlin and Milan Decrees are not repealed; the officers of the Government seize and detain them; and the Plea of having acted upon a confidence in the Imperial word, instead of procuring for them Protection, exposes them to derision; no Order has been passed to save from loss those who confided in the royal Promise; on the contrary their Credulity has been scoffed at, and the Property basely and dishonestly plundered.

Tho' the Virtuous and disinterested, the moderate and benevolent Bonaparte may treat thus contemptuously the friendless and unprotected, the degraded and dispirited Citizens of a free Country, have they nothing to hope from the power and affection, the elevation and generous sentiments of their own Government? Or are Republics an inferior and debased species of Government, whose citizens may with impunity be robbed, imprisoned and scourged by slaves of despotism?

Suppose that one of our Countrymen, who still retains impressions derived from the Examples of better Days, should represent to Congress, that subsequent to the President's Proclamation he had engaged in a voyage of great value to France, that upon his arrival in that Country, instead of finding that the Berlin and Milan Decrees had been repealed and had ceased to operate, as the President had declared would be the case, he found them in full Force, and that his ship and cargo had been seized and confiscated for having violated those Decrees; that as he confided in the official declaration of the President, and in consequence thereof had lost his property, he prayed Congress to compensate him for his losses; what Congress would decide on such an application, we cannot beforehand tell; but looking at the Principles of Justice for an answer, looking at the Example of other Governments, and looking even at the conduct of England, we know what ought to be their decision.

In considering the President's Message and the Documents which accompanied it, the matter which they contain in respect to England, may be divided into two distinct parts; the first, comprehending the charge which the President has made, of a breach of faith on the part of England in not confirming the arrangement signed by Mr. Erskine; and the second, the dismission of Mr. Jackson on the charge of disrespect to the Government of the U. States. Each of these charges are important; the first, however, beyond all comparison is the most weighty and must have been intended, and unless honor be a jewel lost from the British Crown, will be sure to produce the most decisive Consequences.

Between belligerent nations we sometimes hear of mutual charges of a breach of faith — tho' until the perilous and fearful times in which we live, these recriminations were rare even between Enemies and, when made, called for the most authentic expositions of the conduct which occasioned them. Anonymous publications in the newspapers, insolent and unmeasured discourses in popular meetings, and even in legislative bodies, however unpracticed in other countries and disreputable in our own, serve rather to exhibit the coarseness of our manners & vulgarity of our tastes, than to produce the animadversion of foreign Powers.

But the President of the United States is considered by the Constitution, and must therefore be regarded by foreign powers, as the Representative of the Nation — in him are vested the exclusive superintendence, control and direction of our foreign affairs. When he speaks therefore upon this important subject, it is not as an individual, but his voice is the voice of a Nation, heard and considered throughout the world.

We may question the wisdom, the prudence, the value, the wealth, or the power of a Nation. These are attributes worthy of esteem and highly to be prized. But a nation may be deficient in one or all of them, and still be a virtuous, beloved, esteemed by others and honorable nation. But a nation that can suffer its integrity, its public faith and honor to be openly and solemnly impeached, without making every exertion in its power to vindicate its reputation, justly & unavoidably loses its consideration in the estimation of all other nations by her acquiescence, becomes convicted of dishonor and merits the degradation inseparable from so foul a reputation.

Whatever may be believed by certain men in this country, there are myriads of men in Britain, who are neither princes nor nobles, and who neither fill nor desire public offices, who believe with pride and confidence that the integrity and public faith of their nation are as unquestionable and unblemished as the virgin's fame. With the divisions and parties of Parliament and ministers, these men have no share; they belong to their country and not to its factions; they love that country, because they are persuaded it is a virtuous and honorable one. It is not for Ships, Colonies, or Commerce that this body of men would beat their plough-shares into swords. Money never was in their estimation a legitimate cause of war, whether it be thousands or millions. They think, and they think justly, that no nation ought ever to go to war for money, except so far as its acquisition or defence is connected with honor. It is honor, reputation, a good name which are alone worth fighting for — and no nation that will not fight in their defence, can enjoy them.

With the broad shield of England exalted before their eyes, and the object of their affections, what will be their feelings, what will be the sentiments of the whole nation, when they look upon the foul blot that is cast upon it by the President of the United States?

FRENCH DECREES & ENGLISH ORDERS

It may appear to many wholly useless to add to what has been written & spoken upon this subject. The current of almost every thing which has been published, since the Duke of Cadore's Letter, has been of the same tendency, and strengthened by the Decisions of the President & of Congress, have served to produce a general opinion that France has revoked her Decrees, while England, contrary to good faith, refuses to rescind her Orders. If such be the Fact, there is at least, the appearance of an apology for the wretched condition of the country; and our Rulers even may claim to be in some degree exempt from the charge of Ignorance or Corruption.

It is not to be doubted, that the calm & impartial examination of the subject, momentous as it certainly is, and influential as it undoubtedly will be upon the liberties & character of the country, is a task of extreme difficulty, is a labour not only hopeless of reward, but which exposes him who engages in it, to uncandid & disingenuous imputations.

The prejudices, in favour of one, and against another foreign power, have warped, if not destroyed, the impartiality of the public tribunal; and men whose minds remain free are discouraged from making those efforts in favour of Truth & Justice, which the dangers upon whose brink we stand would otherwise impel them to make — quiet men, whose personal prudence is the ruling motive of their conduct, are from the hope of ease deterred from expressing their sentiments — office-seekers & those who desire popular favour, and are unwilling to incur popular displeasure, hold their peace. Men of sound understanding and who perceive the delusions of the times and the gulf which opens to receive us, doubting the impartiality or the capacity of the People, resign themselves to an unmanly despair & like the ignorant clown, call upon Jupiter for help and deliverance.

The ruinous system of Commercial Restrictions commenced in Decr. 1807, — in different modifications, antecedents to May 1810, are for the sake of perspicuity, passed over, in order that we may state as plainly as we are able the origin of things. The law of May 1810 relinquished the prosecution of the Embargo, and non-intercourse schemes, and after closing the Ports of the U.S. against the armed vessels both of France & England, by its fourth section provides "that in case either G. Britain or France should before the 3d day of March 1811, so revoke or modify her Edicts, as that they should cease to violate the neutral Commerce of the U.S., which fact the President should declare by Proclamation, and if the other nation should not in 3 months thereafter so revoke or modify her Edicts in like manner, then the non-importation sections of a former Law were to revive & operate against such other nation, and our ports were thence forth to be opened to the armed vessels of the Power, which by the President's Proclamation should be declared to have so modified or revoked her Decrees."

We forbear to express our opinion of the unconstitutional encroachments which this Law makes upon Executive power; the President acquiesced in it (and acting under a Law of the U.S. or as an agent of Congress and not in virtue of his constitutional power) he, in pursuance of its enactment, communicated the provisions of the Law to both France & England.

It certainly was the right of the U.S., as of every neutral nation, to trade with all nations in times of war as well as peace, with the exception in time of war, of trade with a belligerent in contraband goods, and to blockaded ports. The French Decrees and English orders abridged, not to say destroyed, this Right so far as regards our trade with both of them. Altho' we profess to have a clear, and as we believe, a correct opinion concerning the retaliatory character of these Decrees and Orders, we *decline expressing it*, because it would divert public attention from the important object of this analysis.

MESSAGE OF THE PRESIDENT

So far as regards England, Mr. Pinkney's Letters relate to two points, one the successor of rank and talents to Mr. Jackson, the other the orders in Council.

As to the first every man of honorable feelings and national spirit, must be sick and disgusted with the overtures, intimations, prayers and menaces which have been employed to engage England to send another minister to this country. The apologies and twistings, the alternate hopes and fears which Mr. P. has manifested upon this subject are humiliating and offensive.

The case is a plain one; if the Govt. thinks the omission to send another minister is disrespectful, their remedy is at every moment in their own hands; let them positively instruct Mr. Pinkney to return home; in which case he must do so; without it no one who reads his letters upon this subject, deficient as they are in good manners and becoming language, will believe that he has any intention to leave his post. Endless words and phrases and petty altercations upon a question, which might at any moment be safely, and with dignity decided, are anything but what they should be and evince more than any other course the utter weakness and indecision of these who prefer this course.

With regard to the second point, the Orders in Council, without saying one word respecting their justice or expediency, we are called to give our attention to the provisional promises of Eng. to repeal them as soon as France repeals her Decrees. Mr. P. in his third letter on this point, claims the repeal by England on the principle of good faith, or because she is bound to perform her promise. To prove that the promise is binding, Mr. P. is bound to prove, and contends that he has proved, that the French Decrees are repealed; in other words that their operation has absolutely ceased. It is curious enough to remark the similitude of Mr. P.'s efforts on the present and on a former occasion, in which a question was raised and discussed with much zeal, whether the Berlin and Milan decrees were anything more than mere municipal Regulations, which France was free to make, and which no other nation might complain of.

It will be recollected that this Doctrine was asserted and maintained in their Courts, in order to prove that England, having no ground of complaint, could have no right to retaliate by her Orders in Council.

Unfortunately France was consulted and Bonaparte answered, that as the Decrees were general, and not confined to the Territory, no exceptions could have been intended and therefore that none existed. So on the present occasion, while Mr. Pinkney is labouring to prove that the Berlin and Milan Decrees are unconditionally repealed and have wholly ceased, the Grand Judge, by a letter to the Tribunals, informs them that the American vessels which arrived after the 1st of November are in virtue of those Decrees sequestered, and that in case the U.S. shall have actually performed a Condn. connected with the notification of repeal, they will be discharged from the Principles of these Decrees. It is therefore quite probable, as these letters are inserted in the French newspapers, that they will have reached England before Lord Wellesley answered Mr. P.'s letter. In which case he will have nothing more to do, than to send him a Copy of these Letters by way of answer, and conclusive answer, too, of that Min. Letter.

PART III

THE DIE IS CAST

9

A WAR HAWK'S TESTIMONIAL

 By the end of 1811 opinion in the United States had begun to harden against Britain. A new Congress had been elected and it was profoundly influenced by a group of young, able, and dedicated nationalists who were fast reaching the conclusion that war with Britain was preferable to continued submission to her maritime practices. But before war could be undertaken the nation's military establishment would have to be enlarged and her fiscal resources increased. The fight to do this was led by the War Hawks — men like Henry Clay of Kentucky, Felix Grundy of Tennessee, John C. Calhoun of South Carolina, John A. Harper of New Hampshire, and Peter B. Porter of New York. It was not an easy battle, for there were still many who were plagued by doubts concerning the wisdom of this course of action and fearful of its consequences.

Yet the spokesmen for the War Hawks were eloquent and persuasive. One of the most effective proponents of war was Richard Johnson (1781–1850), a Democrat from Kentucky. In a speech on a bill to increase taxes he vigorously supported the idea of war and forcibly outlined the ways in which it could be successfully pursued. Like Albert Gallatin in 1807, and Henry Clay in 1810, he argued that Canada should be the battle ground in the projected conflict. But his speech had a double significance, for he went beyond a discussion of mere military tactics. By urging the annexation of Canada on the grounds that God and nature had destined that country to become a part of the United States, he foreshadowed the spirit of manifest destiny.

SPEECH IN THE HOUSE OF REPRESENTATIVES

DECEMBER 11, 1811

Richard Johnson

Mr. Richard M. Johnson said he rose to thank the committee for the report which was offered to the House, and the resolutions which were recommended; though the measures fell short of his wishes, and, he believed, of public expectation. The ulterior measures, however, promised by the committee satisfied his mind, and he should give the report his warm support. The chairman had given the views of the committee. The expulsion of the British from their North American possessions, and granting letters of marque and reprisal against Great Britain are contemplated. Look at the Message of the President. At a moment least to be expected, when France had ceased to violate our neutral rights, and the olive branch was tendered to Great Britain, her orders in council were put into a more rigorous execution. Not satisfied with refusing a redress for wrongs committed on our coasts and in the mouths of our harbors, our trade is annoyed, and our national rights invaded; and, to close the scene of insolence and injury, regardless of our moderation and our justice, she has brought home to the "threshold of our territory," measures of actual war. As the love of peace has so long produced forbearance on our part, while commercial cupidity has increased the disposition to plunder on the part of Great Britain, I feel rejoiced that the hour of resistance is at hand, and that the President, in whom the people have so much confidence, has warned us of the perils that await them, and has exhorted us to put on the armor of defence, to gird on the sword, and assume the manly and bold attitude of war. He recommends filling up the ranks of the present military establishment, and to lengthen the term of service; to raise an auxiliary force for a more limited time; to authorize the acceptance of volunteers, and provide for calling out detachments of militia as circumstances may require. For the first time since my entrance into this body, there now seems to be but one opinion with a great majority — that with Great Britain war is inevitable; that the hopes of the sanguine as to a returning sense of British justice have expired; that the prophecies of the discerning have failed; and that her infernal system

FROM *Annals of Congress*, 12th Congress, 1st session, vol. 24, col. 457–67.

has driven us to the brink of a second revolution, as important as the first. Upon the Wabash, through the influence of British agents, and within our territorial sea by the British navy, the war has already commenced. Thus, the folly, the power, and the tyranny of Great Britain, have taken from us the last alternative of longer forbearance.

Mr. J. said we must now oppose the farther encroachments of Great Britain by war, or formally annul the Declaration of our Independence, and acknowledge ourselves her devoted colonies. The people whom I represent will not hesitate which of the two courses to choose; and, if we are involved in war, to maintain our dearest rights, and to preserve our independence, I pledge myself to this House, and my constituents to this nation, that they will not be wanting in valor, nor in their proportion of men and money to prosecute the war with effect. Before we relinquish the conflict, I wish to see Great Britain renounce the piratical system of paper blockade; to liberate our captured seamen on board her ships of war; relinquish the practice of impressment on board our merchant vessels; to repeal her Orders in Council; and cease, in every other respect, to violate our neutral rights; to treat us as an independent people. The gentleman from Virginia (Mr. Randolph) has objected to the destination of this auxiliary force — the occupation of the Canadas, and the other British possessions upon our borders where our laws are violated, the Indians stimulated to murder our citizens, and where there is a British monopoly of the peltry and fur trade. I should not wish to extend the boundary of the United States by war if Great Britain would leave us to the quiet enjoyment of independence; but, considering her deadly and implacable enmity, and her continued hostility, I shall never die contented until I see her expulsion from North America, and her territories incorporated with the United States. It is strange that the gentleman would pause before refusing this force, if destined to keep the negroes in subordination — who are not in a state of insurrection as I understand — and he will absolutely refuse to vote this force to defend us against the lawless aggressions of Great Britain — a nation in whose favor he had said so much.

But, he has a dislike to the Canadian French. French blood is hateful to him. I have no doubt but the Canadian French are as good citizens as the Canadian English, or the refugee tories of the Revolution; nor have I any doubt but a great majority of that vast community are sound in their morals and in their politics, and would make worthy members of the United States.

But, open the sacred pages of the Journals of the Congress of 1774–'75 — that Congress which commenced, and conducted to victory, the American Revolution. Upon the pages of the first volume (from page 54 to 100) we will find letters, addressed to the inhabitants of Canada and the province of Quebec, containing the language of affectionate respect, and, in the warmth of patriotism, inviting them to unite against British tyranny, to make the cause of quarrel common, and to enter into the union of the States on the principles of equality. The encroachments of Great Britain are depicted in the most vivid colors, and then they say "we shall consider the violation of your rights a violation of our own, and you are invited to accede to the confederacy of the States." Thus, the patriots of the Revolution styled the inhabitants of the British provinces friends and fellow-sufferers in 1774; although then but a handful of men compared to their present numbers, and only ten years had elapsed from their first incorporation with the British dominions; and nothing but the want of physical power and means prevented their independence in 1776. The misfortunes of our arms at Quebec, and in that quarter are well known. These overtures of the Old Congress did not stop here. After the Articles of Confederation had been adopted, the door was left open for the reception of the Canadas, and the hope was not lost until British arms riveted the chains of slavery upon them, which at that time could not be broken. Now, sir, these people are more enlightened, they have a great American population among them, and they have correct ideas of liberty and independence, and only want an opportunity to throw off the yoke of their taskmasters.

Let us not think so meanly of the human character and the human mind. We are in pursuit of happiness, and we place a great value upon liberty as the means of happiness. What, then, let me ask, has changed the character of those people, that they are to be despised? What new order of things has disqualified them for the enjoyment of liberty? Has any malediction of Heaven doomed them to perpetual vassalage? Or, will the gentleman from Virginia pretend to more wisdom and more patriotism than the constellation of patriots who conducted the infant Republic through the Revolution? In point of territorial limit, the map will prove its importance. The waters of the St. Lawrence and the Mississippi interlock in a number of places, and the great Disposer of Human Events intended those two rivers should belong to the same people.

But is has been denied that British influence had any agency in the late dreadful conflict and massacre upon the Wabash; and this is said to vindicate the British nation from so foul a charge. Sir, look to the book of the Revolution. See the Indian savages in Burgoyne's army urged on every occasion to use the scalping-knife and tomahawk — not in battle, but against old men, women, and children; in the night, when they were taught to believe an Omniscient eye could not see their guilty deeds; and thus hardened in iniquity, they perpetrated the same deeds by the light of the sun, when no arm was found to oppose or protect. And when this crying sin was opposed by Lord Chatham, in the House of Lords, the employment of these Indians was justified by a speech from one of the Ministry. Thus we see how the principles of honor, of humanity, of Christianity, were violated and justified in the face of the world. Therefore, I can have no doubt of the influence of British agents in keeping up Indian hostility to the people of the United States, independent of the strong proofs on this occasion; and, I hope it will not be pretended that these agents are too moral or too religious to do the infamous deed. So much for the expulsion of Great Britain from her dominions in North America, and their incorporation into the United States of America.

The gentleman from Virginia says we are identified with the British in religion, in blood, in language, and deeply laments our hatred to that country, who can boast of so many illustrious characters. This deep rooted enmity to Great Britain arises from her insidious policy, the offspring of her perfidious conduct towards the United States. Her disposition is unfriendly; her enmity is implacable; she sickens at our prosperity and happiness. If obligations of friendship do exist, why does Great Britain rend those ties asunder, and open the bleeding wounds of former conflicts? Or does the obligation of friendship exist on the part of the United States alone? I have never thought that the ties of religion, of blood, of language, and of commerce, would justify or sanctify insult and injury — on the contrary, that a premeditated wrong from the hand of a friend created more sensibility, and deserved the greater chastisement and the higher execration. What would you think of a man, to whom you were bound by the most sacred ties, who would plunder you of your substance, aim a deadly blow at your honor, and in the hour of confidence endeavor to bury a dagger in your bosom? Would you, sir, proclaim to the world your affection for this miscreant of society, after this conduct, and endeavor to interest your audience with the ties of kindred that bound you to each other? So let it be with nations, and there will be neither surprise nor lamentation that we execrate a Government so hostile to our independence — for it is from the Government that we meet with such multiplied injury, and to that object is our hatred directed. As to individuals of merit, whether British or French, I presume no person would accuse the people of the United States of such hatred to them, or of despising individuals, who might not be instrumental in the maritime despotism which we feel; and this accounts for the veneration we have for Sidney and Russell, statesmen of whom the gentleman has spoken; they are fatal examples why we should love the British Government. The records of that Government are now stained with the blood of these martyrs in freedom's cause, as vilely as with the blood of American citizens; and certainly we shall not be called upon to love equally the murderer and the victim. For God's sake let us not again be told of the ties of religion, of laws, of blood, and of customs, which bind the two nations together, with a view to extort our love for the English Government, and more especially when the same gentleman has acknowledged that we have ample cause of war against that nation — let us not be told of the freedom of that corrupt Government whose hands are washed alike in the blood of her own illustrious statesmen, for a manly opposition to tyranny, and the citizens of every other clime. But I would inquire into this love for the British Government and British institutions, in the gross, without any discrimination. Why love her rulers? Why kiss the rod of iron which inflicts the stripes without a cause? When all admit we have just cause of war, such attachments are dangerous, and encourage encroachment. I will venture to say, that our hatred of the British Government is not commensurate with her depredations and her outrages on our rights, or we should have waged a deadly war against her many years past. The subject of foreign attachments and British hatred has been examined at considerable length. I did not intend to begin that discussion, but I will pursue it, and though I make no charge of British attachments, I will, at all times, at every hazard, defend the Administration and the Republican party against the charge of foreign partialities — French or Spanish, or any other kind, when applied to the measures of our Government. This foreign influence is a dangerous enemy; we should destroy the means of its circulation among us — like the fatal tunic, it destroys where it touches. It is insidious, invisible, and takes advantage of the most unsuspecting hours of social intercourse. I would not deny the good will of France nor of Great Britain to have an undue influence among us. But Great Britain alone has the means of this influence to an extent dangerous to the United States. It has been said that Great Britain was fighting the battles of the world — that she stands against universal dominion threatened by the archfiend of mankind. I should be sorry if our independence depended upon the power of Great Britain. If, however, she would act the part of a friendly power towards the United States, I should never wish to deprive her of power, of wealth, of honor, of prosperity. But if her energies are to be directed against the liberties of this free and happy people, against my native country, I should not drop a tear if the fast-anchored isle would sink into the waves, provided the innocent inhabitants could escape the deluge and find an asylum in a more favorable soil. And as to the power of France, I fear it as little as any other power; I would oppose her aggressions, under any circumstances, as soon as I would British outrages.

The ties of religion, of language, of blood, as it regards Great Britain, are dangerous ties to this country, with her present hostile disposition — instead of pledges of friendship they are used to paralyze the strength of the United States in relation to her aggressions. There are other ties equally efficacious. The number of her commercial traders within our limits, her agents, etc., the vast British capital employed in our commerce and our moneyed institutions, connected with her language, ancestry, customs, habits, and laws. These are formidable means for estranging the affections of many from our republican institutions, and producing partialities for Great Britain. Now I shall attend to the charge of partiality in our measures towards France. It is an insinuation not founded in fact, and can only exist in the imagination of those who may insinuate it. We are not driven to mere declarations — the truth of the assertion is bottomed upon the statute records of the United States; and we appeal to the character of every measure relative to foreign relations, since the adoption of the embargo, in consequence of the violation of neutral rights upon the high seas. The direct object of the Berlin and Milan decrees was the ruin of all trade to British ports — and the object of the Orders in Council was the destruction of all commerce to French ports and ports from which the British flag was excluded.

The gentleman from Virginia has called the military regular forces mercenaries. If by this appellation any reproach or degredation is intended, its justice and propriety is denied. In times like the present, when dangers thicken upon us, at the moment when we are compelled by most wanton tyranny upon the high seas, and upon land may be added, to abandon our peaceful habits for the din of arms, officers and soldiers in this country are governed by the noble feelings of patriotism and valor. The history of the world may be ransacked; other nations may be brought in review before us, and examples of greater heroism cannot be quoted, than shall be performed in battle by our officers and soldiers, military and naval and marine. The deeds of their ancestors would be before them; glory would animate their bosoms, and love of country would nerve the heart to deeds of mighty fame. If, therefore, there should not be a diminution of respect for those who entertain an opinion so degrading to our army, it should at least be understood that such opinions do not lessen the confidence due to those who faithfully serve their country, and who would lay down their life for it. This reflection brings to memory the late memorable conflict upon the Wabash. Governor Harrison pitched his tents near the Prophet's town; and although this fanatic had his followers collected, and the American forces were anxious to finish the work by an open and daylight engagement, if there was a necessity to resort to arms, their impetuous valor was easily stayed, when they were informed that the white flag of peace was to be hoisted next morning, and the effusion of blood was to be spared. But in the silent watches of the night, relieved from the fatigues of valor, and slumbering under the perfidious promises of the savages, who were infuriated and made drunk by British traders, dreaming of the tender smile of a mother, and the fond embraces of affectionate wives, and of prattling children upon their knees, on their return from the fatigues of a campaign! — the destroyers came with the silent instruments of death, the war club, the scalping knife, the tomahawk, and the bow and arrow; with these they penetrate into the heart of our forces — they enter the tents of our officers — many close their eyes in death — it was a trying moment for the rest of our heroes, but they were equal to the dreadful occasion. The American forces flew to arms; they rallied at the voice of their officers, and soon checked the work of death. The savages were successively and successfully charged and driven until day-light, when they disappeared like the mist of morning. In this dreadful conflict many were killed and wounded on both sides; and the volunteers and the regiment under Colonel Boyd acted and fought with equal bravery and to their immortal honor. The volunteers from Kentucky were men of valor and worth — young men of hopeful prospects, and married men of reputation and intelligence, governed by no mercenary views — honor prompted them to serve their country. Some of these fallen heroes were my acquaintances, my friends: one not the least conspicuous lived in my district — Colonel Owens; Colonel Daviess, a neighbor. You, Mr. Speaker, know the worth of some of these men; and I regret that you are not in my place to speak their praise. So long as the records of this transaction remain, the 9th of November will not be forgotten, and time shall only brighten the fame of the deeds of our army, and a tear shall be shed for those who have fallen. But the loss will not be felt by the public alone; the friends of their social hours will regret their loss; the widow will mourn her disconsolate situation; the orphan shall cry for the return of his father in vain; and the mother carry her sorrow to the grave. Let this ornamented hall be clothed with the symbols of mourning, although our army proved victorious in war; and to their memory let a monument be erected in the hearts of a grateful country.

10

A REJECTION
OF FORCE

 If an increasing number of members of Congress was convinced that war was the only alternative to submission, there were still some who felt that to enter the lists against Britain was reckless folly. Their reasons for this were as varied and complex as the issues involved. Some, who were Federalists, felt that Britain was defending stability and good government in a world in turmoil and that to attack her while she was engaged with France would be an act of near treason. Others felt that the United States was not sufficiently prepared for war, and the long and acrimonious debates over the defense establishment and the tax bills gave substance to their views. Still others distrusted President Madison and felt that he had neither the capacity to govern effectively in time of crisis nor the qualities of leadership necessary to lead the country in war. And finally, some believed that, as both Britain and France had shown an equally cavalier disregard for American sovereignty, it was wrong to direct the wrath of the United States against a single culprit.

While all these views were held throughout the nation, they were given their most forceful expression in a speech delivered in Congress by John Randolph (1773–1833) of Virginia, a Democrat who had become increasingly disillusioned and angered by the policies of his party.

SPEECH IN THE HOUSE OF REPRESENTATIVES

DECEMBER 10, 1811

John Randolph

Mr. Randolph rose. He expressed his sense of the motive which had induced the gentleman from Tennessee (Mr. Grundy) to move the adjournment, yesterday, and of the politeness of the House in granting it; at the same time declaring that in point of fact he had little cause to be thankful for the favor, well intended as he knew it to have been — since he felt himself even less capable of proceeding with his argument, than he had been on the preceding day.

It was a question, as it had been presented to the House, of peace or war. In that light it had been argued; in no other light could he consider it, after the declarations made by members of the Committee of Foreign Relations. Without intending any disrespect to the Chair, he must be permitted to say that if the decision yesterday was correct, "That it was not in order to advance any arguments against the resolution, drawn from topics before other committees of the House," the whole debate, nay, the report itself on which they were acting, was disorderly; since the increase of the military force was a subject at that time in agitation by the select committee raised on that branch of the President's Message. But it was impossible that the discussion of a question broad as the wide ocean of our foreign concerns — involving every consideration of interest, of right, of happiness and of safety at home — touching in every point, all that was dear to freedom, "their lives, their fortunes, and their sacred honor!" — could be tied down by the narrow rules of technical routine. The Committee of Foreign Relations had indeed decided that the subject of arming the militia (which he had pressed upon them as indispensable to the public security) did not come within the scope of their authority. On what ground, he had been and still was unable to see, they had felt themselves authorized (when the subject was before another committee) to recommend the raising of standing armies, with a view (as had been declared) of immediate war — a war not of defence, but of conquest, of aggrandizement, of ambition; a war foreign to the interests of this country, to the interests of humanity itself.

FROM *Annals of Congress,* 12th Congress, 1st session, vol. 24, col. 441–55.

He knew not how gentlemen, calling themselves Republicans, could advocate such a war. What was their doctrine in 1798-'9, when the command of the army — that highest of all possible trusts in any Government, be the form what it may — was reposed in the bosom of the Father of his Country, the sanctuary of a nation's love, the only hope that never came in vain! When other worthies of the Revolution — Hamilton, Pinckney, and the younger Washington — men of tried patriotism, of approved conduct and valor, of untarnished honor, held subordinate command under him! Republicans were then unwilling to trust a standing army, even to his hands who had given proof that he was above all human temptation. Where now is the Revolutionary hero to whom you are about to confide this sacred trust? To whom will you confide the charge of leading the flower of our youth to the Heights of Abraham? Will you find him in the person of an acquitted felon? What! then you were unwilling to vote an army where such men as had been named held high command! When Washington himself was at the head — did you then show such reluctance, feel such scruples; and are you now nothing loth, fearless of every consequence? Will you say that your provocations were less than now? When your direct commerce was interdicted — your Ambassadors hooted with derision from the French Court — tribute demanded — actual war waged upon you!

Those who opposed the army then were indeed denounced as the partisans of France; as the same men — some of them at least — are now held up as the advocates of England; those firm and undeviating Republicans who then dared, and now dare, to cling to the ark of the Constitution, to defend it even at the expense of their fame, rather than surrender themselves to the wild projects of mad ambition! There was a fatality attending plenitude of power. Soon or late some mania seize upon its possessors — they fall from the dizzy height through the giddiness of their own heads. Like a vast estate, heaped up by the labor and industry of one man, which seldom survives the third generation — power, gained by patient assiduity, by a faithful and regular discharge of its attendant duties, soon gets above its own origin. Intoxicated with their own greatness the Federal party fell. Will not the same causes produce the same effects now, as then? Sir, you may raise this army, you may build up this vast structure of patronage, this mighty apparatus of favoritism; but — "lay not the flattering unction to your souls" — you will never live to enjoy the succession. You sign your political death warrant.

Mr. R. here adverted to the provocation to hostilities from shutting up the Mississippi by Spain in 1803 — but more fully to the conduct of the House in 1805-'6, under the strongest of all

imaginable provocatives to war; the actual invasion of our country.
He read various passages from the President's public Message of
December 3, 1805.

. . .

Mr. R. said that the peculiar situation of the frontier, at that
time insulted, had alone induced the committee to recommend the
raising of regular troops. It was too remote from the population
of the country for the militia to act, in repelling and chastising
Spanish incursion. New Orleans and its dependencies were separated
by a vast extent of wilderness from the settlements of the United
States; filled with a disloyal and turbulent people, alient to our
institutions, language and manners, and disaffected towards our
Government. Little reliance could be placed upon them, and it was
plain, that if "it was the intention of Spain to advance on our possessions until she should be repulsed by an opposing force," that force
must be a regular army, unless we were disposed to abandon all
the country north of Tennessee. That if "the protection of our citizens
and the spirit and the honor of our country required that force should
be interposed," nothing remained but for the Legislature to grant
the only practicable means, or to shrink from the most sacred of
all its duties — to abandon the soil and its inhabitants to the tender
mercies of hostile invaders.

Yet this report, moderate as it was, had been deemed of too
strong a character by the House. It was rejected: and, at the motion
of a gentleman from Massachusetts, (Mr. Bidwell,) — who had since
taken a great fancy also to Canada, and marched off thither, in
advance of the committee of Foreign Relations — "$2,000,000, were
appropriated towards" (not in full of) "any extraordinary expense
which might be incurred in the intercourse between the United States
and foreign nations:" in other words, to buy off, at Paris, Spanish
aggressions at home.

Was this fact given in evidence of our impartiality towards
the belligerents? — that to the insults and injuries and actual invasions
of one of them we opposed not bullets, but dollars; that to Spanish
invasion we opposed money, whilst for British aggression on the
high seas we had arms; offensive war? But Spain was then shielded,
as well as instigated, by a greater power. Hence our respect for
her. Had we at that time acted as we ought to have done in defence
of our rights, of the *natale solum* itself, we should (he felt confident)
have avoided that series of insult, disgrace, and injury, which had
been poured out upon us in long unbroken succession. We would
not then raise a small regular force for a country where the militia

could not act, to defend our Territory; now, we are willing to levy a great army, for great it must be, to accomplish the proposed object, for a war of conquest and ambition — and, this, too, at the very entrance of the "Northern Hive," of the strongest part of the Union.

An insinuation had fallen from the gentleman from Tennessee, (Mr. Grundy,) that the late massacre of our brethern on the Wabash had been instigated by the British Government. Has the President given any such information? has the gentleman received any such, even informally, from any officer of this Government? Is it so believed by the Administration? He had cause to think the contrary to be the fact; that such was not their opinion. This insinuation was of the grossest kind — a presumption the most rash, the most unjustifiable. Show but good ground for it, he would give up the question at the threshold — he was ready to march to Canada. It was indeed well calculated to excite the feelings of the Western people particularly, who were not quite so tenderly attached to our red brethern as some modern philosophers; but it was destitute of any foundation, beyond mere surmise and suspicion. What would be thought, if, without any proof whatsoever, a member should rise in his place and tell us, that the massacre in Savannah, a massacre perpetrated by civilized savages, with French commissions in their pockets, was excited by the French Government? There was an easy and natural solution of the late transaction on the Wabash, in the well-known character of the aboriginal savages of North America, without resorting to any such mere conjectural estimate. He was sorry to say, that for this signal calamity and disgrace the House was, in part, at least, answerable. Session after session, their table had been piled up with Indian treaties, for which the appropriations had been voted as a matter of course, without examination. Advantage had been taken of the spirit of the Indians, broken by the war which ended in the Treaty of Greenville. Under the ascendency then acquired over them, they had been pent up by subsequent treaties into nooks straightened in their quarters by a blind cupidity, seeking to extinguish their title to immense wildernesses, for which (possessing, as we do already, more land than we can sell or use) we shall not have occasion, for half a century to come. It was our own thirst for a territory, our own want of moderation, that had driven these sons of nature to desperation, of which we felt the effects.

Mr. R., although not personally acquainted with the late Colonel Daviess, felt, he was persuaded, as deep and serious regret for his loss as the gentleman from Tennessee himself. He knew him only through the representation of a friend of the deceased, (Mr. Rowan,) some time a member of that House; a man who, for native force of intellect, manliness of character, and high sense of honor, was not inferior to any that had ever sat there. With him he sympathized in the severest calamity that could befall a man of his cast of character. Would to God they were both then on the floor! From his personal knowledge of the one, he felt confident that he would have his support — and he believed (judging of him from the representation of their common friend) of the other also.

He could but smile at the liberality of the gentleman, in giving Canada to New York, in order to strengthen the Northern balance of power, while at the same time he forwarned her that the Western scale must preponderate. Mr. R. said that he could almost fancy that he saw the Capitol in motion towards the falls of Ohio — after a short sojourn taking its flight to the Mississippi, and finally alighting on Darien; which, when the gentlemen's dreams are realized, will be a most eligible seat of government for the new Republic (or Empire) of the two Americas! But it seemed that "in 1808 we talked and acted foolishly," and to give some color of consistency to that folly, we must now commit a greater. Really he could not conceive of a weaker reason offered in support of a present measure, than the justification of a former folly. He hoped we should act a wiser part — take warning by our follies, since we had become sensible of them, and resolve to talk and act foolishly no more. It was indeed high time to give over such preposterous language and proceedings.

This war of conquest, a war for the acquisition of territory and subjects, is to be a new commentary on the doctrine that Republics are destitute of ambition — that they are addicted to peace, wedded to the happiness and safety of the great body of her people. But it seems this is to be a holiday campaign — there is to be no expense of blood, or treasure, on our part — Canada is to conquer herself — she is to be subdued by the principles of fraternity. The people of that country are first to be seduced from their allegiance, and converted into traitors, as preparatory to the making them good citizens. Although he must acknowledge that some of our flaming patriots were thus manufactured, he did not think the process would hold good with a whole community. It was a dangerous experiment. We were to succeed in the French mode by the system of fraternization — all is French! but how dreadfully it might be retorted on the Southern and Western slaveholding States. He detested this subornation of treason. No — if he must have them, let them fall by the valor of our arms, by fair, legitimate conquest; not become the victims of treacherous seduction.

He was not surprised at the war spirit which was manifesting itself in gentlemen from the South. In the year 1805-'6, in a struggle for the carrying trade of belligerent colonial produce, this country has been most unwisely brought into collision with the great powers of Europe. By a series of most impolitic and ruinous measures, utterly incomprehensible to every rational, sober-minded man, the Southern planters, by their own votes, had succeeded in knocking down the price of cotton to seven cents, and of tobacco (a few choice crops excepted) to nothing — and in raising the price of blankets (of which a few would not be amiss in a Canadian campaign,) coarse woolens, and every article of first necessity, three or four hundred per cent. And now that, by our own acts, we have brought ourselves into this unprecedented condition, we must get out of it in any way, but by an acknowledgement of our own want of wisdom and forecast. But is war the true remedy? Who will profit by it? Speculators — a few lucky merchants, who draw prizes in the lottery — commissaries and contractors. Who must suffer by it? The people. It is their blood, their taxes, that must flow to support it.

But gentlemen avowed that they would not go to war for the carrying trade — that is, for any other but the direct export and import trade — that which carries our native products abroad, and brings back the return cargo; and yet they stickle for our commercial rights, and will go to war for them! He wished to know, in point of principle, what difference gentlemen could point out between the abandonment of this or of that maritime right? Do gentlemen assume the lofty port and tone of chivalrous redressers of maritime wrongs, and declare their readiness to surrender every other maritime right, provided they may remain unmolested in the exercise of the humble privilege of carrying their own produce abroad, and bringing back a return cargo? Do you make this declaration to the enemy at the outset? Do you state the minimum with which you will be contented, and put it in her power to close with your proposal at her option; give her the basis of a treaty ruinous and disgraceful beyond example and expression? and this, too, after having turned up your nose in disdain at the treaties of Mr. Jay and Mr. Monroe! Will you say to England, "end the war when you please, give us the direct trade in our own produce, we are content?" But what will the merchants of Salem, and Boston, and New York, and Philadelphia, and Baltimore, the men of Marblehead and Cape Cod, say to this? Will they join in a war professing to have for its object what they would consider (and justly too) as the sacrifice of their maritime rights, yet affecting to be a war for the protection of commerce?

He was gratified to find gentlemen acknowledging the demoralizing and destructive consequences of the non-importation law — confessing the truth of all that its opponents foretold when it was enacted. And will you plunge yourselves in war, because you have passed a foolish and ruinous law, and are ashamed to repeal it? "But our good friend the French Emperor stands in the way of its repeal," and as we cannot go too far in making sacrifices to him, who has given such demonstration of his love for the Americans, we must, in point of fact, become parties to his war. "Who can be so cruel as to refuse him this favor?" His imagination shrunk from the miseries of such a connection. He called upon the House to reflect whether they were not about to abandon all reclamation for the unparalleled outrages, "insults and injuries" of the French Government, to give up our claim for plundered millions; and asked what reparation or atonement they could expect to obtain in hours of future dalliance, after they should have made a tender of their person to this great deflowerer of the virginity of republics. We had by our own wise (he would not say *wise-acre*) measures, so increased the trade and wealth of Montreal and Quebec, that at last we began to cast a wishful eye at Canada. Having done so much towards its improvement by the exercise of "our restrictive energies," we began to think the laborer worthy of his hire, and to put in claim for our portion. Suppose it ours, are we any nearer to our point? As his Minister said to the King of Epirus, "may we not as well take our bottle of wine before as after this exploit?" Go! march on Canada! leave the broad bosom of the Chesapeake and her hundred tributary rivers — the whole line of seacoast from Machias to St. Mary's unprotected! You have taken Quebec — have you conquered England? Will you seek for the deep foundations of her power in the frozen deserts of Labrador?

"Her march is on the mountain wave,
    Her home is on the deep!"

Will you call upon her to leave your ports and harbors untouched, only just till you can return from Canada to defend them? The coast is to be left defenceless, whilst men of the interior are revelling in conquest and spoil. But grant for a moment, for mere argument's sake, that in Canada you touched the sinews of her strength, instead of removing a clog upon her resources — an encumbrance, but one, which, from a spirit of honor, she will vigorously defend. In what situation would you then place some of the best men of the nation? As Chatham and Burke, and the whole band of her patriots, prayed for her defeat in 1776, so must some of the truest friends to their country deprecate the success of our arms against the only power that holds in check the arch-enemy of mankind.

Mr. R. declared the committee had outstripped the Executive. In designating the power against whom this force was to be employed — as had most unadvisedly been done in the preamble or manifesto with which the resolutions were prefaced — they had not consulted the views of the Executive; that designation was equivalent to an abandonment of all our claims on the French Government. No sooner was the report laid on the table, than the vultures were flocking round their prey, the carcass of a great Military Establishment — men of tainted reputation, of broken fortune (if they ever had any) and of battered constitutions, "choice spirits, tired of the dull pursuits of civil life," were seeking after agencies and commissions; willing to doze in gross stupidity over the public fire; to light the public candle at both ends. Honorable men undoubtedly there were ready to serve their country, but what man of spirit, or of self-respect, would accept a commission in the present army?

The gentleman from Tennessee (Mr. Grundy) had addressed himself, yesterday, exclusively to the "Republicans of this House." Mr. R. knew not whether he might consider himself as entitled to any part of the benefit of the honorable gentleman's discourse. It belonged not, however, to that gentleman to decide. If we must have an exposition of the doctrines of Republicanism, he should receive it from the fathers of the Church, and not from the junior apprentices of the law. He should appeal to his worthy friends from Carolina, (Messrs. Macon and Standford,) "men with whom he had measured his strength," by whose side he had fought during the reign of terror, for it was indeed an hour of corruption, of oppression, of pollution. It was not all to his taste, that sort of Republicanism which was supported on this side of the Atlantic by the father of the sedition law, John Adams, and by Peter Porcupine on the other. Republicanism! of John Adams! and William Cobbett! *Par nobile fratrum,* now united as in 1798, whom the cruel walls of Newgate alone keep from flying to each other's embrace — but whom, in sentiment it is impossible to divide! Gallant crusaders in the holy cause of Republicanism! Such "Republicanism does indeed mean any thing or nothing."

Our people will not submit to be taxed for this war of conquest and dominion. The Government of the United States was not calculated to wage offensive foreign war — it was instituted for the common defence and general welfare; and whosoever should embark in a war of offence, would put it to a test which it was by no means calculated to endure. Make it out that Great Britain had instigated the Indians on the late occasion, and he was ready for battle; but not for dominion. He was unwilling, however, under the present circumstances, to take Canada, at the risk of the constitution — to embark in common cause with France and be dragged at the wheels of the car of some Burr or Bonaparte. For a gentleman from Tennessee or Gennesee, or Lake Champlain, there may be some prospect of advantage. Their hemp would bear a great price by the exclusion of foreign supply. In that too the great importers were deeply interested. The upper country on the Hudson and the Lakes would be enriched by the supplies for the troops, which they alone could furnish. They would have the exclusive market: to say nothing of the increased preponderance from the acquisition of Canada and that section of the Union, which the Southern and Western States had already felt so severely in the apportionment bill.

Mr. R. adverted to the defenceless state of our seaports, and particularly of the Chesapeake. A single spot only, on both shores, might be considered in tolerable security — from the nature of the port and the strength of the population — and that spot unhappily governed the whole state of Maryland. His friend, the late Governor of Maryland, (Mr. Lloyd,) at the very time he was bringing his warlike resolutions before the Legislature of the State, was liable, on any night, to be taken out of his bed, and carried off with his family, by the most contemptible picaroon. Such was the situation of many a family in Maryland and lower Virginia.

Mr. R. dwelt on the danger arising from the black population. He said he would touch this subject as tenderly as possible — it was with reluctance that he touched it at all — but in cases of great emergency, the State physician must not be deterred by a sickly, hysterical humanity, from the probing the wound of his patient — he must not be withheld by a fastidious and mistaken humanity from representing his true situation to his friends, or even to the sick man himself, where the occasion called for it. What was the situation of the slaveholding States? During the war of the Revolution, so fixed were their habits of subordination, that when the whole southern country was overrun by the enemy, who invited them to desert, no fear was ever entertained of an insurrection of the slaves. During the war of seven years, with our country in possession of the enemy, no such danger was ever apprehended. But should we therefore be unobservant spectators of the progress of society, within the last twenty years — of the silent and powerful change wrought by time and chance, upon its composition and temper? When the fountains of the great deep of abomination were broken up, even the poor slaves had not escaped the general deluge. The French Revolution

had polluted even them. Nay, there had not been wanting men in
that House, witness their Legislative *Legendre,* the butcher who once
held a seat there, to preach upon that floor those imprescriptible
rights to a crowded audience of blacks in the galleries — teaching
them that they are equal to their masters; in other words, advising
them to cut their throats. Similar doctrines were disseminated by
pedlers from New England and elsewhere, throughout the southern
country — and masters had been found so infatuated, as by their
lives and conversation, by a general contempt of order, morality,
and religion, unthinkingly to cherish these seeds of self-destruction
to them and their families. What was the consequence? Within the
last ten years, repeated alarms of insurrection among the slaves —
some of them awful indeed. From the spreading of this infernal
doctrine, the whole southern country had been thrown into a state
of insecurity. Men dead to the operation of moral causes, had taken
away from the poor slave his habits of loyalty and obedience to
his master, which lightened his servitude by a double operation;
beguiling his own cares and disarming his master's suspicions and
severity; and now, like true empirics in politics, you are called upon
to trust to the mere physical strength of the fetter which holds him
in bondage. You have deprived him of all moral restraints, you have
tempted him to eat the fruit of the tree of knowledge, just enough
to perfect him in wickedness; you have opened his eyes to his
nakedness; you have armed his nature against the hand that has
fed, that has clothed him, that has cherished him in sickness; that
hand, which before he became a pupil of your school, he had become
accustomed to press with respectful affection. You have done all
this — and then show him the gibbet and the wheel, as incentives
to a sullen, repugnant obedience. God forbid, sir, that the Southern
States should ever see an enemy on their shores, with these infernal
principles of French fraternity in the van! While talking of taking
Canada, some of us were shuddering for our own safety at home.
He spoke from facts, when he said that the night-bell never tolled
for fire in Richmond that the mother did not hug her infant more
closely to her bosom. He had been a witness of some of the alarms
in the capital of Virginia.

Mr. R. then proceeded to notice the unjust and illiberal imputa-
tion of British attachments, against certain characters in this country,
sometimes insinuated in that House, but openly avowed out of it.
Against whom were these charges brought? Against men, who in
the war of the Revolution were in the councils of the nation, or
fighting the battles of your country. And by whom were they made?
By runaways, chiefly from the British dominions, since the breaking

out of the French troubles. He indignantly said — it is insufferable. It cannot be borne. It must, and ought, with severity, be put down in this House, and, out of it, to me the lie direct. We have no fellow feeling for the suffering and oppressed Spaniards! Yet even them we do not reprobate. Strange! that we should have no objection to any people or Government civilized or savage, in the whole world. The great Autocrat of all the Russias receives the homage of our high consideration. The Dey of Algiers and his Divan of Pirates are very civil, good sort of people, with whom we find no difficulty in maintaining the relations of peace and amity — "Turks, Jews, and Infidels;" Mellimelli, or the little Turtle; barbarians and savages of every clime and color, are welcome to our arms. With chiefs of banditti, negro or mulatto, we can treat and can trade. Name, however, but England, and all our antipathies are up in arms against her. Against whom? Against those whose blood runs in our veins; in common with whom we claim Shakespeare, and Newton, and Chatham, for our countrymen; whose form of government is the freest on earth, our own only excepted; from whom every valuable principle of our own institutions has been borrowed — representation, jury trial, voting the supplies, writ of habeas corpus — our whole civil and criminal jurisprudence — against our fellow Protestants indentified in blood, in language, in religion with ourselves. In what school did the worthies of our land, the Washingtons, Henrys, Hancocks, Franklins, Rutledges of America learn those principles of civil liberty which were so nobly asserted by their wisdom and valor? And American resistance to British usurpation had not been more warmly cherished by these great men and their compatriots; not more by Washington, Hancock, and Henry, than by Chatham and his illustrious associates in the British Parliament. It ought to be remembered, too, that the heart of the English people was with us. It was a selfish and corrupt Ministry, and their servile tools, to whom we were not more opposed than they were. He trusted that none such might ever exist among us — for tools will never be wanting to subserve the purposes, however ruinous or wicked, of Kings and Ministers of State.

He acknowledged the influence of a Shakespeare and Milton upon his imagination, of a Locke upon his understanding, of a Sidney upon his political principles, of a Chatham upon qualities which, would to God! he possessed in common with that illustrious man — of a Tillotson, a Sherlock, and a Porteus, upon his religion. This was a British influence which he could never shake off. He allowed much to the just and honest prejudices growing out of the Revolution. But by whom had they been suppressed when they ran counter to the interests of his country? By Washington. By whom, would you listen to them, are they most keenly felt? By felons escaped from the jails of Paris, Newgate, and Kilmainham, since the breaking out of the French Revolution — who, in this abused and insulted country, have set up for political teachers, and whose disciples give no other proof of their progress in Republicanism, except a blind devotion to the most ruthless military despotism that the world ever saw. These are the patriots, who scruple not to brand with the epithet of tory the men (looking towards the seat of Col. Stuart) by whose blood your liberties have been cemented. These are they, who hold in so keen remembrance the outrages of the British armies, from which many of them were deserters. Ask these self-styled patriots where they were during the American war, (for they are for the most part old enough to have borne arms,) and you strike them dumb — their lips are closed in eternal silence. If it were allowable to entertain partialities, every consideration of blood, language, religion, and interest, would incline us towards England; and yet, shall they be alone extended to France and her ruler, whom we are bound to believe a chastening God suffers as the scourge of a guilty world! On all other nations he tramples — he holds them in contempt — England alone he hates; he would, but he cannot despise her — fear cannot despise. And shall we disparage our ancestors? — shall we bastardize ourselves by placing them even below the brigands of St. Domingo? with whom Mr. Adams had negotiated a sort of treaty, for which he ought to have been and would have been impeached, if the people had not previously passed sentence of disqualification for their services upon him. This antipathy to all that is English must be French.

But the outrages and injuries of England, bred up in the principles of the Revolution, he could never palliate, much less defend them. He well remembered flying with his mother, and her new-born child, from Arnold and Philips — and how they had been driven by Tarleton and other British pandoors from pillar to post, while her husband was fighting the battles of his country. The impression was indelible on his memory — and yet (like his worthy old neighbor, who added seven buck-shot to every cartridge at the battle of Guilford, and drew a fine sight at his man) he must be content to be called a tory by a patriot of the last importation. Let us not get rid of one evil (supposing it to be possible) at the expense of a greater — *mutatis mutandis.* Suppose France in possession of the British naval power — and to her the trident must pass should England be unable to wield it — what would be your condition? What would be the situation of your seaports and their seafaring inhabitants?

Ask Hamburg, Lubec. Ask Savannah. What, sir! when their privateers are pent up in our harbors by the British bull-dogs, when they receive at our hands every rite of hospitality; from which their enemy is excluded, when they capture within our waters, interdicted to British armed ships, American vessels; when such is their deportment towards you, under such circumstances, what could you expect if they were the uncontrolled lords of the ocean? Had those privateers at Savannah borne British commissions, or had your shipments of cotton, tobacco, ashes, and what not, to London and Liverpool, been confiscated, and the proceeds poured into the English Exchequer — my life upon it! you would never have listened to any miserable wire-drawn distinctions between "orders and decrees affecting our neutral rights," and "municipal decrees," confiscating in mass your whole property. You would have had instant war! The whole land would have blazed out in war.

And shall republicans become the instruments of him who had effaced the title of Attilla to the "Scourge of God!" Yet even Attilla, in the falling fortunes of civilization, had, no doubt, his advocates, his tools, his minions, his parasites in the very countries that he overran — sons of that soil whereon his horse had trod; where grass could never after grow. If perfectly fresh, Mr. Randolph said (instead of being as he was — his memory clouded, his intellect stupified, his strength and spirits exhausted) he could not give utterance to that strong detestation which he felt towards (above all other works of the creation) such characters as Zingis, Tamerlane, Kouli-Khan, or Bonaparte. His instincts involuntarily revolted at their bare idea. Malefactors of the human race, who ground down man to a mere machine of their impious and bloody ambition. Yet, under all the accumulated wrongs, and insults, and robberies of the last of these chieftains, are we not in point of fact about to become a party to his views, a partner in his wars?

But before this miserable force of ten thousand men was raised to take Canada, he begged them to look at the state of defence at home — to count the cost of the enterprize before it was set on foot, not when it might be too late — when the best blood of the country should be split, and naught but empty coffers left to pay the cost. And the bounty lands to be given in Canada? It might lessen his repugnance to that part of the system, to granting these lands, not to those miserable wretches who sell themselves to slavery for a few dollars and a glass of gin, but in fact to the clerks of our offices, some of whom, with an income of fifteen hundred or two thousand dollars, lived at the rate of four or five thousand,

and yet grew rich — who perhaps at that moment were making out blank assignments for these land rights.

He would beseech the House, before they ran their heads against this post, Quebec, to count the cost. His word for it, Virginia planters would not be taxed to support such a war — a war which must aggravate their present distresses; in which they had not the remotest interest. Where is the Montgomery, or even the Arnold, or the Burr, who is to march to Point Levi?

He called upon those professing to be republicans to make good the promises held out by their republican predecessors when they came into power — promises which, for years afterwards, they had honestly, faithfully fulfilled. We had vaunted of paying off the national debt, or retrenching useless establishments; and yet had now become as infatuated with standing armies, loans, taxes, navies, and war, as ever were the Essex Junto. What Republicanism is this?

11

THE NECESSITY OF WAR

In June, 1812, the United States finally declared war upon Great Britain. But it was done only after a long, bitter, and unhappy debate over the President's War Message. When the vote was finally tallied it revealed that a powerful minority in both the Senate and the House of Representatives still opposed taking this final and fateful step. This was in marked contrast to the situation after Pearl Harbor in 1941 when there was a universal conviction that Japan's aggression must be met and repelled by force.

But in 1812 the issues were less clear cut and some still felt profoundly that peaceful alternatives lay at hand and that an inventive executive should be able to exploit them. Yet a majority believed otherwise, and it won the day. The views of the majority were brilliantly expressed in a report of the committee on foreign affairs of the House of Representatives. This body, whose chairman was John C. Calhoun (1782–1850), a Democrat from South Carolina, reached its conclusions and presented them to the House on June 3, 1812. The document presents in precise and powerful language the case against Great Britain and argues that the United States could only defend its interests by the use of force.

REPORT ON FOREIGN RELATIONS

THE HOUSE OF REPRESENTATIVES, JUNE 3, 1812

Mr. Calhoun, from the Committee on Foreign Relations, to whom was referred the Message of the President of the United States of the first instant, made a report, stating at large the causes and reasons of a war with Great Britain, which was read as follows.

That, after the experience which the United States have had of the great injustice of the British Government towards them, exemplified by so many acts of violence and oppression, it will be more difficult to justify to the impartial world their impatient forbearance to which it has become necessary to resort, to avenge the wrongs, and vindicate the rights and honour of the nation. Your committee are happy to observe, on a dispassionate view of the conduct of the United States, that they see in it no cause for censure.

If a long forbearance under injuries ought ever to be considered a virtue in any nation, it is one which peculiarly becomes the United States. No people ever had stronger motives to cherish peace; none have ever cherished it with greater sincerity and zeal.

But the period has now arrived, when the United States must support their character and station among the nations of the earth, or submit to the most shameful degradation. Forbearance has ceased to be a virtue. War on the one side, and peace on the other, is a situation as ruinous as it is disgraceful. The mad ambition, the lust of power, and commercial avarice of Great Britain, arrogating to herself the complete dominion of the ocean, and exercising over it an unbounded and lawless tyranny, have left to neutral nations an alternative only between the base surrender of their rights, and a manly vindication of them. Happily for the United States, their destiny, under the aid of Heaven, is in their own hands. The crisis is formidable only by their love of peace. As soon as it becomes a duty to relinquish that situation, danger disappears. They have suffered no wrongs, they have received no insults, however great, for which they cannot obtain redress.

From *Annals of Congress,* 12th Congress, 1st session, vol. 25, col. 1546–54.

More than seven years have elapsed since the commencement of this system of hostile aggression by the British government, on the rights and interests of the United States. The manner of its commencement was not less hostile than the spirit with which it has been prosecuted. The United States have invariably done every thing in their power to preserve the relations of friendship with Great Britain. Of this disposition they gave a distinguished proof at the moment when they were made the victims of the opposite policy. The wrongs of the last war had not been forgotten at the commencement of the present one. They warned us of dangers, against which it was sought to provide. As early as the year 1804, the Minister of the United States at London was instructed to invite the British government to enter into a negotiation on all the points on which a collision might arise between the two countries, in the course of the war, and to propose to it an arrangement of their claims on fair and reasonable conditions. The invitation was accepted. A negotiation had commenced, and was depending, and nothing had occurred to excite a doubt that it would not terminate to the satisfaction of both parties. It was at this time, and under these circumstances, that an attack was made by surprise, on an important branch of the American commerce, which affected every part of the United States, and involved many of their citizens in ruin.

The commerce on which this attack was so unexpectedly made, was that between the United States and the colonies of France, Spain, and other enemies of Great Britain. A commerce just in itself; sanctioned by the example of Great Britain, in regard to the trade with her own colonies; sanctioned by a solemn act between the two Governments in the last war; and sanctioned by the practice of the British Government in the present war; more than two years having then elapsed, without any interference with it.

The injustice of this attack could only be equalled by the absurdity of the pretext alleged for it. It was pretended by the British Government that, in case of war, her enemy had no right to modify its colonial regulations, so as to mitigate the calamities of war to the inhabitants of its colonies. This pretension, peculiar to Great Britain, is utterly incompatible with the rights of sovereignty in every independent state. If we recur to the well-established, and universally admitted law of nations, we shall find no sanction to it in that venerable code. The sovereignty of every State is co-extensive with its dominions, and cannot be abrogated, or curtailed in its rights, as to any part, except by conquest. Neutral nations have a right to trade to every port of either belligerents, which is not legally blockaded, and in all articles which are not contraband of war. Such is the absurdity of this pretension, that your committee are aware, especially after the able manner in which it is been heretofore refuted and exposed, that they would offer an insult to the understanding of the House, if they enlarged on it; and if any thing could add to the high sense of injustice of the British Government in this transaction, it would be the contrast which her conduct exhibits in regard to this trade, and in regard to a similar trade by neutrals, with her own colonies. It is known to the world, that Great Britain regulates her own trade, in war and in peace, at home and in her colonies, as she finds for her interest; that in war she relaxes the restraints of her colonial system in favor of the colonies, and that it never was suggested that she had not a right to do it, or that a neutral, in taking advantage of the relaxation, violated a belligerent right of her enemy. But with Great Britain every thing is lawful. It is only in trade with her enemies, that the United States can do wrong: with them, all trade is unlawful.

In the year 1793, an attack was made by the British Government on the same branch of our neutral trade, which had nearly involved the two countries in war. The difference, however, was amicably accommodated. The pretension was withdrawn, and reparation made to the United States for the losses which they had suffered by it. It was fair to infer from that arrangement, that the commerce was deemed by the British Government lawful, and that it would not be again disturbed.

Had the British Government been resolved to contest this trade with neutrals, it was due to the character of the British nation, that the decision should be known to the Government of the United States. The existence of a negotiation which had been invited by our Government, for the purpose of preventing differences, by an amicable arrangement of their respective pretensions, gave a strong claim for the notification, while it afforded the fairest opportunity for it. But, a very different policy animated the then Cabinet of England. Generous sentiments were unknown to it. The liberal confidence and friendly overtures of the United States were taken advantage of to ensnare them. Steady to its purpose, and inflexibly hostile to this country, the British Government calmly looked forward to that moment when it might give the most deadly wound to our interest. A trade, just in itself, which was secured by so many strong and sacred pledges, was considered safe. Our citizens, with their usual industry and enterprise, had embarked in a vast proportion of their shipping and of their capital, which were at sea under no other protection than the law of nations, and the confidence which they reposed in the justice and friendship of the British nation. At this period, the unexpected blow was given. Many of our vessels were seized, carried into port, and condemned by a tribunal, which, while it professes to respect the law of nations, obeys the mandate of its own Government in opposition to all law. Hundreds of other vessels were driven from the ocean, and the trade itself in a great measure suppressed.

The effect produced by this attack on the lawful commerce of the United States, was as might have been expected from a virtuous, independent, and highly-injured people. But one sentiment pervaded the whole American nation. No local interests were regarded, no sordid motive felt. Without looking to the parts which suffered most, the invasion of our rights was considered a common cause, and from one extremity of our Union to the other, was heard the voice of a united people, calling on their Government to avenge their wrongs, and vindicate the rights and honor of the country.

From this period, the British Government has gone on in a continued encroachment on the rights and interests of the United States, disregarding in its course, in many instances, obligations which have heretofore been held sacred by civilized nations.

In May, 1806, the whole coast of the continent, from the Elbe to the Brest, inclusive, was declared to be in a state of blockade. By this act, the well-established principles of the law of nations, principles which have served for ages as guides, and fixed the boundary between the rights of belligerents and neutrals, were violated. By the law of nations, as recognized by Great Britain herself, no blockade is lawful, unless it be sustained by the application of an adequate force; and that an adequate force was applied to this blockade, in its full extent, ought not to be pretended. Whether Great Britain was able to maintain legally so extensive a blockade, considering the war in which she is engaged, requiring such extensive naval operations, is a question which is not necessary at this time to examine. It is sufficient to be known, that such force was not applied, and this is evident, from the terms of the blockade itself, by which, comparatively, an inconsiderable portion of the coast only was declared to be in a state of strict and rigorous blockade. The objections to the measure is not diminished by that circumstance. If the force was not applied, the blockade was unlawful, from whatever cause the failure might proceed. The belligerent who institutes the blockade, cannot absolve himself from the obligation to apply the force, under any pretext whatever. For a belligerent to relax a blockade which it could not maintain, with a view to absolve itself from the obligation to maintain it, would be a refinement in injustice, not less insulting to the understanding, than repugnant to the law of nations. To claim merit for the mitigation of evil which the party either had not the power, or found it inconvenient to inflict, would be a new mode of encroaching on neutral rights. Your committee think it just to remark, that this act of the British Government does not appear to have been adopted in the sense in which it has since been construed. On consideration of all the circumstances attending the measure, and particularly the character of the distinguished statesmen who announced it, we are persuaded that it was conceived in a spirit of conciliation and intended to lead to an accommodation of all differences between the United States and Great Britain. His death disappointed that hope, and the act has since become subservient to other purposes. It has been made, by his successors, a pretext for that vast system of usurpation, which has so long oppressed and harassed our commerce.

The next act of the British Government which claims our attention, is the Order of Council of January 7, 1807, by which neutral powers are prohibited trading from one port to another of France, or her allies, or any other country with which Great Britain might not freely trade. By this order, the pretensions of England, heretofore disclaimed by every other power, to prohibit neutrals disposing of parts of their cargoes at different ports of the same enemy, is revived, and with vast accumulation of injury. Every enemy, however great the number, or distant from each other, is considered one, and the like trade, even with powers at peace with England, who, from motives of policy, had excluded or restrained her commerce was also prohibited. In this act, the British Government evidently disclaimed all regard for neutral rights. Aware that the measures authorized by it could find no pretext in any belligerent right, none was urged. To prohibit the sale of our produce, consisting of innocent articles, in any port of a belligerent, not blockaded; to consider every belligerent as one, and subject neutrals to the same restraints with all as if there was but one, were bold encroachments. But to restrain, or in any manner interfere with our commerce with neutral nations, with whom Great Britain was at peace, and against whom she had no justifiable cause of war, for the sole reason that restrained or excluded from their ports her commerce, was utterly incompatible with the pacific relations subsisting between the two countries.

We proceed to bring into view the British Order in Council of November 11, 1807, which superseded every other order, and consummated that system of hostility on the commerce of the United States, which has been since so steadily pursued. By this order all France and her allies, and every other country at war with Great

Britain, or with which she was not at war, from which the British flag was excluded, and all the colonies of her enemies, were subject to the same restrictions as if they were actually blockaded in the most strict and rigorous manner; and all trade in articles, the produce and manufacture of the said countries and colonies, and the vessels engaged in it, were subject to capture and condemnation as lawful prize. To this order certain exceptions were made, which we forbear to notice, because they were not adopted from a regard to neutral rights, but were dictated by policy, to promote the commerce of England, and so far as they related to neutral powers, were said to emanate from the clemency of the British Government.

It would be superfluous in your committee to state, that, by this order, the British Government declared direct and positive war against the United States. The dominion of the ocean was completely usurped by it, all commerce forbidden, and every flag driven from it, or subjected to capture and condemnation, which did not subserve the policy of the British Government, by paying it a tribute, and sailing under its sanction. From this period, the United States have incurred the heaviest losses, and most mortifying humiliations. They have borne the calamities of war without retorting them on its authors.

So far your committee has presented to the view of the House the aggressions which have been committed, under the authority of the British Government, on the commerce of the United States. We will now proceed to other wrongs, which have been still more severely felt. Among these is the impressment of our seamen, a practice which has been unceasingly maintained by Great Britain in the wars to which she has been a party since our Revolution. Your committee cannot convey in adequate terms the deep sense which they entertain of the injustice and oppression of this proceeding. Under the pretext of impressing British seamen, our fellow-citizens are seized in British ports, on the high seas, and in every other quarter to which the British power extends; are taken on board British men-of-war, and compelled to serve there as British subjects. In this mode our citizens are wantonly snatched from their country and their families; deprived of their liberty, and doomed to an ignominious and slavish bondage; compelled to fight the battles of a foreign country, and often to perish in them. Our flag has given them no protection; it has been unceasingly violated, and our vessels exposed to dangers by the loss of the men taken from them. Your committee need not remark that, while this practice is continued, it is impossible for the United States to consider themselves an independent nation. Every new case is a new proof of their degradation. Its continuance is the more unjustifiable, because the United States have repeatedly proposed to the British Government an arrangement which would secure to it the control of its own people. An exemption of the citizens of the United States from this degrading oppression, and their flag from violation, is all that they have sought.

This lawless waste of our trade, and equally unlawful imprisonment of our seamen, have been much aggravated by the insults and indignities attending them. Under the pretext of blockading the harbors of France and her allies, British squadrons have been stationed on our own coast, to watch and annoy our own trade. To give effect to the blockade of European ports, the ports and harbors of the United States have been blockaded. In executing these orders of the British Government, or in obeying the spirit which was known to animate it, the commanders of these squadrons have encroached on our jurisdiction, seized our vessels, and carried into effect impressments within our limits, and done other acts of great injustice, violence, and oppression. The United States have seen, with mingled indignation and surprise, that these acts, instead of procuring to the perpetrators the punishment due to unauthorized crimes, have not failed to recommend them to the favor of their Government.

Whether the British Government has contributed by active measures to excite against us the hostility of the savage tribes on our frontiers, your committee are not disposed to occupy much time in investigating. Certain indications of general notoriety may supply the place of authentic documents, though these have not been wanting to establish the fact in some instances. It is known that symptoms of British hostility towards the United States have never failed to produce corresponding symptoms among those tribes. It is also well known that, on all such occasions, abundant supplies of the ordinary munitions of war have been afforded by the agents of British commercial companies, and even from British garrisons, wherewith they were enabled to commence that system of savage warfare on our frontiers, which has been at all times indiscriminate in its effect, on all ages, sexes, and conditions, and so revolting to humanity.

Your committee would be much gratified if, they could close here the detail of British wrongs; but it is their duty to recite another act of still greater malignity than any of those which have been already brought to your view. The attempt to dismember our Union, and overthrow our excellent constitution, by a secret mission, the object of which was to foment discontents and excite insurrection against the constituted authorities and laws of the nation, as lately disclosed by the agent employed in it, affords full proof that there is no bound to the hostility of the British Government towards the

United States; no act, however unjustifiable, which it would not commit to accomplish their ruin. This attempt excites the greater horror, from the consideration that it was made while the United States and Great Britain were at peace, and an amicable negotiation was depending between them for the accommodation of their differences, through public Ministers, regularly authorized for the purpose.

The United States have beheld, with unexampled forbearance, this continued series of hostile encroachments on their rights and interests, in the hope that, yielding to the force of friendly remonstrances, often repeated, the British Government might adopt a more just policy towards them; but that hope no longer exists. They have, also weighed impartially the reasons which have been urged by the British Government in vindication of those encroachments, and found in them neither justification nor apology.

The British Government has alleged, in vindication of the Orders in Council, that they were resorted to as a retaliation on France for similar aggressions committed by her on our neutral trade with the British dominions. But how has this plea been supported? The dates of British and French aggressions are well known to the world. Their origin and progress have been marked with too wide and destructive a waste of the property of our fellow-citizens to have been forgotten. The decrees of Berlin, of November 21st, 1806, was the first aggression of France in the present war. Eighteen months had then elapsed after the attack made by Great Britain on our neutral trade with the colonies of France and her allies, and six months from the date of the proclamation of May, 1806. Even on the 7th of January, 1807, the date of the first British Order in Council, so short a term had elapsed after the Berlin decree, that it was hardly possible that the intelligence of it should have reached the United States. A retaliation which is to produce its effect, by operating on a neutral power, ought not to be resorted to till the neutral had justified it by a culpable acquiescence in the unlawful act of the other belligerent. It ought to be delayed until after sufficient time had been allowed to the neutral to remonstrate against the measures complained of, to receive an answer, and to act on it, which had not been done in the present instance. And, when the order of November 11th was issued, it is well known that a Minister of France had declared to the Minister Plenipotentiary of the United States at Paris, that it was not intended that the decree of Berlin should apply to the United States. It is equally well known, that no American vessel had been condemned under it, or seizure been made, with which the British Government was acquainted. The facts prove incontestably, that the measures of France, however unjustifiable in themselves, were nothing more than a pretext for those of England. And of the insufficiency of that pretext, ample proof has already been afforded by the British Government itself, and in the most impressive form. Although it was declared that the Orders in Council were retaliatory on France for her decrees, it was also declared, and in the orders themselves, that, owing to the superiority of the British navy, by which the fleets of France and her allies were confined within their own ports, the French decrees were considered only as empty threats.

It is no justification of the wrongs of one power, that the like were committed by another; nor ought the fact, if true, to have been urged by either, as it could afford no proof of its love of justice, of its magnanimity, or even of its courage. It is more worthy the Government of a great nation to relieve than to assail the injured. Nor can a repetition of the wrongs by another power repair the violated rights or wounded honor of the injured party. An utter inability alone to resist could justify a quiet surrender of our rights, and degrading submission to the will of others. To that condition the United States are not reduced, nor do they fear it. That they ever consented to discuss with either power the misconduct of the other, is a proof of their love of peace, of their moderation, and of the hope which they still indulged, that friendly appeals to just and generous sentiments would not be made to them in vain. But the motive was mistaken, if their forbearance was imputed either to the want of a just sensibility to their wrongs, or a determination, if suitable redress was not obtained, to resent them. The time has now arrived when this system of reasoning must cease. It would be insulting to repeat it. It would be degrading to hear it. The United States must act as an independent nation, and assert their rights, and avenge their wrongs, according to their own estimate of them, with the party who commits them, holding it responsible for its misdeeds, unmitigated by those of another.

For the difference made between Great Britain and France, by the application of the non-importation act against England only, the motive has been already too often explained, and is too well known to require further illustration. In the commercial restrictions to which the United States resorted as an evidence of their sensibility, and a mild retaliation of their wrongs, they invariably placed both powers on the same footing, holding out to each, in respect to itself, the same accommodation, in case it accepted the condition offered, and, in respect to the other, the same restraint if it refused. Had the British Government confirmed the arrangement which was entered into with the British Minister in 1809, and France maintained her decrees, with France would the United States have had to resist, with the firmness belonging to their character, the continued violation of their rights. The committee do not hesitate to declare, that France has greatly injured the United States, and that satisfactory reparation has not yet been made for many of those injuries. But that is a concern which the United States will look to and settle for themselves. The high character of the American people is a sufficient pledge to the world that they will not fail to settle it, on conditions which they have a right to claim.

More recently, the true policy of the British Government towards the United States, has been completely unfolded. It has been publicly declared by those in power, that the Orders in Council should not be repealed until the French Government had revoked all its internal restraints on the British commerce; and that the trade of the United States with France and her allies, should be prohibited, until Great Britain was also allowed to trade with them. By this declaration, it appears that, to satisfy the pretensions of the British Government, the United States must join Great Britain in the war with France, and prosecute the war until France should be subdued; for without her subjugation, it were in vain to presume on such a concession. The hostility of the British Government to these States has been still further disclosed. It has been made manifest that the United States are considered by it as the commercial rival of Great Britain, and that their prosperity and growth are incompatible with her welfare. When all these circumstances are taken into consideration, it is impossible for your committee to doubt the motives which have governed the British Ministry in all its measures towards the United States since the year of 1805. Equally it is impossible to doubt, longer, the course which the United States ought to pursue towards Great Britain.

From this review of the multiplied wrongs of the British Government since the commencement of the present war, it must be evident to the impartial world, that the contest which is now forced on the United States, is radically a contest for their sovereignty and independence. Your committee will not enlarge on any of the injuries, however great, which have had a transitory effect. They wish to call the attention of the House to those of a permanent nature only, which intrench so deeply on our most important rights, and wound so extensively and vitally our best interests, as could not fail to deprive the United States of the principal advantages of their Revolution, if submitted to. The control of our commerce by Great Britain, in regulating, at pleasure, and expelling it almost from the ocean; the oppressive manner in which these regulations have been carried into effect, by seizing and confiscating such of our vessels, with their cargoes, as were said to have violated her edicts, often without previous warning of their danger; the impressment of our citizens from on board our own vessels on the high seas, and elsewhere, and holding them in bondage till it suited the convenience of their oppressors to deliver them up; are encroachments of that high and dangerous tendency, which could not fail to produce that pernicious effect; nor would these be the only consequences that would result from it. The British Government might, for a while, be satisfied with the ascendency thus gained over us, but its pretensions would soon increase. The proof which so complete and disgraceful a submission to its authority would afford of our degeneracy, and could not fail to inspire confidence, that there was no limit to which its usurpations, and our degradation, might not be carried.

Your committee, believing that the free-born sons of America are worthy to enjoy the liberty which their fathers purchased at the price of so much blood and treasure, and seeing in the measures adopted by Great Britain, a course commenced and persisted in, which must lead to a loss of national character and independence, feel no hesitation in advising resistance by force; in which the Americans of the present day will prove to the enemy and to the world, that we have not only inherited that liberty which our fathers gave us, but also the will and power to maintain it. Relying on the patriotism of the nation, and confidently trusting that the Lord of Hosts will go with us to battle in the righteous cause, and crown our efforts with success, your committee recommend an immediate appeal to arms.

PART IV

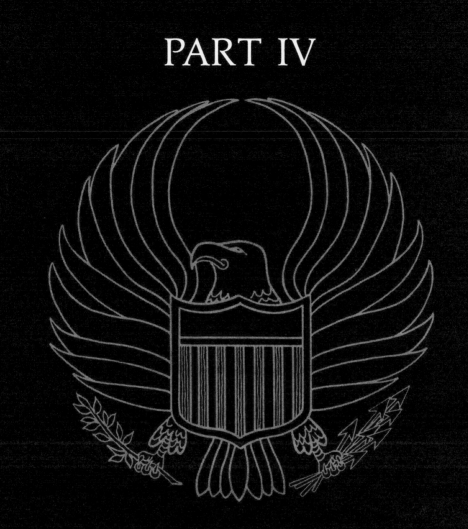

THE QUEST
FOR PEACE

12
AN UNJUST WAR

When the United States entered into war with Great Britain in 1812, most Americans believed that it would be fought to a swift and successful conclusion. But the early months of campaigning dashed the hopes of those who had thought that the taking of Canada would be a mere matter of marching and confirmed the worst expectations of those who had argued that the declaration of war was an act of wanton and dangerous folly. The surrender of William Hull at Detroit, the defeat at Queenston Heights, and the failure of thousands of Americans living in Canada to rise up in support of the invaders cast a pall of gloom over Washington. While it is true that the American military posture improved by 1814, the continued and intensified blockade of the Atlantic coastline and the failure to occupy Canada made dissent widespread and opposition to Madison deep and bitter.

Much of this discontent centered in New England where hostility to the war had always been deep seated. As the conflict progressed sentiment against it hardened and achieved its final expression in the Hartford Convention which called for a revision of the Constitution that would have restricted the power and flexibility of the national government.

One of the most articulate exponents of New England's attitude was Daniel Webster. In a speech delivered in Congress on a bill to enlarge the army he gave forceful expression to his views. He argued passionately that the war was endangering the unity of the nation, that the attempt to conquer Canada was both hazardous and dishonorable, and that a reasonable and just peace should be sought at the earliest opportunity.

SPEECH IN THE HOUSE OF REPRESENTATIVES

JANUARY 14, 1814

*Daniel
Webster*

Mr. Speaker, it was not my intention to offer myself to your notice on this question. I have changed my purpose only in consequence of the course which the debate took yesterday, on an amendment proposed by me to one of the subordinate provisions of this bill. The observations to which that occasion gave rise, have induced me to prefer assigning my own reasons for my own vote, rather than trust to the justice or charity of the times to assign reasons for me.

The design of this bill is to encourage, by means of a very extraordinary bounty, enlistments into the regular army. Laws already existing, and other bills now in progress before the House, provide for the organization of an army of sixty-three thousand men. For the purpose of filling the ranks of that army, the bill before us proposes to give to each recruit a bounty of one hundred and twenty-four dollars, and three hundred and twenty-acres of land. It offers also a premium of eight dollars to every person, in or out of the army, citizen or soldier, who shall procure an able-bodied man to be enlisted.

Before, sir, I can determine for myself whether so great a military force should be raised, and at so great an expense, I am bound to inquire into the object to which that force is to be applied. If the public exigency shall in my judgment demand it; if any object connected with the protection of the country, and the safety of its citizens, shall require it; and if I shall see reasonable ground to believe that the force, when raised, will be applied to meet that exigency, and yield that protection, I shall not be restrained by any considerations of expense from giving my support to the measure. I am aware that the country needs defence, and I am anxious that defence should be provided for it to the fullest extent, and in the promptest manner. But what is the object of this bill? To what service is this army destined, when its ranks shall be filled? We are told, sir, that the frontier is invaded, and that troops are wanted to repel that invasion. It is too true that the frontier is invaded — that the war,

From *Annals of Congress,* 13th Congress, 1st and 2nd sessions, vol. 27, col. 940–51.

with all its horrors, ordinary and extraordinary, is brought within our own territories — and that the inhabitants near the country of the enemy are compelled to fly, lighted by the fires of their own houses, or stay and meet the foe, unprotected by an adequate aid of Governments. But show me that by any vote of mine, or any effort of mine, I can contribute to the relief of such distress; show me that the purpose of Government, in this measure, is to provide defence for the frontiers. I aver I see no evidence of any such intention. I have no assurance that this army will be applied to any such object. There are, as was said by my honorable friend from New York, (Mr. Grosvenor,) strong reasons to infer the contrary, from the fact that the forces hitherto raised have not been so applied, in any suitable or sufficient proportion. The defence of our own territory seems hitherto to have been regarded as an object of secondary importance — a duty of a lower order than the invasion of the enemy. The army raised last year was competent to defend the frontier. To that purpose Government did not see fit to apply it. It was not competent, as the event proved, to invade with success the provinces of the enemy. To that purpose, however, it was applied. The substantial benefit which might have been obtained, and ought to have been obtained, was sacrificed to a scheme of conquest, in my opinion a wild one, commenced without means, prosecuted without plan or concert, and ending in disgrace. Nor is it the inland frontier only that has been left defenceless. The seacoast has been, in many places, wholly exposed. Give me leave to state one instance: the mouth of one of the largest rivers in the eastern section of the Union is defended by a fort mounting fourteen guns; this fort, for a great part of the last season, was holden by one man and one boy only. I state the fact on the authority of an honorable gentleman of this House. Other cases, almost equally flagrant, are known to have existed, in some of which interests of a peculiar character and great magnitude have been at stake. With this knowledge of the past, I must have evidence of some change in the purposes of the Administration before I can vote for this bill, under an expectation that protection will thereby be afforded to either frontier of the Union. Of such change there is no intimation. On the contrary, gentlemen tell us explicitly that the acquisition of Canada is still deemed to be an essential object, and the vote of the House within the last half hour has put the matter beyond doubt. An honorable gentleman from Virginia (Mr. Sheffey) has proposed an amendment to the bill, limiting the service of the troops to be raised by its provisions, to objects of defence. To the bill thus amended he offered his support, and would have been cheerfully followed by his friends.

The amendment was rejected. It is certain, therefore, that the real object of this proposition to increase the military force to an extraordinary degree, by extraordinary means, is to act over again the scenes of the two last campaigns. To that object I cannot lend my support — I am already satisfied with the exhibition. Give me leave to say, sir, that the tone on the subject of the conquest of Canada seems to be not a little changed.

Before the war, that conquest was represented to be quite an easy affair. The valiant spirits who meditated it were only fearful lest it should be too easy to be glorious. They had no apprehension, except that resistance would not be so powerful as to render the victory splendid. These confident expectations were, however, accompanied with a commendable spirit of moderation, the true mark of great minds, and it was gravely said that we ought not to make too large a grasp for dominion, but to stop in our march of conquest northward, somewhere about the line of perpetual congelation, and leave to our enemies or others the residue of the continent to the pole.

How happens it, sir, that this country, so easy of acquisition, and over which, according to the prophecies, we were to have been by this time legislating, dividing it into States and Territories, is not yet ours? Nay, sir, how happens it that we are not even free of invasion ourselves; but gentlemen here call on us, by all the motives of patriotism, to assist in the defence of our own soil, and portray before us the state of the frontier, by frequent and animated allusion to all those topics which the modes of Indian warfare usually suggest?

This, sir, is not what we were promised. This is not the entertainment to which we were invited. This is no fulfillment of those predictions which it was deemed obstinacy itself not to believe. This is not the harvest of greatness and glory, the seeds of which were supposed to be sown with the declaration of war.

When we ask, sir, for the causes of these disappointments, we are told that they are owing to the opposition which the war encounters in this House and among the people. All the evils which afflict the country are imputed to opposition. This is the fashionable doctrine, both here and elsewhere. It is said to be owing to opposition that war became necessary; and owing to opposition, also, that is has been prosecuted with no better success.

This, sir, is no new strain. It has been sung a thousand times; it is the constant tune of every weak or wicked Administration. What Minister ever yet acknowledged that the evils which fell on his country were the necessary consequences of his own incapacity, his own folly, or his own corruption? What possessor of political power ever yet failed to charge the mischiefs resulting from his own measures, upon those who had uniformly opposed those measures? The people of the United States may well remember the administration of Lord North. He lost America to his country. Yet he could find pretences of throwing the odium upon his opponents. He could throw it upon those who had forewarned him of the consequences from the first, and who had opposed him, at every stage of his disastrous policy, with all the force of truth, and reason, and talent. It was not his own weakness, his own ambition, his own love of arbitary power, which disaffected the Colonies. It was not the Tea act, the Stamp act, or the Boston Port bill, that severed the empire of Great Britain. Oh, no! It was owing to no fault of Administration; it was the work of opposition. It was the impertinent boldness of Chatham; the idle declamation of Fox; and the unseasonable sarcasm of Barre! These men, and men like them, would not join the Minister in his American war. They would not give the name and character of wisdom to that which they believed to be the extreme of folly. They would not pronounce those measures just and honorable, which their principles led them to detest. They declared the Minister's war to be wanton. They foresaw its end, and pointed it out plainly both to the Minister and to the country. He pronounced the opposition to be selfish and factious; he persisted in his course, and the result is in history.

This example of Ministerial justice seems to have become a model for these times, and this country. With slight shades of difference, owing to different degrees of talent and ability, the imitation is sufficiently exact. It requires little imagination to fancy one's self sometimes to be listening to a recitation of the captivating orations of the occupants of Lord North's Treasury bench. We are told that our opposition has divided the Government, and divided the country. Remember, sir, the state of the Government and of the country when war was declared. Did not difference of opinion then exist? Do we not know that this House was divided? Do we not know that the other House was still more divided? Does not every man, to whom the public documents are accessible, know, that in that House one single vote, having been given otherwise than it was, would have rejected the declaring war, and adopted a different course of measures? A parental, guardian Government, would have regarded that state of things. It would have weighed such considerations; it would have inquired coolly and dispassionately into the state of public opinion in the State of this Confederacy; it would have looked especially to those States most concerned in the professed objects of the war, and whose interests were to be most deeply affected by it. Such a Government, knowing that its strength consisted in the union of opinion among the people, would have taken no step of such importance without that union; nor would it have mistaken mere party feeling for national sentiment.

That occasion, sir, called for a liberal view of things. Not only the degree of union in the sentiments of the people, but the nature and structure of the Government; the general habits and pursuits of the community; the probable consequences of the war, immediate and remote, on our civil institutions; the effect of a vast military patronage; the variety of important local interests and objects; — these were considerations essentially belonging to the subject. It was not enough that Government could make out its cause of war on paper, and get the better of England in the argument. This was requisite, but not all that was requisite. The question of war or peace, in a country like this, is not to be compressed into the compass that would befit a small litigation. It is not to be made to turn upon a pin. Incapable in its nature of being decided upon technical rules, it is unfit to be discussed in the manner which usually appertains to the forensic habit. It should be regarded as a great question, not only of right, but also of prudence and expediency. Reasons of a general nature, considerations which go back to the origin of our institutions, and other considerations which look forward to our hopeful progress in future times, all belong, in their just proportions and gradations, to a question, in the determination of which the happiness of the present and of future generations may be so much concerned.

I have heard no satisfactory vindication of the war on grounds like those. They appear not to have suited the temper of that time. Utterly astonished at the declaration of war, I have been surprised at nothing since. Unless all history deceived me, I saw how it would be prosecuted when I saw how it was begun. There is in the nature of things an unchangeable relation between rash counsels and feeble execution.

It was not, sir, the minority that brought on the war. Look to your records from the date of the embargo in 1807, to June 1812. Every thing that men could do, they did, to stay your course. When at last they could effect no more, they urged you to delay your measures. They entreated you to give yet a little time for deliberation, and to wait for favorable events. As if inspired for the purpose of arresting your progress, they laid before you the consequences of your measures, just as we have seen them since take place. They predicted to you their effects on public opinion. They told you that, instead of healing, they would inflame political dissensions. They pointed out to you also what would and what must happen on the frontier. That which since has happened there, is but their prediction turned into history. Vain is the hope then of escaping just retribution, by imputing to the minority of the Government, or to the opposition among the people, the disasters of these times. Vain is the attempt to impose thus on the common sense of mankind. The world has had too much experience of ministerial shifts and evasions. It has learned to judge of men by their actions, and of measures by their consequences.

If the purpose be, by casting these implications upon those who are opposed to the policy of the Government, to check their freedom of inquiry, discussion, and debate, such purpose is also incapable of being executed. That opposition is constitutional and legal. It is also conscientious. It rests in settled and sober conviction, that such policy is destructive to the interests of the people, and dangerous to the being of the Government. The experience of every day confirms these sentiments. Men who act from such motives are not to be discouraged by trifling obstacles nor awed by any dangers. They know the limit of constitutional opposition — up to that limit, at their own discretion will they walk, and walk fearlessly. If they should find, in the history of their country, a precedent for going over, I trust they will not follow it. They are not of a school, in which insurrection is taught as a virtue. They will not seek promotion through the paths of sedition, nor qualify themselves to serve their country in any of the high departments of its Government, by making rebellion the first element in their political science.

Important as I deem it to discuss, on all proper occasions, the policy of the measures at present pursued, it is still more important to maintain the right of such discussion, in its full and just extent. Sentiments lately sprung up, and now growing fashionable, make it necessary to be explicit on this point. The more I perceive a disposition to check the freedom of inquiry by extravagant and unconstitutional pretences, the firmer shall be the tone in which I shall assert, and the freer the manner in which I shall exercise it. It is the ancient and undoubted prerogative of this people to canvass public measures and the merits of public men. It is a "home-bred right," a fireside privilege. It has ever been enjoyed in every house, cottage, and cabin, in the nation. It is not to be drawn into controversy. It is as undoubted as the right of breathing the air, or walking on the earth. Belonging to private life as a right, it belongs to public life as a duty; and it is the last duty which those whose representative I am, shall find me to abandon. Aiming at all times to be courteous and temperate in its use, except when the right itself shall be questioned, I shall then carry it to its extent. I shall then place myself on the extreme boundary of my right, and bid defiance to any arm that would move me from my ground. This high constitutional privilege I shall defend and exercise within this House, and without this House, and in all places: in time of war, in time of peace, and at all times. Living I shall assert it, dying I shall assert it; and, should I leave no other inheritance to my children, by the blessing of God I will still leave them the inheritance of free principles, and the example of a manly, independent, and constitutional defence of them.

Whoever, sir, would discover the causes which have produced the present state of things, must look for them not in the efforts of opposition, but in the nature of the war in which we are engaged, and in the manner in which its professed objects have been attempted to be obtained. Quite too small a portion of public opinion was in favor of the war, to justify it, originally. A much smaller portion is in favor of the mode in which it has been conducted. This is the radical infirmity. Public opinion, strong and united, is not with you, in your Canada project. Whether it ought to be, or ought not to be, the fact that it is not, should by this time be evident to all; and it is the business of practical statesmen, to act upon the state of things as it is, and not to be always attempting to prove what it ought to be. The acquisition of that country is not an object generally desired by the people. Some gentlemen indeed say it is not their ultimate object; and that they wish it only as the means of effecting other purposes. But, sir, a large portion of the people believe that a desire for the conquest and final retention of Canada is the main spring of public measures. Nor is the opinion without ground. It has been distinctly avowed by public men, in a public manner. And if this be not the object, it is not easy to see the connection between your means and ends. At least that portion of the people, that is not in the habit of refining far, cannot see it. You are, you say, at war for maritime rights, and free trade. But they see you lock up your commerce and abandon the ocean. They see you invade an interior province of the enemy. They see you involve yourselves in a bloody war with the native savages; and they ask you, if you have, in truth, a maritime controversy with the Western Indians, and are really contending for sailor's rights with the tribes of the Prophet? In my judgment the popular sentiment, in this case, corresponds with the soundest political discretion. In my humble opinion, you are not only not able to travel in the road you have taken, but, if you were, it would not conduct you to your object.

I am aware, sir, that both the professed objects of the war, and the manner of prosecuting it, may receive the nominal approbation of a great majority of those who constitute the prevailing party. But I know also how extremely fallacious any influence from that circumstance would be, in favor of the real popularity of the measure. In times like these, a great measure of a prevalent party becomes incorporated with the party interest. To quarrel with the measure would be to abandon the party. Party considerations, therefore, induce an acquiescence in that on which the fate of party is supposed to depend. Gentlemen, sir, fall into strange inconsistencies on this subject. They tell us that the war is popular; that the invasion of Canada is popular, and that it would have succeeded before this time, had it not been for the force of opposition. Sir, what gives force to opposition in this country? Certainly nothing but the popularity of the cause of opposition, and the numbers who espouse it. Upon this argument, then, in what an unprecedented condition are the people of these States? We have on our hands a most popular war; we have also a most popular opposition to that war. We cannot push the measure, the opposition is so popular. We cannot retract it, the measure itself is so popular. We can neither go forward, nor backward. We are at the very centre of gravity — the point of perpetual rest.

The truth is, sir, that party support is not the kind of support necessary to sustain the country through a long, expensive, and bloody contest; and this should have been considered before the war was declared. The cause, to be successful, must be upheld by other sentiments, and higher motives. It must draw to itself the sober approbation of the great mass of the people. It must enlist, not their temporary or party feelings, but their steady patriotism, and their constant zeal. Unlike the old nations of Europe, there are in this country no dregs of population, fit only to supply the constant waste of war, and out of which an army can be raised, for hire, at any time, and for any purpose. Armies of any magnitude can here be nothing but the people embodied — and if the object be one for which the people will not embody, there can be no armies.

It is, I think, too plain to be doubted, that the conquest of Canada is such an object. They do not feel the impulse of adequate motive. Not unmindful of military distinction, they are yet not sanguine of laurels in this conquest. The harvest, thus far, they perceive has not been great. The prospect of the future is no greater. Nor are they altogether reconciled to the principle of this invasion. Canada, they know, is not to be conquered, but by drenching its soil in the blood of its inhabitants. They have no thirst for that blood. The borderers, on the line, connected by blood and marriage, and all the ties of social life, have no disposition to bear arms against one another. Merciless indeed has been the fate of some of these people. I understand it to be a fact, that in some of the affairs which we call battles, because we have had nothing else to give the name to, brother has been in arms against brother. The bosom of the parent has been exposed to the bayonet of his own son. Sir, I honor the people that shrink from a warfare like this. I applaud their sentiments and their feelings. They are such as religion and humanity dictate, and such as none but cannibals would wish to eradicate from the human heart.

You have not succeeded in dividing the people of the Provinces from their Government. Your commanders tell you that they are universally hostile to your cause. It is not, therefore, to make war on their Government, it is to make war, fierce, cruel, bloody war on the people themselves, that you call to your standard the yeomanry of the Northern States. The experience of the two campaigns should have taught you, that they will not obey that call. Government has put itself in every posture. It has used supplication and entreaty; it has also menaced, and it still menaces compulsion. All is in vain. It cannot longer conceal its weakness on this point. Look to the bill before you. Does not that speak a language exceeding every thing I have said? You last year gave a bounty of sixteen dollars, and now propose to give a bounty of one hundred and twenty-four dollars, and you say you have no hope of obtaining men at a lower rate. This is sufficient to convince me, it will be sufficient to convince the enemy and the whole world, yourselves only excepted, what progress your Canada war is making in the affections of the people.

It is to no want of natural resources, or natural strength in the country, that failures can be attributed. The Northern States alone are able to overrun Canada in thirty days, armed or unarmed, in any cause which should propel them by inducements sufficiently powerful. Recur, sir, to history. As early as 1745, the New England Colonies raised an army of five thousand men, and took Louisburg from the troops of France. On what point of the enemy's territory, let me ask, have you brought an equal force to bear in the whole course of two campaigns? On another occasion, more than half a century ago, Massachusetts alone, although its population did not exceed one-third of its present amount, had an army of twelve thousand men. Of these, seven thousand were at one time employed against Canada. A strong motive was then felt to exist. With equal exertion that Commonwealth could now furnish an army of forty thousand men.

You have prosecuted this invasion for two campaigns. They have cost you vastly more, upon the average, than the campaigns of the Revolutionary war. The project has already cost the American people nearly half as much as the whole price paid for independence.

The result is before us. Who does not see and feel that this result disgraces us? Who does not see in what estimation our martial prowess must be by this time holden by the enemy and by the world? Administration has made its master effort to subdue a province, three thousand miles removed from the mother country; scarcely equal in natural strength to the least of the States of this confederacy, and defended by external aid to a limited extent. It has persisted two campaigns, and it has failed. Let the responsibility rest where it ought. The world will not ascribe the issue to want of spirit or patriotism in the American people. The possession of those qualities, in high and honorable degrees, they have heretofore illustriously evinced, and spread out proof on the record of their Revolution. They will be still true to their character, in any cause which they feel to be their own. In all causes they will defend themselves. The enemy, as we have seen, can make no permanent stand in any populous part of the country. Its citizens will drive back his forces to the line. But at that line, at the point where defence ceases and invasion begins, they stop. They do not pass it, because they do not choose to pass it. Offering no serious obstacle to their actual power, it rises, like a Chinese wall, against their sentiments and their feelings.

It is natural, sir, such being my opinion, on the present state of things, that I should be asked what, in my judgment, ought to be done. In the first place, then, I answer, withdraw your invading armies and follow counsels which the national sentiment will support. In the next place, abandon the system of commercial restriction. That system is equally ruinous to the interests, and obnoxious to the feelings of whole sections and whole States. They believe you have no constitutional right to establish such systems. They protest to you that such is not, and never was, their understanding of your powers. They are sincere in this opinion, and it is of infinite moment that you duly respect that opinion, although you may deem it to be erroneous. These people, sir, resisted Great Britain, because her Minister, under pretence of regulating trade, attempted to put his hand into their pockets and take their money. There is that, sir, which they then valued, and which they still value, more than money. That pretence of regulating trade they believed to be a mere cover for tyranny and oppression. The present embargo, which does not vex, and harass, and embarrass their commerce, but annihilates it, is also laid by color of a power to regulate trade. For if it be not laid by virtue of this power, it is laid by virtue of no power. It is not wonderful, sir, if this should be viewed by them as a state of things, not contemplated when they came into the national compact.

The humble aid which it would be in my power to render to measures of Government, shall be given cheerfully, if Government will pursue measures which I can conscientiously support. Badly as I think of the original grounds of the war, as well as of the manner in which it has been hitherto conducted, if even now, failing in an honest and sincere attempt to procure just and honorable peace, it will return to measures of defence and protection, such as reason, and common sense, and the public opinion all call for, my vote shall not be withholden from the means. Give up your futile projects of invasion. Extinguish the fires that blaze on your inland frontiers. Establish perfect safety and defence there, by adequate force. Let every man that sleeps on your soil, sleep in security. Stop the blood that flows from the veins of unarmed yeomanry and women and children. Give to the living time to bury and lament their dead, in the quietness of private sorrow. Having performed this work of beneficence and mercy on your inland border, turn, and look with the eye of justice and compassion on your vast population along the coast. Unclench the iron grasp of your embargo. Take measures for that end before another sun sets upon you. With all the war of the enemy on your commerce, if you would cease to war on it yourselves, you would still have some commerce. That commerce would give you some revenue. Apply that revenue to the augmentation of your navy. That navy, in turn, will protect your commerce. Let it no longer be said that not one ship of force, built by your hands since the war, yet floats upon the ocean. Turn the current of your efforts into the channel which national sentiment has already worn broad and deep to receive it. A naval force, competent to defend your coast against considerable armaments, to convoy your trade, and perhaps raise the blockade of your rivers, is not a chimera. It may be realized. If, then, the war must be continued, go to the ocean. If you are seriously contending for maritime rights, go to the theatre where alone those rights can be defended. Thither every indication of your fortune points you. There the united wishes and exertions of the nation will go with you. Even our party divisions, acrimonious as they are, cease at the water's edge. They are lost in attachment to national character on the element where that character is made respectable. In protecting naval interests by naval means, you will arm yourselves with the whole power of national sentiment, and may command the whole abundance of the national resources. In time you may enable yourselves to redress injuries, in the place where they may be offered, and, if need be, to accompany your own flag throughout the world, with the protection of your own cannon.

13

A CALL FOR VICTORY

 The rising tide of dissent in the United States and the growing opposition to the war did not dissuade the administration's supporters from pressing for vigorous military action. Men like Felix Grundy of Tennessee argued that an enlarged army, led daringly and imaginatively, could turn the tide in favor of America. And indeed, if the United States could occupy Canada, she would put herself in a formidable position at the bargaining table. But it had to be done quickly, for the war in Europe was approaching its end. And when that happened Britain would be free to send Wellington's veterans to Canada. These seasoned, disciplined, and confident troops would be capable of inflicting heavy punishment on the United States.

It was, therefore, essential that the government unite the country and increase its military forces. Grundy, a War Hawk in 1812, spoke vigorously in support of raising money for the army and he spoke equally harshly of those who opposed the government's policies. Open dissent in a democratic society was perfectly natural, but a conscious attempt by a minority to thwart the will of a majority was intolerable. Action of that kind would endanger the existence of the Union and jeopardize the bright hopes which the future held for the new nation.

SPEECH IN THE HOUSE OF REPRESENTATIVES

FEBRUARY 18, 1814

Felix Grundy

Mr. Grundy addressed the Chair as follows:

Mr. Chairman, I had determined to remain silent during this discussion, and nothing but the extraordinary course pursued by gentlemen on the other side of the House could have induced me to relinquish that determination. Not satisfied with replying to the arguments urged by the majority at the present, they have assailed sentiments advanced by me at the last session; nor has this been done by one or two only, but by all who have addressed you; yes, sir, from the greatest to the least — from the venerable gentleman from Massachusetts, (Mr. Pickering,) down to the gentlemen from North Carolina, (Messrs. Culpeper and Pearson,) who spoke a short time since — this has constituted the burden of their song. But for this, I should have been saved the trouble of speaking, and you the fatigue of hearing me.

Before I proceed to an examination of their arguments, the committee will indulge me a few moments in taking a view of the subjects under consideration, different from any yet presented.

The Committee of Ways and Means have recommended to the House the adoption of a bill providing for a loan of twenty-five millions of dollars; the majority seem disposed to grant the supply asked for, the minority say it ought not be granted — the question then is, which party is right? This can best be decided by an examination into the effects which will result from the adoption of the one course or the other. If more public good will result from the passage of the bill than from its rejection, the minority are acting erroneously. If, on the other hand, more evil will arise from its passage than from its rejection, the minority are acting correctly. You are engaged, Mr. Chairman, in a war with a powerful nation, on whose magnanimity and justice, judging from past experience, you can place no reliance. Should this bill pass, you will be prepared to arm the American people, and (should negotiation fail) meet your enemy in the field of battle; you will be prepared to assert your rights by the sword; you will exhibit your Government in the attitude which is most commanding, with the sword in the one hand, and the olive

FROM *Annals of Congress,* 13th Congress, 1st and 2nd sessions, vol. 28, col. 1532–42.

branch in the other, saying to the enemies of your country — Choose ye which to select. This is what the majority recommend. What is the course advocated by the minority? Disarm the American people, lay down your weapons of warfare, and do what? Ask pardon and forgiveness for your transgressions, and accept of such terms as the enemy will accord to you. Is this a course worthy of a great and free people? Would you not by this demonstrate to the world that you are unworthy of that liberty which you enjoy? I confess, Mr. Chairman, I am almost tempted to doubt the sincerity of gentlemen's declarations, when I look at the low and degraded state to which the country would be reduced, should the opposition to this bill succeed. Further, sir, by the money contemplated to be raised under the authority of this bill, you can comply with all your engagements; you can pay the officers and soldiers already in your service; you can support that navy of which all parties claim to be the patrons; you can pay the stipulated portion of former debts; in short, you will support the public credit; reject it, and you cannot pay those at present in your employment; your navy must rot, your ability to obtain loans at any future period will be entirely annihilated; for, once let it be ascertained that your punctuality is not to be depended on, rely on it, it will be idle to attempt to borrow. What, sir, has hitherto kept up the price of American stock at home and abroad? It has been that rigid regard to justice and good faith which has at all times characterized this Government. There are cases in which, probably, a government might fail punctually to comply with its engagements, and still the public credit might not be greatly affected. This would not, however, be one of those cases; because, in this instance, there would not only be a failure, but it would be unaccompanied with an honest exertion towards compliance. If, sir, the idea shall ever meet with public sanction, that one political party may incur a debt and their political opponents stand justified in refusing to discharge it, I pronounce that public credit is at an end, and this form of government will soon follow it. At the last session, a gentleman from New York (Mr. Oakley) furnished the best apology that could be made for his vote against the loan bill; but I have heard nothing of the kind from others; and even his apology was not very satisfactory. After the passage of that bill, he declared he would have voted for it, only he knew the majority were bound to pass it. He seemed justly to appreciate the importance of preserving the public faith. I thought the sentiment honorable to him; but I confess it did occur to me that he had adopted too easy a method to get clear of the trouble of doing his duty for himself. I did suppose that the better way was for each individual to do that which appeared right to himself, and not leave it to others to perform it for him. If, however, that gentleman can reconcile such conduct to his own conscience, it is not for me to censure or condemn. Who, Mr. Chairman, complain most of the defenceless state of the country? The very men who refuse to grant men and money for its defence. They say they need protection, and criminate the Government for the want of it; and at the same time use all their exertions to withhold from the Administration the means of protecting them.

Sir, members venerable for their age and experience, and more so for their pursuits in life, (for they profess to be the interpreters of the word of truth,) have said in debate that this is a wicked and irreligious war: and quote the expressions "Thou shall not kill," &c., "Love thy neighbor as thyself," &c., in support of this charge. Do these gentlemen suppose that the book to which they refer, the authority of which all admit, is so little understood that misrepresentations of this kind can be practised successfully? Can it be believed that that Deity, who, on many occasions, expressly commanded wars to be made; he who led his favorite people to battle, and was a shield and defence to them in the hour of danger, should condemn all wars as unlawful? These gentlemen have forgotten that the British Government, which they consider as the great promoter of Christianity, is in the habit of shedding human blood by her wars. Yes, that moral and religious nation is more frequently engaged in war than any other; not defensive wars only, but offensive foreign wars. Examine her history, and you will find that within the last six hundred and ten years she has been at war two hundred and sixty-one years with a single nation; and during that period she has never been invaded, though at particular periods greatly threatened. The same gentlemen affect to value the blessings of civil liberty, as enjoyed by us, and to revere the Constitution of the United States: and can they not remember that these are the effects of the war of the Revolution? If all wars are forbidden by the law of God, the Revolution was an immoral and wicked thing, and those who achieved it are liable to censure, rather than entitled to that praise which all parties unite in bestowing on them.

It is also alleged that it is unjust to invade Canada. In the Revolutionary war it was invaded: and I defy those who pretend they are the disciples of Washington, to show any difference in principle between the propriety of an invasion then, and an invasion now. Yet at that period the illustrious man who commanded the American armies, and all those who were united with him in rescuing this country from the unfeeling grasp of a foreign tyrant, decided that the conquest of the Canadas was just and expedient.

I come now, Mr. Chairman, to speak on that point which produced the necessity of my addressing you: Moral treason — that sentiment expressed by me at a former session, which has excited so much sensibility, and given rise to so much censure. To whom have I ascribed it? Not to those who exercise their constitutional privilege of opposing measures before they are adopted by the constituted authorities; not to those who shall, even after their adoption, deliver their sentiments freely against them; not to those who shall fail to join the army themselves, or decline to loan their money; but to those who shall exert their influence to prevent others from enlisting, and shall combine together for the purpose of preventing loans from being filled. Men of the latter description, I did say, were, in my judgment, guilty of treason in a moral point of view. I say so still. It is an opinion which reflection has doubly confirmed; it is an opinion I shall never retract. So far from it, would to God it were written in letters of sunshine in the very centre of Heaven, that all the world might read. It is opposing the laws after they are constitutionally enacted; it is attempting to prevent the operation of the laws by other means than a repeal of them; and the latter is the only way in which I believe the effect of any law can with propriety be defeated.

Gentlemen who are so very sensitive on this subject had better look back a few years, and see how they thought and acted when in power, and perhaps a review of this kind will show them the true difference between us on this point. We say such conduct as I have described is unjustifiable. We advise, we admonish, we entreat those who practise it, to desist. Not so in 1798. The party then in power acted; they passed their Sedition law; they recorded their disapprobation of such conduct; and a republican member of Congress, from Vermont, suffered the penalties imposed. And, sir, recollect, this took place in what is called the quasi war with France, and not at a period when dangers assailed the nation on every side, as at present.

Let us recur to that law, and see whether its provisions would not punish those guilty of such conduct as I have censured:

AN ACT IN ADDITION TO THE ACT, ENTITLED "AN ACT FOR THE PUNISHMENT OF CERTAIN CRIMES AGAINST THE UNITED STATES."

SEC. 1 Be it enacted by the Senate and House of Representatives of the United States of America, in Congress assembled, That if any person shall unlawfully combine or conspire together, with intent to oppose any measure or measures of the Government of the United States, which are or shall be directed by proper authority, or to impede the operation of any law of the United States, or to intimidate or prevent any person holding a place or office in or under the Government of the United States, from undertaking, performing, or executing his trust or duty; and if any person or persons, with intent as aforesaid, shall counsel, advise, or attempt to procure any insurrection, riot, unlawful assembly, or combination, whether such conspiracy, threatening, counsel, advice, or attempt, shall have the proposed effect or not, he or they shall be deemed guilty of high misdemeanor, and, on conviction before any court of the United States having jurisdiction thereof, shall be punished by a fine not exceeding five thousand dollars, and by imprisonment during a term not less than six months, nor exceeding five years; and further, at the discretion of the court, may be holden to find sureties for his good behavior in such sum, and for such time, as the said court may direct.

Sec. 2 And be it further enacted, That if any person shall write, print, utter, or publish, or shall cause or procure to be written, printed, uttered, or published, or shall knowingly and willingly assist or aid in writing, printing, uttering, or publishing any false, scandalous, and malicious writing or writings against the Government of the United States, or either House of the Congress of the United States, or the President of the United States, with intent to defame the said Government, or either House of the said Congress, or the said President, or to bring them, or either of them, into disrepute; or to excite against them, or either, or any of them, the hatred of the good people of the United States, or to stir up sedition within the United States, or to excite any unlawful combinations therein, for opposing or resisting any law of the United States, or any act of the President of the United States, done in pursuance of any such law, or of the powers in him vested by the Constitution of the United States, or to resist, oppose, or defeat any such law or act; or to aid, encourage, or abet any hostile designs of any foreign nation against the United States, their people, or Government, then such person, being thereof convicted before any court of the United States having jurisdiction thereof, shall be punished by a fine not exceeding two thousand dollars, and by imprisonment not exceeding two years.

Now, sir, examine the extent of the provisions I have read. It is declared, that if any persons shall unlawfully combine or conspire together, with intent to oppose any measure or measures of the General Government, which are or shall be directed by proper authority, or to impede the operation of any law of the United States, &c. Suppose the first branch of the sentence should be construed to extend to cases only where open force was intended to be applied, yet the terms "to combine or conspire together, with intent to impede the operation of any law of the United States," would clearly embrace those who combine and conspire together to prevent the filling of the loans, and the ranks of the army. Observe, Mr. Chairman, in the second section, how careful those who now talk so much about the liberty of speech and of the press were to guard themselves from the attacks of their opponents. "To defame either House of Congress, or the President of the United States, with intent to bring them into contempt or disrepute," was made punishable. And this bill passed the Senate of the United States, containing only the two sections I have read, and without any provision that the truth might be given in evidence on the trial. Thus far I speak of the facts as the public records prove them to be. I examined them on yesterday. And I am informed by a venerable gentleman, then and now a member of this House, that, with great difficulty, a predecessor of mine (Mr. Claiborne) procured, in the House of Representatives, the insertion of the third section, which declares that the truth may be given in evidence on the trial. Without this provision, what would have been the condition of men prosecuted under that law? The principles of the common law would have been applied, and every gentleman of the law will admit, that in cases of libels, the truth could not be given in evidence in justification of the defendant. Here, then, according to the act of the Senate, the President and each House of Congress had effectually secured their conduct from investigation; and to the citizen who should arraign them before the bar of public opinion, truth afforded no protection. Have any attempts of this kind been made since the commencement of the Republican Administration? No, sir. And have not the President and both Houses of Congress been slandered, and basely slandered? The present majority wish not to hide their conduct from public view and scrutiny. All that is wished for is, that those who are opposed to them should so act as not to injure the public service. Those whose object is the public good need not the aid of sedition laws. They only need them whose actions cannot bear the light of truth. We wish to effect our object, not by fines and imprisonments, as our predecessors did, but by making it disreputable in the public estimation to injure the country by indirect means.

So fully, Mr. Chairman, am I satisfied of the correctness of the sentiments I have at all times entertained on this subject, that should it be my lot to be placed in a minority, however freely I might express my opinions of measures, no impediment should ever be thrown by me in the way of the execution, or operations of the laws, when once enacted, except so far as an attempt to repeal them might have that tendency.

A gentleman from New York (Mr. Grosvenor) had certainly not well considered the application of a sentiment expressed by him, or sure I am he would not have relied on it as a justification of the conduct of the minority in this House. He says, that opposition is useful and beneficial, and to prove this, he declares that had it not been for the opposition members of the British Parliament, the American Revolution would never have been effected. Grant it. We are in the habit of admiring and praising those who opposed the British Ministry during that struggle, because much good has resulted to the American people from their opposition. But if the interest of Great Britain required that she should retain the then colonies as a part of her dominions, have the labors of these men benefited their own country — have the people of Great Britain any cause to thank them for their exertions? Suppose the Opposition here should so far prevail as to compel the Administration to yield the great points in controversy between the two nations and surrender essential American rights — the same language we now use in relation to the Opposition in England, during our struggle for independence, might be applied to the Opposition in this country by Englishmen; but the American people could feel under no obligations to them.

Another gentleman from New York (Mr. Shipard) said that we, the majority, are prejudiced against the religion of England. Sir, this is the unkindest cut of all. I had hoped that the vanity of the minority would have been satisfied in claiming for their party all the talents and political integrity of the country; but, not contented with depriving us of all respectability and comfort in this life, they even attempt to deprive us of every hope for happiness in the world to come. This charge we repel with indignation. If we do not make as many religious professions, it does not therefore follow that we possess less true religion than our political opponents. Sir, what does the gentleman mean by the religion of England? I presume he means what is generally understood to be the Protestant, in contradiction to the Catholic faith. If so, how small a portion of the American people profess the latter? They are few in number and respectable, considering their number; but, they neither have the ability nor disposition to excite prejudices against the religion of England. The great body of the people composing the present political majority, profess the religion of that country from which they descended, and cannot therefore on that account feel any prejudices against Great Britian.

We not only feel no prejudices against that nation, but we feel our partialities for it. It is the land of our fathers, and therefore we are partial to it; the English language is our language, and therefore we are partial to it; all our institutions, except those of a political kind, derive their origin from that country, and therefore we are partial to it; we are taught knowledge from English sources, and therefore we are partial to it. I confess, Mr. Chairman, I am under the influence of these partialities. But shall I, on that account, forget my own country? Shall I be actuated by such feelings so far as to permit that nation to trample under foot the sovereignty of the United States? No, sir, I love my country better than I love England.

The same gentleman has said, that the Government has done more to christianize the world than all other nations. Sir, look to India, and the crimsoned flood of the sacred Ganges will tell you what that Government has done to christianize the world. View the idol of Juggernaut, and the mass of human misery and death which is produced by an idolatrous superstition, which is not only permitted, but promoted, by this christianizing Government, for the express purpose of raising a revenue for the British Crown. Sir, a strong British guard is there kept to encourage superstition, and exact a tax from the deluded pilgrims who resort to that place to worship. That there are many associations of pious men in England, who have done much to benefit mankind, is readily admitted; but their acts are not the acts of the Government; nor has the Government at all times approved of them, else how did it happen that the missionaries Gordon, Morrison, and Lee, were not permitted to depart for India and China in British vessels, but were compelled to come to America to obtain passage in an American ship, in the execution of their mission? Sir, these things I should not have brought to the view of the committee, had not the strange course in debate taken by gentlemen on the other side of the House rendered it necessary.

Mr. Chairman, it is insinuated that the Indian war has been produced by the conduct of the Government of the United States. I ask gentlemen to show in what manner this has been done. It cannot be shown; so far from it every exertion has been used to ameliorate the condition of that unfortunate people, and save them from that destruction which a war with the United States must inevitably bring upon them. You have sent your agents amongst them to teach them the arts of civilization, and while your Government was thus engaged, the agents and traders of Great Britain were employed in preventing the progress of your labors. You sent your teachers, your bibles, and your testaments; they sent their rum, their trinkets, and their baubles.

Sir, during the last Indian war, and after the treaty of peace between the United States and Great Britain, the agents of that Government furnished the Indians with supplies to carry on their savage warfare, and ever since they have been busied in inculcating on their minds sentiments hostile to the people of the United States. They have been told, as the public documents abundantly prove, to be prepared to strike the blow, whenever a rupture should take place between Great Britain and the United States; and it was owing to their being overcharged with sentiments of this kind, that induced them to commence hostilities in the Indiana Territory, before the declaration of war.

Mr. Chairman, look at that Indian war which is now raging in all its fury in the Southwest, and account for its origin. What cause of complaint has the Creek Nation ever had against the United States? None is pretended; it originated in the manner pointed out to me by the captive chief of that nation, who is now confined in the town in which I live. When asked why his people had made war on the United States, he replied: "A letter came from the North; a council of the chiefs was held; we were promised arms and every thing else necessary, if we could make war on the United States; we were told that the British would assist us in recovering our lands and driving the people of the United States from them, and that the ancient order of things should be restored — upon these conditions war was decided on." This, sir, is the way in which Great Britain christianizes the world.

A gentleman from Connecticut (Mr. Pitkin) says, that the Administration has abandoned the ground first taken with regard to impressment, and an arrangement on that subject is all that is now expected, and not a formal relinquishment of the right on the part of Great Britain. Sir, a security against impressment is all that was ever asked; and to us it is altogether immaterial, whether it be by a renunciation of the right, or an arrangement by which the officers of the British navy shall be prohibited from entering American vessels and taking from them American citizens. And it only requires that this point should be fairly stated, to prove that the enemy can settle it whenever he is disposed to act justly towards this nation. It has been alleged by Great Britain, that her seafaring subjects, whose services she needs, escape from her employment and enter into the service of the United States; and to reclaim them, she has been compelled to permit her officers to enter American vessels and seize them. By the passage of a bill, commonly called the seamen's bill, this Government has declared that this pretext for impressment shall no longer exist, for British seamen shall not be engaged in the American service, and adequate provisions are made to effectuate the object professed. If then Great Britain is disposed for peace, this subject can form no obstacle.

It is said that England and her allies, since the late great events in Europe, are omnipotent. On this point, gentlemen may calculate too strongly; it is one on which no man in this country can speak with confidence; but it seems to me not improbable that the influence of England on the Continent of Europe has already or will soon cease. Hitherto the power of France, which threatened to annihilate the Northern powers, united them with England in opposing the Emperor of the French. But now, when France is reduced almost, if not entirely to its ancient limits, and ceases to be a terror to them, is there not every reason to believe, that having humbled the tyrant of the land, they will turn their attention to the tyrant of the ocean? Sir, I cannot believe that Alexander the Mediator, or Deliverer, if you please, will consent to surrender to Great Britain those maritime rights for which his Government has at all times contended. True, sir, while Russia was struggling for her existence, while a powerful invasion threatened the capital of her Empire, her maritime claims were permitted to rest, but they were never abandoned; and let it be recollected, that her maritime claims at all times have equalled, if not exceeded those of the United States.

Another gentleman from New York (Mr. Sherwood) has told you that the subject of impressment was never considered as a cause of war. This has often been said before and as often refuted — need I refer you to the uniform sentiment of this Government for upwards of twenty years, and under every Administration?

Sir, all parties when in power have concurred in declaring it to be an evil not to be borne. It is somewhat remarkable, that however great the differences of opinion on other political subjects, in this all concurred. Mr. Washington, Mr. Pickering, Mr. Marshall, Mr. Adams, Mr. Stoddart, Mr. McHenry, Mr. Jefferson, Mr. Madison, Mr. Monroe, Mr. King, have each in their turn declared the impressment of our citizens as practised by Great Britain to be a sufficient cause of war — and if persisted in, it would result in an open rupture between the two countries; and although gentlemen now say that this formed no inducement for the declaration of war, at the session when it was declared, yet examine the public documents of that period, and it will be discovered that it was considered and treated as a prominent cause of war. Indulge me in reading a paragraph from the first report made by the Committee of Foreign Affairs at that session; the language of the Committee is:

Your committee are not, however, of that sect whose worship is at the shrine of a calculating avarice; and, while we are laying before you the just complaints of our merchants against the plunder of their ships and cargoes, we cannot refrain from presenting to the justice and humanity of our country the unhappy case of our impressed seamen. Although the groans of those victims of barbarity for the loss of (what should be dearer to Americans than life) their liberty; although the cries of their wives and children in the privation of protectors and parents have of late been drowned in louder clamors at the loss of property; yet is the practice of forcing our mariners into the British navy, in violation of the rights of our flag, carried on with unabated vigor and severity. If it be our duty to encourage the fair and legitimate commerce of this country by protecting the property of the merchants; then indeed, by as much as life and liberty are more estimable than ships and goods, so much more impressive is the duty to shield the persons of our seamen, whose hard and honest services are employed, equally with those of the merchants, in advancing under the mantle of its laws the interests of this country.

I could refer you to other documents of that session containing sentiments of the same kind, but this I deem sufficient to do away the effect of insinuations made by those who were not then members, and know but little on the subject. A gentleman from Virginia (Mr. Sheffey) has said, that the number of American seamen impressed by the British has been exaggerated. How is this proved? By bare assertion, and not otherwise. The official reports from the American Government, show the number to be 6,257: this statement I will rely on until its incorrectness is shown. But admit it to be incorrect, Lord Castlereagh, in the British Parliament, admitted that 1,600 American citizens had been impressed; this admission is surely good evidence against the British Government; and recollect these are admitted to be native American citizens, not British subjects, naturalized in this country. Now let me ask the gentleman from Virginia, whether if 1,600 men were forcibly taken from his district by any foreign power, he would not say it was sufficient cause of war, and would not condemn the Government that would refuse them protection? I am bound to believe he would; if so, is the principle changed when they are taken from any other quarter? Sir, so long as we are one nation, the same protection must be extended to every portion of the community.

One word more in reply to that gentleman, in behalf of my friend from Kentucky, (Mr. Sharpe,) who is detained by sickness from his seat in this House. I understand the gentleman from Virginia as saying that his (Mr. Sharpe's) constituents were so uninformed on political subjects as not to have known of the existence of the Orders in Council until last year.

[Mr. Sheffey here explained, by saying that what he had said was in reference to a statement made by a member from Maryland at the last session, and not intending to make such charge himself.]

Mr. Grundy proceeded. It is then a matter of very little consequence; I will, however, suggest to the gentleman from Virginia, that he perhaps should be the last member on the floor, who should provoke an inquiry into the comparative degree of intelligence and information which is to be found in different districts. I well know that my friend's district would have nothing to fear from such a comparison with the district represented by the gentleman from Virginia.

We are told, that before the declaration of war, the minority warned the majority of the consequences that were to follow, and predicted all the unfortunate events which have taken place; true, sir, they did, and much more; they told us that Boston, New York, Philadelphia, Baltimore, Norfolk, and Charleston, would immediately be reduced to ashes, and the whole seaboard laid waste. What, sir, has been done? Havre de Grace, Frenchtown, and a few other inconsiderable villages have been destroyed; what else? "Let the blushing streets of Hampton answer!" Sir, the enemy has made no solid impression on the country; they have carried on a kind of warfare calculated to irritate and unite the American people in the prosecution of the war.

A gentleman from New York asserted that we are waging this war to protect a set of renegado Irishmen. Sir, he is mistaken. It is an American war, carried on to secure American rights, and I have the fullest confidence that the nation will support the majority in every measure calculated to give vigor to it, until it can be brought to a just and honorable termination.

14
THE WAR'S END

The peace negotiations that terminated the War of 1812 were long and difficult. Early efforts to arrange a truce shortly after the outbreak of hostilities collapsed abruptly, and the subsequent attempt by Czar Nicholas to act as a mediator between the warring parties was equally unsuccessful. It was not until 1814, when American and British commissioners met at Ghent, that serious efforts were undertaken to end the war. The desire for peace sprang from a mutual recognition that neither side was capable of securing a victory. Events had shown that the United States was incapable of taking Canada. Events had shown, too, that Great Britain was unable to launch a successful invasion of American territory. Two war-weary governments then concluded that peace was desirable and necessary.

It took months of hard bargaining before this could be achieved. The reason for this lay in the extravagant terms which each side first put forward. Great Britain demanded a neutral Indian barrier state carved out of American territory, an end to the fishing liberties granted to the United States in the Treaty of 1783, and a new boundary giving to each side that territory which it currently occupied. The United States, for her part, insisted upon a resolution of all the maritime disputes in her favor (including the abolition of impressment), the retention of the fisheries, and a return to the pre-war boundary. The annexation of Canada was also suggested but soon dropped. Of course, the military posture of neither side justified such demands. The Duke of Wellington advised Lord Liverpool, the British Prime Minister, that the army in Canada had fought honorably and that the government should end the war on the basis of the *status quo ante bellum*. The American commissioners grudgingly reached the same conclusion. And so a treaty was signed that called for a return to the situation as it had existed before the outbreak of the war and provided for the creation of commissions to negotiate current boundary disputes.

It was an honorable peace that the country was happy to accept. The war had provided a harsh test to the nation, but it had risen to the challenge. A republican form of government, which many had thought too fragile to survive a conflict with Britain, had proved its worth. The economy, which some had believed was dependent upon Britain for its survival, had revealed a capacity to stand on its own and indeed, to even flourish in the face of adversity. And, as Gallatin observed, the nation had developed a new sense of purpose and dedication. These were no mean accomplishments for a new nation.

THE AMERICAN COMMIS-SIONERS TO THE SECRETARY OF STATE

Ghent, December 25, 1814

Sɪʀ:

We have the honor of transmitting herewith one of the three copies of the treaty of peace between Great Britain and the United States, signed last evening by the plenipotentiaries of His Britannic Majesty and by us.

The papers, of which copies are likewise now forwarded, will exhibit to you so fully the progress of the negotiation since the departure of the Chauncey, that few additional remarks from us will be necessary. It may be proper for us, however, to state that, in the interval between the time when our first *projet* of a treaty was sent to the British plenipotentiaries and that when they communicated to us the answer to it, the despatches which we had sent by Mr. Dallas, and the instructions to us, which had been published

Fʀᴏᴍ *American State Papers,* Foreign Relations, vol. 3, pp. 732–33.

in the United States, were republished in England. In declining to insist on the articles respecting impressment and indemnities, we made a formal declaration that the rights of both parties on the subject of seamen and the claims to indemnities for losses and damages sustained prior to the commencement of the war should not be affected or impaired by the omission in the treaty of a specific provision on these two subjects.

From the time when the *projet* of the treaty presented by us was returned with the proposed alterations, it was apparent that, unless new pretensions on the part of Great Britain should be advanced, the only important differences remaining to be discussed were those relating to the mutual restoration of territory taken during the war, to the navigation of the Mississippi by British subjects, and to the right of the people of the United States to the fisheries within the British jurisdiction. Instead of a general restitution of captured territory, which we had proposed, the British Government at first wished to confine it to the territory taken by either party belonging to the other. On our objecting that this would make each party the judge whether territory taken did or did not belong to the other, and thereby occasion new disputes, they acknowledged it to be their object that each party should, until a decision had taken place with respect to the title, retain possession of all the territory claimed by both parties, which might have been taken by such party during the war. They proposed, however, to limit the exception from mutual restitution to the islands in the bay of Passamaquoddy. As it had been on both sides admitted that the title to these islands was disputed, and as a method of settling amicably those disputes was provided for in the treaty, we had not expected that the British Government would adhere to the demand of retaining the temporary possession of those islands. We insisted, therefore, on their being included in the general restoration, until we had reason to believe that our further perseverance would have hazarded the conclusion of the peace itself. We finally consented, as an alternative preferable to the continuance of the war, to this exception, upon condition that it should not be understood as impairing in any manner the right of the United States to these islands. We also urged for a stipulation requiring an ultimate decision upon the title within a limited time; but to this we also found opposed an insuperable objection, and we were finally induced to accept in its stead a declaration of the British plenipotentiaries, that no unnecessary delay of the decision should be interposed on the part of Great Britain.

At the first conference, on the 8th of August, the British plenipotentiaries had notified to us that the British Government did not intend henceforth to allow the people of the United States, without an equivalent, the liberties to fish and to dry and cure fish within the exclusive British jurisdiction, stipulated in their favor by the latter part of the third article of the treaty of peace of 1783. And in their note of the 19th of August, the British plenipotentiaries had demanded a new stipulation, to secure to British subjects the right of navigating the Mississippi; a demand which, unless warranted by another article of that same treaty of 1783, we could not perceive that Great Britain had any colorable pretence for making. Our instructions had forbidden us to suffer our right to the fisheries to be brought into discussion, and had not authorized us to make any distinction in the several provisions of the third article of the treaty of 1783, or between that article and any other of the same treaty. We had no equivalent to offer for a new recognition of our right to any part of the fisheries, and we had no power to grant any equivalent which might be asked for it by the British Government. We contended that the whole treaty of 1783 must be considered as one entire and permanent compact, not liable, like ordinary treaties, to be abrogated by a subsequent war between the parties to it; as an instrument recognising the rights and liberties enjoyed by the people of the United States as an independent nation, and containing the terms and conditions on which the two parts of one empire had mutually agreed, thenceforth, to constitute two distinct and separate nations. In consenting, by that treaty, that a part of the North American continent should remain subject to the British jurisdiction, the people of the United States had reserved to themselves the liberty, which they had ever before enjoyed, of fishing upon that part of its coasts, and of drying and curing fish upon the shores, and this reservation had been agreed to by the other contracting party. We saw not why this liberty, then no new grant, but the mere recognition of a prior right always enjoyed, should be forfeited by war, any more than any other of the rights of our national independence; or why we should need a new stipulation for its enjoyment more than we needed a new article to declare that the King of Great Britain treated with us as free, sovereign, and independent States. We stated this principle in general terms to the British plenipotentiaries, in the note which we sent to them with our *projet* of the treaty, and we alleged it as the ground upon which no new stipulation was deemed by our Government necessary to secure to the people of the United States all the rights and liberties stipulated in their favor by the treaty of 1783. No reply to that part of our note was given by the British plenipotentiaries, but, in returning our *projet* of a treaty, they added a clause to one of the articles, stipulating a right for British subjects to navigate the Mississippi. Without adverting to the ground of prior and immemorial usage, if the principle were just that the treaty of 1783, from its peculiar character, remained in force in all its parts, notwithstanding the war, no new stipulation was necessary to secure to the subjects of Great Britain the right of navigating the Mississippi, so far as that right was secured by the treaty of 1783, as, on the other hand, no stipulation was necessary to secure to the people of the United States the liberty to fish, and to dry and cure fish, within the exclusive jurisdiction of Great Britain. If they asked the navigation of the Mississippi as a new claim, they could not expect we should grant it without an equivalent; if they asked it because it had been granted in 1783, they must recognise the claim of the people of the United States to the liberty to fish and to dry and cure fish, in question. To place both points beyond all future controversy, a majority of us determined to offer to admit an article confirming both the rights, or we offered at the same time to be silent in the treaty upon both, and to leave out altogether the article defining the boundary from the Lake of the Woods westward. They finally agreed to this last proposal, but not until they had proposed an article stipulating for a future negotiation for an equivalent to be given by Great Britain for the navigation of the Mississippi, and by the United States for the liberty as to the fisheries within British jurisdiction. This article was unnecessary with regard to its professed object, since both Governments had it in their power, without it, to negotiate upon these subjects if they pleased. We rejected it, although its adoption would have secured the boundary of the forty-ninth degree of latitude west of the Lake of the Woods, because it would have been a formal abandonment, on our part, of our claim to the liberty as to the fisheries, recognised by the treaty of 1783.

You will perceive by the correspondence, that the ninth article was offered us as a *sine qua non* and an ultimatum. We accepted it, not without much hesitation, as the only alternative to a rupture of the negotiation; and with a perfect understanding that our Government was free to reject it, as we were not authorized to subscribe to it.

To guard against any accident which might happen in the transmission of a single copy of the treaty to the United States, the British plenipotentiaries have consented to execute it in triplicate; and, as the treaty with the British ratification may be exposed to the same danger, the times for the cessation of hostilities, the restoration of captures at sea, and the release of prisoners, have been fixed, not from the exchange of ratifications, but from the ratification on both sides, without alteration by either of the contracting parties. We consented to the introduction of this latter provision at the desire of the British plenipotentiaries, who were willing to take a full, but were unwilling to incur the risk of a partial, ratification, as the period from which the peace should be considered as concluded.

We are informed by them that Mr. Baker, their secretary, is to go out to America with the British ratification.

We have the honor to be, very respectfully, sir, your most humble and obedient servants,

JOHN QUINCY ADAMS,
J. A. BAYARD,
H. CLAY,
JONATHAN RUSSELL,
ALBERT GALLATIN.

PRESIDENT MADISON TO CONGRESS

WASHINGTON, FEBRUARY 18, 1815

*James
Madison*

TO THE SENATE AND HOUSE OF REPRESENTATIVES OF THE UNITED STATES:

I lay before Congress copies of the treaty of peace and amity between the United States and His Britannic Majesty, which was signed by the commissioners of both parties, at Ghent, on the 24th of December, 1814, and the ratifications of which have been duly exchanged.

While performing this act, I congratulate you and our constituents upon an event which is highly honorable to the nation, and terminates, with peculiar felicity, a campaign signalized by the most brilliant successes.

FROM *A Compilation of the Messages and Papers of the Presidents, 1789–1897* (Washington, 1896) vol. 2, pp. 537–39.

The late war, although reluctantly declared by Congress, had become a necessary resort to assert the rights and independence of the nation. It has been waged with a success which is the natural result of the wisdom of the legislative councils, of the patriotism of the people, of the public spirit of the militia, and of the valor of the military and naval forces of the country. Peace, at all times a blessing, is peculiarly welcome, therefore, at a period when the causes for the war have ceased to operate; when the Government has demonstrated the efficiency of its powers of defence; and when the nation can review its conduct without regret and without reproach.

I recommend to your care and beneficence the gallant men, whose achievements in every department of military service, on the land and on the water, have so essentially contributed to the honor of the American name, and to the restoration of peace. The feelings of conscious patriotism and worth will animate such men under every change of fortune and pursuit; but their country performs a duty to itself, when it bestows those testimonials of approbation and applause which are at once the reward and the incentive to great actions.

The reduction of the public expenditures to the demands of a peace establishment, will doubtless engage the immediate attention of Congress. There are, however, important considerations which forbid a sudden and general revocation of the measures that have been produced by the war. Experience has taught us that neither the pacific dispositions of the American people, nor the pacific character of their political institutions, can altogether exempt them from that strife which appears, beyond the ordinary lot of nations, to be incident to the actual period of the world; and the same faithful monitor demonstrates that a certain degree of preparation for war is not only indispensable to avert disasters in the onset, but affords also the best security for the continuance of peace. The wisdom of Congress will, therefore, I am confident, provide for the maintenance of an adequate regular force; for the gradual advancement of the naval establishment; for improving all the means of harbor defence; for adding discipline to the distinguished bravery of the militia; and for cultivating the military art, in its essential branches, under the liberal patronage of Government.

The resources of our country were at all times competent to the attainment of every national object; but they will now be enriched and invigorated by the activity which peace will introduce into all the scenes of domestic enterprise and labor. The provision that has been made for the public creditors, during the present session of

Congress, must have a decisive effect in the establishment of the public credit, both at home and abroad. The reviving interests of commerce will claim the legislative attention at the earliest opportunity, and such regulations will, I trust, be seasonably devised as shall secure to the United States their just proportion of the navigation of the world. The most liberal policy towards other nations, if met by corresponding dispositions, will, in this respect, be found the most beneficial policy toward ourselves. But there is no subject that can enter with greater force and merit into the deliberations of Congress than a consideration of the means to preserve and promote the manufactures which have sprung into existence, and attained an unparalleled maturity throughout the United States during the period of the European wars. This source of national independence and wealth I anxiously recommend, therefore, to the prompt and constant guardianship of Congress.

The termination of the legislative sessions will soon separate you, fellow-citizens, from each other, and restore you to your constituents. I pray you to bear with you the expressions of my sanguine hope that the peace which has been just declared will not only be the foundation of the most friendly intercourse between the United States and Great Britain, but that it will also be productive of happiness and harmony in every section of our beloved country. The influence of your precepts and example must be everywhere powerful, and while we accord in grateful acknowledgments for the protection which Providence has bestowed upon us, let us never cease to inculcate obedience to the laws, and fidelity to the Union, as constituting the palladium of the national independence and prosperity.

JAMES MADISON

BIBLIOGRAPHICAL ESSAY

GENERAL WORKS

To conserve space, data concerning the publisher's name and place of publication have been omitted.

Books available in paperback editions are shown with an asterisk [*] following the title.

The standard bibliographical work on American foreign policy is S. F. Bemis and G. C. Griffin, *Guide to the Diplomatic History of the United States, 1775-1921* (1925). A more recent work is Oscar Handlin, et al. (eds.), *Harvard Guide to American History** (rev. ed., 1967). The most useful compilation of treaties is D. H. Miller (ed.), *Treaties and Other International Acts of the United States of America* (8 vols., 1931-1948). For a supplemental work see W. M. Mallory (comp.), *Treaties, Conventions, International Acts, Protocols and Agreements between the United States of America and Other Powers, 1776-1923* (3 vols., 1910-1923). Briefer, but very helpful compilations of documents are R. J. Bartlett (ed.), *The Record of American Foreign Policy* (3rd. ed., 1954) and R. A. Divine (ed.), *American Foreign Policy* (1960). An indispensable collection is J. B. Moore, *A Digest of International Law* (8 vols., 1906). A more modern work is G. H. Hackworth, *Digest of International Law* (8 vols., 1940-1944). See also J. B. Moore, *History and Digest of the International Arbitrations* (6 vols., 1948). For the most effective discussion of international law see W. H. Phillips and A. H. Reede, *Neutrality* (1936) and C. C. Cheyney, *International Law Chiefly as Interpreted and Applied by the United States* (3 vols., 1947).

THE PROBLEMS OF NEUTRALITY

A chronological and favorable account of Washington's foreign policy is to be found in L. M. Sears, *George Washington and the French Revolution* (1960). Felix Gilbert, *To the Farewell Address** (1961) examines events leading to Washington's statement and Hamilton's influence on it. The standard work on Jay's Treaty is Samuel F. Bemis, *Jay's Treaty**

(1925). The findings of Bemis are modified in A. L. Burt, *The United States, Great Britain and British North America* (1940). A more recent study is Bradford Perkins, *The First Rapprochement; England and the United States, 1795-1805* (1955). J. C. Miller, *The Federalist Era, 1789-1801** (1960) and *Alexander Hamilton: Portrait in Paradox* (1953), in paperback as *Alexander Hamilton and the Growth of the New Nation*, examine the role Hamilton played in making foreign policy. The best biographies of President Adams are Gilbert Chinard, *Honest John Adams** (1933) and Page Smith, *John Adams* (1962). See also Stephen G. Kurtz, *The Presidency of John Adams** (1957). Alexander DeConde, *The Entangling Alliance* (1958) and *The Quasi-War: The Politics and Diplomacy of the Undeveloped War with France, 1797-1801** (1966) are perceptive and valuable studies of the period. Articles of significance include S. F. Bemis, "Washington's Farewell Address: A Foreign Policy of Independence," *American Historical Review*, XXXIX (1934), 250-68; Alexander DeConde, "Washington's Farewell Address, the French Alliance, and the Election of 1796," *Mississippi Valley Historical Review*, XLIII (1957), 641-58; Joseph Charles, "The Jay Treaty: The Origins of the American Party System," *William and Mary Quarterly*, XII, 3rd ser. (1953), 581-630.

THE SEARCH FOR SECURITY

The history of the Louisiana Purchase is briefly told in A. B. Darling, *Our Rising Empire, 1763-1803* (1940). The western aspects of the purchase are fully examined in Arthur P. Whitaker, *The Mississippi Question, 1795-1803* (1934). Other studies include E. W. Lyons, *The Louisiana Purchase in French Diplomacy, 1759-1804* (1934) and George Dangerfield, *Chancellor Robert R. Livingston of New York, 1746-1813* (1960). Lawrence S. Kaplan, *Jefferson and France* (1966) is a stimulating study of Jefferson's changing relationship to France. The issue of neutral rights is most effectively found in A. L. Burt, *The United States, Great Britain and British North America*, previously cited; W. H. Phillips and A. H. Reede, *Neutrality*, previously cited; and E. F. Hecksher, *The Continental System* (1922). The two most detailed studies of the embargo are L. M. Sears, *Jefferson and the Embargo* (1927) and W. W. Jennings, *The American Embargo, 1807-1809* (1921). For a treatment of Madison's reaction to French policy see Irving Brant, *James Madison; The President, 1809-1812* (1956). Relevant articles on the period include Bradford Perkins, "George Canning, Great Britain and the United States," *American Historical Review*, LXIII (1957), 1-22; L. S. Kaplan, "Jefferson, the Napoleonic Wars, and the Balance of Power," *William and Mary Quarterly*, XIV (1957), 196-217; and R. D. S. Higham, "The Port of Boston and the Embargo of 1807-1809," *The American Neptune*, XVI (1957). The classic accounts of the War of 1812 are Henry Adams, *History of the United States of America during the Administrations of Jefferson* and Madison (9 vols., 1891) and A. T. Mahan, Sea Power in Its Relations to the War of 1812 (2 vols., 1905). J. W. Pratt, Expansionists of 1812 (1925) stresses the important role played by the West in bringing on the war. A. L. Burt, The United States, Great Britain and British North America, previously cited, is a wise and balanced treatment of the subject which emphasizes the importance of maritime issues and neutral rights. Bradford Perkins, Prologue to War* (1961) deals extensively with maritime causes and is critical of the leadership provided by Jefferson and Madison. Reginald Horsman, The Causes of the War of 1812* (1962) contains a balanced analysis of the issues leading Madison into war. Roger Brown, The Republic in Peril (1964) suggests that party division played a significant role in the events leading up to the outbreak of the conflict. Marshall Smelser, The Democratic Republic, 1801–1815* (1968) is a lucidly written and valuable addition to the study of the period. Irving Brant, James Madison: The President, 1809–1812, previously cited, argues, not wholly successfully, that Madison's skills as a leader have been underestimated. A general and popular account of the war is to be found in A. Z. Carr, The Coming of the War (1960). An excellent biography of one of the leading advocates of war is Bernard Mayo, Henry Clay (1937). The most recent study of the war is P. C. T. White, A Nation on Trial: America and the War of 1812* (1965). An admirable summary of various interpretations of the war may be read in W. H. Goodman, "The Origins of the War of 1812: A Survey of Changing Interpretations," Mississippi Valley Historical Review, XXVIII (1941), 171–186. A careful study of the effects of British policies upon the South and West is G. R. Taylor, "Agrarian Discontent in the Mississippi Valley Preceding the War of 1812," Journal of Political Economy, XXXIX (1931), 471–505. N. K. Risjord, "1812: Conservatives, War Hawks, and the Nation's Honor," William and Mary Quarterly, XVIII (1961), 196–210, suggests that the desire to preserve the nation's honor was a critical factor in leading to the war. Additional articles of value include Margaret K. Latimer, "South Carolina — A Protagonist of the War of 1812," American Historical Review, LXI (1956), 914–29; Abbot Smith, "Mr. Madison's War: An Unsuccessful Experiment in the Conduct of National Policy," Political Science Quarterly, LVII (1942), 229–46; Reginald Horsman, "Western War Aims, 1811-1912," Indiana Magazine of History, LIII (1957), 1–18 and "British Indian Policy in the Northwest, 1807–1812, Mississippi Valley Historical Review, XLV (1958), 51–66; and L. M. Hacker, "Western Land Hunger and the War of 1812," Mississippi Valley Historical Review, X (1924), 365–95.

The best accounts of the negotiations leading to the Treaty of Ghent are A. T. Mahan, Sea Power in Its Relations to the War of 1812, previously cited, and Henry Adams, History of the United States during the Ad-

THE DIE IS CAST

THE QUEST FOR PEACE

ministrations of Jefferson and Madison, vol. IX. The fullest treatment is F. A. Updyke, *The Diplomacy of the War of 1812* (1915). The most recent study of the period is Bradford Perkins, *Castlereagh and Adams: England and the United States, 1812-1823* (1964). Reginald Horsman, *The War of 1812* (1969) provides an admirable account of the war years and the negotiations at Ghent. Briefer examinations of the peace making are to be found in Patrick C. T. White, *A Nation on Trial: America and the War of 1812*,* previously cited and A. L. Burt, *The United States, Great Britain and British North America,* previously cited. A popular account which emphasizes the skill of the American negotiators is F. L. Engelman, *The Peace of Christmas Eve* (1962). The role of Adams is effectively and sympathetically studied in S. F. Bemis, *John Quincy Adams and the Foundations of American Foreign Policy* (1949). Irving Brant, *James Madison: Commander in Chief, 1812-1836* (1961) is an effort to portray the President as a successful war leader who brought his country through to victory. Raymond Walters, *Albert Gallatin: Jeffersonian Financier and Diplomat** (1957) is an admirable study of the contributions made to the peace settlement by Gallatin. See also J. H. Powell, *Richard Rush, Republican Diplomat, 1780-1859* (1942). Articles of interest include W. D. Jones, "A British View of the War of 1812 and the Peace Negotiations," *Mississippi Valley Historical Review,* XLV (1958) 481-7 and J. I. Shulim, "The United States Views Russia in the Napoleonic Age," *Proceedings of the American Philosophical Society,* CII (1958), 148-59.

DATE DUE

MAR 1 3 '74			
GAYLORD			PRINTED IN U.S.A.